An Exact Mystery

THE POETIC LIFE OF VERNON WATKINS

An Exact Mystery

THE POETIC LIFE OF VERNON WATKINS

by

Richard Ramsbotham

> A secret law contrives
> To give time symmetry:
> There is, within our lives,
> An exact mystery.
>
> 'The Precision of the Wheel'
> by Vernon Watkins.

THE CHOIR PRESS

Copyright © 2020 Richard Ramsbotham

All rights reserved. No part of this publication may be reproduced or transmitted in any form or by any means, electronic or mechanical including photocopying, recording or any information storage or retrieval system, without prior permission in writing from the publishers.

The right of Richard Ramsbotham to be identified as the author of this work has been asserted by him in accordance with the Copyright, Designs and Patents Act 1988

First published in the United Kingdom in 2020 by
The Choir Press

ISBN 978-1-78963-119-7

Contents

List of Illustrations		vii
Acknowledgements		ix
Foreword – By Gwen Watkins		xiii
Introduction		xv
Chapter One	Birth and Early Years (1906–1920)	1
Chapter Two	Repton (1920–1924)	15
Chapter Three	Cambridge (1924–1925)	38
Chapter Four	Cardiff (1925–1928)	59
	'Beyond Time's Chain'	86
Chapter Five	'Pivotal Crisis In Time' (1929)	90
Chapter Six	Second Apprenticeship (1930–1934)	97
Chapter Seven	Swansea's Other Poet (1935–1936)	113
Chapter Eight	'Wales' And Ireland (1937–1938)	146
Chapter Nine	A Death and a Birth (1938–1939)	165
Chapter Ten	'Sailors on the Moving Land' (1939–1941)	185
Appendix	Unpublished Poems by Vernon Watkins	226
Endnotes		239

Illustrations

1. The Cambria Daily Leader – on the day of Vernon Watkins's birth. https://ichef.bbci.co.uk/news/320/media/images/61168000/jpg/_61168016_61168013.jpg
2. Pentrych Iron Works and the Garth, 1905. http://www.pentyrch.cc/hanesm/images/stories/gwaelodygarth/gwaelodortaf.jpg
3. Vernon Watkins with a tennis racket, c. 1910.
4. Vernon Watkins in Tyttenhanger Lodge uniform, aged 11 or 12.
5. The Watkins family, c. 1920.
6. Christopher Isherwood, aged 17 (photograph by Eric Falk).
7. Vernon Watkins at Repton, Summer 1923 (Repton School Library).
8. Headmaster of Repton, Geoffrey Fisher (photograph by Vernon Watkins).
9. Armistice Day Memorial at Repton, 11th November, 1922 (photograph by Mr. G.B. Smith).
10. Vernon Watkins, aged 17 or 18 (photograph by Eric Falk).
11. Caswell Bay taken from above Redcliffe House (postcard).
12. Vernon Watkins at Cambridge.
13. John Keats' grave in the Protestant Cemetary, Rome (photograph by David Lown – 'picturesfromitaly.com').
14. From Vernon Watkins's Rome Notebook – 1927 (NLW MS 22443C – supplied by Llyfrgell Genedlaethol Cymru/The National Library of Wales).
15. South Wales News, Friday 13th April, 1928 (Cardiff Public Library – printed from microfiche).
16. Postcard to VW from David Cochrane from Greece, Easter Sunday, 1931.
17. Interior of the Lorenzkirche, Nuremberg (© iStock.com/Alizada Studios).

18. Nazi book-burning, Hamburg, May 1933 (© BPK Bildagentur).
19. Portrait of Dylan Thomas by Alfred Janes – 1934
    (National Museum of Wales/© The Estate of Alfred Janes/Bridgeman Images).
20. Portrait of Vernon Watkins by Alfred Janes – 1949
    (Glynn Vivian Art Gallery/© The Estate of Alfred Janes/Bridgeman Images).
21. Vernon Watkins on the Gower Cliffs
    (photograph by Bernard Mitchell).
22. Dylan Thomas overlooking the estuary in Laugharne
    (photograph belonging to John Idris Jones).
23. Vernon Watkins's poem 'Griefs of the Sea', in 'Wales 1', altered by Dylan Thomas and changed back again, by hand, by VW
    (Jeff Towns Archive).
24. Vernon Watkins at Hunt's Bay, July 1937.
25. Francis Dufau-Labeyrie (photograph by Vernon Watkins).
26 William Butler Yeats (photograph by Vernon Watkins).
27. Back cover of 'Wales' – October 1939
    (Swansea Central Library – photocopy).
28. Dylan Thomas and Vernon Watkins – probably 1936
    (photographer unknown).
29. Dylan Thomas, Wyn Lewis and Vernon Watkins
    (photograph by J.C. Wyn Lewis).
32. Central Swansea after the Blitz, 1941 (© War History Online).

(Images 3-6, 8, 10, 12, 16, 24 and 25 are from the archives of Gwen Watkins.)

Acknowledgements

I am deeply grateful to the following people, without whom this book could either not have been written at all or would have been much poorer.

Gwen Watkins - for her patience and unstinting generosity over many years.

Rhiannon, Gareth, Dylan and Conrad Watkins – for their friendly help and generous support in many ways.

Elizabeth Ramsbotham – whose shared love of Vernon Watkins's poetry and all our shared time in the Gower were the ground the book built on.

Danièle Dufau-Labeyrie – Vernon Watkins's goddaughter – for so generously providing me with photocopies of all the letters between Vernon Watkins and her father, Francis Dufau-Labeyrie.

John O'Meara – for his kind help with the above, his critical appraisal of the manuscript and his friendship.

Glen Williamson – for joyfully tracking down T.S. Eliot's letters to Vernon Watkins in the New York Public Library.

Nancy Fulford – Project Archivist of the T.S. Eliot Collection – for providing me with copies of Vernon Watkins's 151 letters to T.S. Eliot.

John Haffenden – for opening the door for me to these letters – and for generously reading my entire manuscript and commenting on it.

The late Ruth Pryor – for passing on to me her bibliography of Vernon Watkins's poetry.

Jeff Towns – for first introducing me to Gwen Watkins – and for much help since – including his unearthing of a copy of 'Wales 1' containing Watkins's handwritten changes to 'Griefs of the Sea'.

David Woolley – and others at the Dylan Thomas Centre, Swansea – for their strong initial support of the project.

ACKNOWLEDGEMENTS

Brian Keeble – for his beautifully produced *Collected Poems of Vernon Watkins*, where all Watkins's published poems are to be found, and for the conversations we have had.

Emma Harris – for arranging for the book to be written as a Ph.D. in Warsaw, when no publisher was interested. The Ph.D. was never completed, but it helped!

Gary Gregor – for picking the project up again and for his diligent care in enabling it to reach this point.

Mick Felton at Seren Books – for initially agreeing to publish the book, without which it would never have been written when it was.

Godlind Gädeke – for selflessly creating the circumstances and the home in which this first part of the book was written.

Warren Bouwer, Gabriella Schilthuis, Jonathan Stedall and Laura Sheldon – for the friendly encouragement they offered as the book's first readers.

Paul Stevens, librarian at Repton College – for exploring the archives at Repton, leading to the discovery of Vernon Watkins's house photograph and, most importantly, of Vernon Watkins's first printed poems. (See Appendix.)

The librarian at Magdalene College, Cambridge, for making available their file on Vernon Watkins and the passages in A.C. Benson's diaries on Watkins.

The librarians of the National Library of Wales - for help on many occasions in relation to their vast Vernon Watkins archive.

Miles Bailey and the Choir Press for all their help and warm efficiency in publishing the book.

Acknowledgements

I am deeply grateful to the following people, without whom this book could either not have been written at all or would have been much poorer.

Gwen Watkins - for her patience and unstinting generosity over many years.

Rhiannon, Gareth, Dylan and Conrad Watkins – for their friendly help and generous support in many ways.

Elizabeth Ramsbotham – whose shared love of Vernon Watkins's poetry and all our shared time in the Gower were the ground the book built on.

Danièle Dufau-Labeyrie – Vernon Watkins's goddaughter – for so generously providing me with photocopies of all the letters between Vernon Watkins and her father, Francis Dufau-Labeyrie.

John O'Meara – for his kind help with the above, his critical appraisal of the manuscript and his friendship.

Glen Williamson – for joyfully tracking down T.S. Eliot's letters to Vernon Watkins in the New York Public Library.

Nancy Fulford – Project Archivist of the T.S. Eliot Collection – for providing me with copies of Vernon Watkins's 151 letters to T.S. Eliot.

John Haffenden – for opening the door for me to these letters – and for generously reading my entire manuscript and commenting on it.

The late Ruth Pryor – for passing on to me her bibliography of Vernon Watkins's poetry.

Jeff Towns – for first introducing me to Gwen Watkins – and for much help since – including his unearthing of a copy of 'Wales 1' containing Watkins's handwritten changes to 'Griefs of the Sea'.

David Woolley – and others at the Dylan Thomas Centre, Swansea – for their strong initial support of the project.

ACKNOWLEDGEMENTS

- Brian Keeble – for his beautifully produced *Collected Poems of Vernon Watkins*, where all Watkins's published poems are to be found, and for the conversations we have had.
- Emma Harris – for arranging for the book to be written as a Ph.D. in Warsaw, when no publisher was interested. The Ph.D. was never completed, but it helped!
- Gary Gregor – for picking the project up again and for his diligent care in enabling it to reach this point.
- Mick Felton at Seren Books – for initially agreeing to publish the book, without which it would never have been written when it was.
- Godlind Gädeke – for selflessly creating the circumstances and the home in which this first part of the book was written.
- Warren Bouwer, Gabriella Schilthuis, Jonathan Stedall and Laura Sheldon – for the friendly encouragement they offered as the book's first readers.
- Paul Stevens, librarian at Repton College – for exploring the archives at Repton, leading to the discovery of Vernon Watkins's house photograph and, most importantly, of Vernon Watkins's first printed poems. (See Appendix.)
- The librarian at Magdalene College, Cambridge, for making available their file on Vernon Watkins and the passages in A.C. Benson's diaries on Watkins.
- The librarians of the National Library of Wales - for help on many occasions in relation to their vast Vernon Watkins archive.
- Miles Bailey and the Choir Press for all their help and warm efficiency in publishing the book.

ACKNOWLEDGEMENTS

I am very grateful to the following people, who all knew Vernon Watkins, for the conversations I have had with them, as well as for generously providing me with letters from, writings about and images of Watkins:

Elizabeth Iorwerth-Jones
Glenys Cour
Wyn Lewis
Irene Lewis
John Heath-Stubbs
Michael Hamburger
Neville Masterman
Kathleen Raine
Philip Hobsbaum
Tony Curtis
Bernard Mitchell.
Rhiannon Watkins
Gareth Watkins
Dylan Watkins
Conrad Watkins

Four events I participated in relating to Vernon Watkins were also helpful towards this book. I am grateful to the following people involved in these events for their lively conversation, help and encouragement:

Phoenix Fires, Stourbridge, 2004 (A celebration of Kathleen Raine – her life and artistic friendships): the late Alan Clodd; Edwin Llowerch; Louise Watkins; Jeremy Naydler; Grevel Lindop; Jeremy Reed.
Swansea's Other Poet, Radio 3, 2012: Rowan Williams; Johannah Smith.
Coffee with the Kardomah Boys, (live Radio 3 event at Laugharne) 2014: Ian McMillan; Hilly Janes; Peter Stead.
Great Welsh Writers – Vernon Watkins (BBC Wales TV) 2014: Alan Golding.

For generously permitting me to include photographs of theirs, I am grateful to:

Bernard Mitchell
John Idris Jones
David Lown

I also acknowledge the quotation of extracts from the following published sources:

The Arms of the Infinite by Christopher Barker (Pomona, 2006).
BOY – Tales of Childhood by Roald Dahl (Puffin, 2013).
Victor Gollancz – A Biography by Ruth Dudley Edwards (Faber 2012)
Lions and Shadows – An Education in the Twenties by Christopher Isherwood (Four Square, 1963)
Dylan Thomas. The Biography by Paul Ferris. (Phoenix, 1999).
Dylan Remembered. Volume 2. Interviews by Colin Edwards. Edited by David N. Thomas (Seren, 2004).
Yeats the Initiate by Kathleen Raine (The Dolmen Press/George Allen & Unwin, 1986).
Portrait of a Friend by Gwen Watkins (Gomer, 1983).

I also gratefully acknowledge:

The *Dylan Thomas Estate* and *The Dylan Thomas Trust* for permission to include the quotations by Dylan Thomas in the book; and *Faber Permissions* and *Faber and Faber Ltd* for permission to include the quotations by T.S. Eliot in the book.

Foreword

I first met Richard many years ago when he was a young man, and was struck by how immersed he was in Vernon's poetry. The verse seemed to speak to him in a way no other poet could. Among the many people who have written about Vernon over the years, Richard has impressed me most with his deep affinity for the poetry emanating from a profoundly spiritual spring.

Vernon often remarked that he could not remember a time when he did not intend to write poetry. His childish scribblings were all in verse. An early love of Keats and Shelley emerged, and he supplied himself with all the English poets, not least through the neat trick of giving books he wished to read to his family for birthdays and Christmas. His parents were Welsh speaking but the language was not passed on to the children, although his father would read the Welsh poets aloud to him, and he became attuned to the native rhythm and lyricism. It was a source of regret in his later life that, although he came to translate French, Italian and German poetry, of which he had a wide knowledge, he never learned the language of his birth.

Vernon is often remembered as the ever-forgiving friend of Dylan Thomas; the mild-mannered bank clerk striding his beloved Gower cliffs, the inspiration for so much of his poetry; but still waters ran very deep indeed, and many poets trod the windy cliffs to speak with him. He used to say that he 'heard' lines of poems in his head, as if by dictation, and 'Griefs of the Sea' came to him in its entirety.

Richard is a close friend whose knowledge of Vernon's verse, culminating in editing 'Vernon Watkins: New Selected Poems', and his rigorous research uncovering events and details hitherto unknown by his family, makes him the ideal biographer of a life devoted to poetry from beginning to end.

Gwen Watkins
January, 2020

Introduction

In my early twenties, in extreme crisis, and wholly unable to come to terms with the fact that after the joyful and exalted experiences of my earlier days I seemed, like Icarus, to have crashed ignominiously to earth, I read the following four lines of a poem:

> *Why, then, complain of evil days*
> *If days you knew before were good?*
> *That is a shallow kind of praise*
> *Which cannot thrive on bitter food.*

I felt that I was being directly addressed and read amazedly on:

> *I know too great a recompense*
> *For any tempest to destroy;*
> *When joy has lost its last defence,*
> *Then is the time to learn of joy.*
>
> *Let discord beat about my ears,*
> *I know too well what time may bring;*
> *Nor can it touch the truest tears,*
> *Such is the secret of their spring.*

The poem had a life-changing effect on me and offered me, just in the substance of its twelve lines, a way through what I had been struggling with, which I had barely considered possible.

I also wondered, of course, who the poet was who had written this. Vernon Watkins. I could hardly believe I had never heard of him. Literature and above all poetry had been the greatest influence in my life for almost as long as I could remember. I had done a degree in English Literature at Cambridge. I had by no means confined my reading to the syllabus. And yet in all my reading and in all the lectures I had attended

I had never even heard his name. How was this possible? Nor was my incredulity based merely on one poem. The *Collected Poems of Vernon Watkins* had just been published (in 1986) and poem after poem in its 480 pages only deepened my wonder at his poetry. In the years that followed I read his poetry for no other reason than the love of it and the immediacy with which it spoke to me.

I did eventually begin speaking about Vernon Watkins, as a lecturer in English Literature at Warsaw University, and later, having completed a Speech and Drama training, gave several poetry performances of his work. The riddle about his unknownness, though, had not gone away. The *Collected Poems* gave no biographical information about him nor any notes to his poems. Kathleen Raine stated on the dustjacket: "*Vernon Watkins is a poet of European stature, and as such he will come to be known*", which I immediately acknowledged, but there seemed to be nothing setting him in a true context. The person who could say: "publication is a very marginal thing, really" was clearly not someone who sought for attention. Yet every remark I had found by Vernon Watkins on poetry spoke with an extraordinary sureness of voice, as Philip Larkin witnessed: "there was something hard and brilliant about his attachment to poetry: he never hesitated. It was something there, tangible and palpable".

Having established from poems and letters that Vernon Watkins had lived on the Gower Peninsula the wish soon grew to visit it. I went there on holiday with my wife and was amazed to see how his poetry, which I had responded to purely on its own terms, also related in such intimate detail to this landscape. I also quickly found my way to 'Dylan's' bookshop in Salubrious Passage, Swansea and talked with its owner, Jeff Towns, about Vernon Watkins and must have said something about my journey with his work that had finally brought me here. "Look" said Jeff, "I don't normally do this, but maybe you should meet Gwen Watkins, his widow", and he gave me her telephone number.

I had never known Watkins was married, let alone imagined his wife might still be alive if he had been, and even had I done so the idea of meeting her would never have occurred to me. The idea seemed at the time almost as unreal as if someone had suggested I meet the wife of Novalis or Shelley or Baudelaire. With encouragement, though, I got myself into a telephone box and, with my hand shaking so badly I could hardly hold the receiver, spoke with Gwen and arranged to meet. We went round to see her soon afterwards in her small flat in the Mumbles. The shock of great poetry breaking into the realm of daily life took its toll, however, and on our way back to where we were staying, I soon needed to stop the car and I vomited violently over the Gower cliffs. I wrote to Gwen to thank her for the meeting and told her what had happened after leaving her, and whether or not my foolish honesty played any part in it, a wonderful and enriching friendship began that has continued till today.

Six or seven years after first meeting Gwen, she suggested that I write Vernon Watkins's biography. "A biography!?" – I replied. I had wanted to write something about him but had never contemplated this. I did eventually, however, take up the challenge.

Vernon Watkins

From having known nothing about his life, but merely having been a lover of his poetry for its own sake, I began to discover almost all there was to know about him.

I learned of his daily work in the bank; of the transformative experience he had gone through aged 22; of his uncompromising devotion to poetry; of his family life; of his athleticism and fitness; of his active and intimate connection with the landscape of Gower; and of his zany humour and absent-mindedness, leading the poet Hugo Williams to say of him at the end of his life: "Like Don Quixote, he was a cock-eyed optimist, lovable and rare."

Above all, though, I discovered that he had been, to an extent I could not have imagined, a significant and often inspiring presence amidst many of the greatest 20th Century poets in English. On account of his loving sensitivity to poetry of all kinds – ("he has … an ear for all music" said Dylan Thomas) – and his selfless encouragement of others, he had friendships with a remarkably wide range of poets. He had profound connections with both W.B. Yeats and T.S. Eliot. This is already unusual, though a few others, like Ezra Pound, also bridged the gap between these two opposite poetic giants of the early 20th Century. To this must be added, however, with Vernon Watkins, close friendships with Dylan Thomas *and* with Philip Larkin. *And* with the poet and painter David Jones and the painter Ceri Richards. In the latter part of his life he also had friendships with such diverse poets as W.H. Auden, R.S. Thomas, Kathleen Raine and Marianne Moore, among others.

The secret of what made this possible is perhaps to be found in those wide and generous ears, so visible in Alfred Janes's portrait of him, as well as in what he wrote to Philip Larkin, inviting him to stay: "Come down soon. *No competition here*, except for our one good chair." As well of course as simply in how he was, attested to by Michael Hamburger, who called him: "one of the most admirable and lovable men it has been my good fortune to know."

But unlike Crabb Robinson, the diarist who seemed to know every Romantic poet in Europe and yet was no poet himself, Vernon Watkins was a poet through and through, and his poetry, from the time of its first appearance until today, has received extraordinary praise. W.B. Yeats, three years before Watkins's first book was published, told him: "I am not quite certain that I always get your meaning, but I always find beauty." The usually reticent T.S. Eliot called one of his early poems: "a magnificent *tour de* force … it takes one's breath away." Dylan Thomas joked with him that he was: "the only other poet except me whose poetry I really like today". Stephen Spender referred to him as: "one of the most dedicated, admirable and scrupulous living poets". Marianne Moore addressed him in a poem: "O imagnifico,/ wizard in words." And after his death Kathleen Raine called him: "the greatest lyric poet of my generation."

Why so unknown?

So why has he remained so unknown?

There are three answers, at the very least, to this question.

The first has to do with how he lived his life and practised his art, and one cannot possibly wish for him to have done so any differently. They reveal Vernon Watkins's "unknownness", in fact, to be a positive rather than a negative. For he neither desired nor sought for fame or reputation. As he wrote in the title-poem of his last book: "For me neglect and world-wide fame were one." ('Fidelities') Or in an earlier poem:

> Let the world offer what it will,
> Its bargains I refuse;
> Those it rewards are greedy still,
> I serve a stricter Muse. ('Rewards of the Fountain')

He never wavered in relation to this.

One consequence, however, is that as two of his close friends were extremely famous and since that time have become even more so – Dylan Thomas and Philip Larkin – he has often been known for his supporting role in *their* lives and is usually assumed to have been a lesser poetic light around their greater ones, with these relationships hardly ever being viewed from his perspective. I am perhaps one of the few people, of whom there will, I imagine, be many more, who first developed a genuine interest in Dylan Thomas on learning that he had been a friend of Vernon Watkins.

The second answer also has to do with Vernon Watkins's relationship to his own art, though in this case one is, I believe, justified in wishing for this now to be corrected. For Vernon Watkins said very little about the background of his poetry and about the circumstances that gave rise to his poems. As he wrote: "*What matters is to get poems down. What matters is not to waste time on comment.*"

When one contemplates the enormous number of poems he wrote, each of which might go through up to fifty drafts, as well as all his other writing, which he managed on top of a full-time job in the bank and, in the last two decades of his life, with a large family in a very small house, it is easy to see how his prime need was "to get poems down". In approaching his poetry now, however, we are in a different situation.

It was not his task to describe the context out of which he wrote and nor did it matter much during his lifetime that he didn't do so. His readers were living through the same times that he was, he was known by the poets of his day, Faber brought out nine books of his poetry, which were widely reviewed – and thus there *was* a context in which his work could be recognized and received. Fifty years after his death that context has disappeared and we must rediscover it, at least to some degree, in order to recognize him as one of the major poets of his time.

This is *not* to say that great poetry should be reduced to the context of the poet's lifetime. Like all art that of Vernon Watkins must ultimately be able to speak to people beyond the life-circumstances that gave rise to it. But if these are completely unknown, his work may remain without context for many people, preventing them from finding their way to the true gifts of his poetry.

There *is*, in other words, a need for his biography to be written, which is the reason for attempting this book.

The third answer has been a considerable surprise and will, I think, surprise others too, who know Watkins's work. It is one of the main reasons for writing this biography in two volumes.

It had been known, previously, that Vernon Watkins had a transformative inner experience around the age of 23, after which he made a wholly new beginning. It was after this experience that he became the selfless mature poet who refused to "waste time on comment" or to concern himself with fame or reputation. As a result, almost his entire biography *before* this experience disappeared from view completely. This *caesura* in his life therefore led to less being known about Vernon Watkins than perhaps about any other poet of similar stature.

What had *not* been expected was how rich and fascinating that first untold part of his life was. It is too much to say that he had been sitting on a "bombshell", which we had known nothing about, yet his biography certainly looks dramatically different when we not only know what followed from his great crisis but also all that led up to it. His true poetry did indeed only begin after this watershed experience – but his journey towards that watershed is like a brief biography in itself of a young, ambitious, intensely fascinating Romantic poet we had never heard of. For all the immaturity of that early life, which he then so radically overcame, it is filled with the turbulent and passionate striving we are more used to finding in artists' biographies. We gain a far more comprehensive picture of his biography when we know this part of his life. By knowing the original direction of his poetic striving, we also gain a much clearer sense of what he achieved in his mature poetry and hence of his unique place in 20th Century poetry in English.

There were in fact two poets named Vernon Watkins, the first one ending with his transformational experience and the second one beginning from it. The first poet (who usually signed himself V.P. Watkins or Vernon P. Watkins) was quite different from the selfless, unassuming, spiritually mature poet he later became. Philip Larkin understandably expressed his amazement that Vernon Watkins burned as many as 2000 poems written by the first poet: "which meant nothing to me now". This is more than most poets write in their lifetime.

Luckily, however, whether on purpose or through incompetence, Vernon Watkins failed to destroy all his early poetry, and enough of it has survived to be able to tell the tale of the birth, growth and demise of that first poet. This first volume of his biography tells the whole of this story – then describes his transformational experience itself and the changes this led to in his life and in his poetry, and ends with Vernon Watkins fully established as the mature second poet he became, with the publication of his first book, aged 35.

Poetry and biography

There has, for all this, been a particular challenge in writing Vernon Watkins's biography, because of the kind of poet he was, which he could hardly have expressed more forthrightly: *"Do not look for a poet's raison d'être in his biography, for you are bound to be baffled."* Some artists' lives lend themselves easily to biography and some do not, and Vernon Watkins's life was undeniably of the latter variety. Andrew Motion threw down a gauntlet in relation to this, in a review of Vernon Watkins's *Collected Poems*, by claiming that his biography would be impossible to write: "One way of redeeming Watkins from neglect would be to socialize the work by showing how it related to the life ... But in the sense that biographers use the phrase, Watkins didn't have much of a life."

About his friend David Jones, however, Vernon Watkins made a very different kind of statement: *"The history of one man's experience, if intensely recorded, contains the history of the race.*" The words might equally well have been written about himself. For the "history" of Vernon Watkins's "experience", of all he underwent and witnessed in his life, was "intensely recorded" by him in the greatest detail. The place where he did so was *in his poetry.* Even in this first volume, therefore, it has been necessary to go to Watkins's poems as primary documents with regard to all he lived through and experienced. This could be said to make the book more of an inner than an outer biography, but what makes an artist's life different from that, say, of an explorer or political leader, is precisely in the intensity of their inner experience. This is certainly the case with Vernon Watkins.

It is essential to state, however, that *none* of the poems quoted in the first six chapters of this book were seen by Vernon Watkins as belonging to his mature poetry. He saw them as unfit to publish and never chose to do so. He did publish some of the poems quoted in the last four chapters, but even these belong to his earliest work.

Readers new to his work, therefore, who are interested to read more of his poetry, are recommended to look at *New Selected Poems of Vernon Watkins* (Carcanet, 2006), which has a detailed introduction and notes to many of his poems, and/or at the *Collected Poems of Vernon Watkins* (Golgonooza, 1986) which contains all ten of his published books of poetry.

"Fifty years or a hundred"

Soon after being asked to write this book, in 2000, someone advised me to get all the research done as soon as possible, even if it might be ten years or more before the book could actually be written. The words have proved almost disturbingly true.

A year later we moved to Gower for nine months and I completed much of the research for the book, but failed to interest a publisher. In 2006, for the hundredth anniversary of Vernon Watkins's birth, I edited *New Selected Poems of Vernon Watkins* for Carcanet. In 2017, for the 50th anniversary of his death, a publisher in Wales was happy to bring out a biography, but asked that it not be longer than 78,000 words. By the agreed deadline I had only completed half of Vernon Watkins's life but had already reached the set word-limit, at which the publisher agreed, in principle, to publishing the book in two parts – Part One in time for the anniversary, later to be followed by Part Two.

Sadly we then met a hitch. The publisher wanted me to provide far greater detail on the Welsh environment and context Watkins had grown up in, so that it could be seen how this had shaped him and his poetry. Such an amount of extra detail, as I saw it, would greatly have narrowed the interest of the book. The poetry of Vernon Watkins, like the work of any great artist, is able to speak in a way that reaches far beyond the particular circumstances in which they grew up. Wonderful though it is that in the places where Watkins lived in Wales there is considerable interest in him as a local poet, I see it as ultimately more important that his poetry, like all great poetry, may be read and enjoyed by all who can respond to it, wherever they may be from. I did not wish, therefore, to include all the accidental details of Watkins's life, *because they happened*, but only to include them if they added something to our understanding of either Vernon Watkins, his poetry, or of the circumstances or people around him. I was, as a result, unwilling to make the requested additions, and the publisher was unwilling to publish the book unless I did so. The 50th anniversary of Watkins's death therefore passed without the book being published.

My wish to address a wider audience may be said to have prevented the book being published in the only place where there was a genuine, pre-existing interest in it. Perhaps. I have not changed my views on this, however. But what certainly is unfortunate is that during the time I was under contract I was only able to complete Part One, and since then I have found neither the time nor the funding needed to write Part Two. I am nevertheless delighted that *An Exact Mystery – Part One* is now being published, and hope it may somehow help bring about the writing of Part Two, which would cover the last 26 years of Watkins's life, during which his life and poetry had their true flowering and bore their greatest fruit.

The present volume can also well stand on its own, having an important, untold story to tell. A biography of Vernon Watkins is long overdue, and this is the case in a special way with regard to the time-period covered in this first part – his early life and his most formative years, both experientially and poetically, leading up to the publication of his first book in 1941, aged 35. About these early years and experiences next to nothing has been written in any detail, and the book, I hope, may therefore help provide a context for Vernon Watkins's poetry which has not previously existed.

It is now 52 years since Vernon Watkins's death on a tennis court in Seattle, on October 8th 1967. It seems scarcely credible that Gwen Watkins, who was with him in Seattle, with three of their five children, the oldest two having long since left school, is still here with us and has been able to grace this book with her foreword. She is a warm, wise, life-filled and life-giving human being, who has written several books of her own, as well as helping constantly, over five decades, in all manner of ways, with bringing forward Vernon Watkins's life and work. She has been extremely generous with me – as when we once, over several weeks, went through every one of Watkins's 350+ *Collected Poems* together, with her telling me all she knew of the biographical circumstances behind them. She has also been a wonderful friend and for her sake I greatly wish I had finished this whole biography many years ago. As for Vernon Watkins, happily, I'm not so sure he would have minded, never having had much time for literary biographies, always being more concerned with the true manifestation of an artist's genius, their art – or in his case his poetry – and in relation to this he appears to have had infinite patience:

"a poet … mustn't really mind if even fifty years or a hundred go by before his work is felt by people exactly attuned to it, because that's happened to very great poets in the past."

Richard Ramsbotham
January, 2020

CHAPTER ONE

Birth and Early Years (1906–1920)

When I was born on Amman hill
A dark bird crossed the sun.

('The Collier')

On the morning of June 27th, 1906, the day when Vernon Phillips Watkins was born in Maesteg, Glamorgan, the whole of South Wales was shaken by one of the strongest earthquakes in its history. The tremors were felt as far off as Bristol, Birmingham and Liverpool. The South Wales Daily Post reported:

"At Bridgend people walking in the street were nearly thrown off their feet ... At Mumbles people, frightened out of their wits, rushed into the streets and began to wander about as though they were almost beside themselves ... All the bells of Carmarthen Prison were set ringing by the earth heaving ... A heap of boulders in the centre of Ammanford 'became as if alive and rolled about in extraordinary fashion.' ... At Dowlais, 1,500 miners stopped work after the shock." It added: "An awful possibility is opened up should a really violent shock occur in South Wales, with the enormous number of men employed underground, who would be entombed alive by a great upheaval."[1]

As for Maesteg itself, 12 miles from the earthquake's epicentre offshore from Swansea[2]: "A rumbling noise and a distinct tremor was Maesteg's experience ... an old lady of 96 and the little daughter of Mr. Beynon ... were thrown out of bed." In Lloyds Bank House, Talbot Street, where the one soon to be named Vernon Watkins was entering the world, his mother recalled how "the windows and the crockery rattled".

The Cambria Daily Leader – on the day of Vernon Watkins's birth

> O why was I born of two?
> Why had I not one
> To feed me, to dress me,
> The moon or the sun? ('Ballad of the Gravestone')

Vernon Watkins's parents, William and Sarah, had come from two very different worlds and cultural climates about 40 miles to the East and West of Swansea, respectively. William Watkins had grown up in difficult family circumstances in the harsh, mining, Welsh-speaking environment around the ancient site of the Garth Hill, near Cardiff. Sarah (Sally) Watkins, née Phillips, had grown up in the gentler landscape of Carmarthenshire on a 144 acre farm, with several servants, into a world enjoying literature, culture and a certain cosmopolitan scope.

The Garth

The Garth – on whose slopes stand the interlinked villages of Pentyrch, Gwaelod-y-Garth and Taff's Well – has played a central role in the landscape around Cardiff since at least 2000 BC, the date usually given for the several ancient tumuli – or burial mounds – on its top.

BIRTH AND EARLY YEARS (1906–1920)

The Garth Hill could be said to contain in miniature the whole history of Wales. Around 500 AD the Celtic Saint Catwg (Cadoc) "the wise and the good" is said to have founded a church and village around a healing well in Pentyrch. Despite the invasions that followed – from the Romans, the Normans and the English – a native Welsh stream has continued to run here. Even when the English language filled the underlying valley the Garth's villages remained strongly Welsh-speaking. Ancient Welsh customs and rituals such as that of the "Mari Lwyd" (the ribboned skull of a white horse), which was carried from house to house on New Year's Eve, survived undisturbed here until the 1940s, when Vernon Watkins himself would link onto it and give it a resonance far beyond the places and times of its origins, in the title-poem of his first book – the '*Ballad of the Mari Lwyd*'.

> *Mari Lwyd, Lwyd Mari,*
> *A sacred thing through the night they carry.*

Iron ore had already been mined from the Garth's slopes in Roman times, but in the Industrial Revolution of the 18th and 19th Centuries it was extracted on a massive scale. The Iron Works at Pentyrch were initially developed in order to supply the tinplate works nearby. Thomas Watkins (Tomos o'r Lan) – Vernon's great grandfather – had been a farmer in Llantwit Vardre, not far from Pentyrch. His son Evan Watkins

Pentyrch Iron Works and the Garth (1905)

(1833-1895), Vernon's grandfather, joined the Iron Industry and was the Furnace Manager at the Pentyrch Iron Works during its difficult final decade between 1875 and 1885. In December 1875, a terrible explosion in the coalmine next-door at Gwaelod-y-Garth had killed 16 miners. In 1879, iron ore production having drastically decreased,[3] the Iron Works went into liquidation; the Iron Mine was abandoned in 1884; and in 1885 the last of the smelting furnaces managed by Evan Watkins was put out.

Evan Watkins's family life – in his house Ty Newydd at Pentrych – was almost equally difficult. His wife Sarah (née Richards) bore him 11 children (5 boys and 6 girls) in 18 years.[4] Her first daughter Catherine died as a baby. Her second daughter Mary died in 1882 aged 17. A year later, she died herself, aged 46. Evan Watkins married again – to Catherine (née Evans) – but the challenge of looking after Evan and his 7 youngest children (between 6 and 16 years-old), in the house that had clearly known happier days, took its toll and she is reported to have turned increasingly to alcohol. Evan remained closely involved in the local community and was a deacon of the Gwaelodygarth Congregational Church.[5] In 1895, 12 years after his wife Sarah died and 10 years after the Iron Furnace closed, Evan Watkins died aged 62.

Vernon's father, William Watkins, born in 1872, was Evan and Sarah's 8th child and the 4th son. William had been 10 when his mother died and, his oldest two brothers having emigrated to America, he soon took on responsibility for providing for his six remaining brothers and sisters, which became a necessity after his father died. William gave up his hopes to study law and as soon as he left school, aged 17, in June 1890, he made the short journey to Cardiff and found employment as a clerk in Brecon Old Bank, which Lloyds Bank soon took over. He was quiet and hardworking, but was also: "a man of judgement and great intellect."[6] His abilities and his "tremendous power of mind" were soon noticed and he rose swiftly, becoming Manager in Bridgend in 1902, aged 29, purportedly the youngest Manager anywhere in Lloyds Bank at the time. On a visit to Carmarthen, he met and fell in love with Vernon's mother-to-be, Sarah (Sally) Phillips, five years his younger.

BIRTH AND EARLY YEARS (1906-1920)

Llangynog

She had been born and brought up at Cowin Grove Farm, Llangynog, Carmarthenshire, in the landscape sung of in idyllic terms by Dylan Thomas in 'Fern Hill', a farm just three miles from Cowin Grove.[7] Sally, with her one sibling, her older sister Mary, enjoyed a happy and privileged upbringing there[8], until when she was 13 her mother Esther, widely loved in the area, had died aged 45. Her father, James Phillips, the only grandparent Vernon would ever know, then retired from farming and moved with his daughters in 1891 to a comfortable town house overlooking the countryside, "Llywn Onn" in Penllwyn Park, Carmarthen. A warm-hearted and devout Welsh-speaking man, who is said to have known large parts of the Welsh Bible by heart, he exchanged farming for religion and become a lay Congregationalist Minister. Sarah went to the Girl's Congregational School in Carmarthen and, with a gift for languages and literature had been sent, aged 18, as a student-teacher to a school in the Regensbürg Mountains in Germany for 2 years.[9] This clearly gave her a wider outlook than many of her age in Wales at the time, and on top of her privileged upbringing and an innate feisty self-assurance, made her not only into a slightly formidable presence but also into someone with far-reaching ambitions, both for herself and later for her children.

Two different worlds were therefore brought together in William and Sarah, and the marriage between them, which took place on 30th April, 1902 in Carmarthen, was to be a happy one. Their first child, Marjorie, was born in 1903, in Bridgend. Not long afterwards William was sent to the coalmining town of Maesteg to open a new branch of Lloyds Bank. There, in their unimaginatively named house, Lloyds Bank House, Talbot Street, on June 27th, 1906, accompanied by the earthquake, their second child, Vernon (Phillips Watkins) was born.

Earliest experiences and memories

Inspired, as far as he could be, by his own experience, Vernon Watkins would write about the earliest months and years of childhood:

"Gifted with fiery enthusiasm and perceptions of boundless wonder, we run naked until aged ignorance, as in Blake's engraving, clips our wings. We have all the greedy vices in miniature, but we forgive quickly and are forgiven, and the kingdom of heaven is ours.

While we are children we are not at all concerned with ourselves; we simply *are* … The sun and trees, grass and flowers, birds and beasts, insects and fishes, are seen … by the first wonder, which accepts them as gifts. Their presence is immediate … When children reflect, they become involved in a deeper myster than thought could possibly unravel or truly penetrate, so much more does their unconscious mind know than they do."[10]

The world he drank in unconsciously during his first three years was that of inland South Wales – first the coalmining hills around Maesteg and then Bridgend, where his younger sister Dorothy was born in 1909 in their house "Quarella", Vernon's home between the ages of 2 and 5, not far from the places of his father's upbringing on the Garth Hill and its deep veins not only of metal ore but also of Welsh life and ancient culture.

Like the Welsh language, which "from the first I was accustomed to hear"[11], but which he could not speak, this whole world would lie outside the reach of his conscious mind and memory, yet nonetheless lay deeply within him and would be intuitively accessible. Speaking of the "finest early poetry in Britain", that of Aneurin, Taliesin and Llywarch Hen, which he could not read in Welsh, he would say: "I feel the affinity with these poets which does not come from study, or history, but from instinct. Their roots go very deep."[12] Of his own poetry he would say: "my verse is characteristically Welsh in the same way that the verse of Yeats is characteristically Irish … because rhythm and cadence are born in the blood."[13] And it is certainly telling that the opening poem of his first book casts himself as 'The Collier', is set in the inland hills of Wales where he was born, and concerns a fatal mining disaster:

> *I heard mouths pray in the after-damp,*
> *When the picks would not break through.*

His first book's second poem depicts the life of a 'Pit-Boy', and the book's title-poem *The Ballad of the Mari Lwyd* was inspired by what rose up in him, intuitively, on hearing from his father's home village the ancient New Year's ritual of the 'Mari Lwyd'.

It is perhaps too early to be talking of the poetry the very small boy would one day write. Yet looking back years later Vernon Watkins once attempted to recall the origins of his work:

"I must try to think back to the very beginning, to my first idea of writing poetry at all. I find this very difficult. I cannot remember a time when I did not mean to write poetry ... I am fairly confident that the ultimate need of poetry is either there or not there, from the first."[14]

Vernon Watkins with a tennis racket, c. 1910

When Vernon was 3, in 1909 or 1910, the family moved to the other side (Sarah's side) of Swansea – to Llanelli[15] – where Sarah and the children would often visit her father, James Phillips, in his house "Goleufryn" at 8, Picton Terrace, Carmarthen. From these visits, among other things, Vernon would recall hearing "the faint leavening music of first Welsh words".[16] In 1912, when Vernon was 6, the family arrived at the final goal of their wanderings, Swansea. William Watkins, aged 40, became Manager of the main Wind Street branch of Lloyds Bank and the family lived at 5, Eaton Grove, in the Uplands area of the town.

The move coincided with the shift in Vernon from his first unconscious experiences to his first awakenings of consciousness and his first memories:

"In childhood, especially, we cannot choose the moments we afterwards remember ... a hundred thousand moments of transience are recorded in minute detail, moments that we might today dismiss as unimportant, but they remain ineffaceable … Why, if I close my eyes, do I find myself breaking a stem off a tall privet-hedge in Eaton Crescent and hearing the noise of a hoop and heels clattering? Yet any one picture, if it could be seen completely, would restore an entire world."[17]

Even in Swansea Vernon continued to encounter the sufferings of the coal-mining world of his earliest years. In the streets, aged 7 or 8, he was startled by the sight of a "soot-grimed man" yelling "Coal, Coal!" The coalseller's face would not leave him alone and so, having been sent to buy flowers, he kept seeing "through the glistening petals his red mouth calling 'Coal'", and the image stayed with him throughout the day.[18] Another of his indelible memories, says Gwen Watkins, was of a horse's pain, being harshly thrashed by a collier to the ground.

Young children, wrote Watkins, live in a world quite foreign to adults, though they can be "won over at any time by favour and love. When we are not won over, when we are left to our own devices, we enter a jungle of fear and illusion, delight and savagery."[19] This is true, Vernon reckoned, of every child. His younger sister Dorothy, who slept in the same room as him in Eaton Grove, indeed recalled: "only his heightened imagination and sensitivity marked him out from any other small boy of his age."[20] At night, she says, "Vernon would call up various imaginary characters, giving a different voice and accent to each, all of whom became quite real to me; I would listen spell-bound." He was able to read, she says, "well before the age of five" and tells that "the first and greatest influence on Vernon as a little boy were the stories of King Arthur and the Knights of the Round Table", which they "enacted endlessly" and that among their favourite books were *The Adventures of Prince Prigio* and *The Pied Piper of Hamelyn*, "which we soon knew by heart."

"I wrote poetry continuously from the age of about seven"

Vernon Watkins began writing poetry aged seven or eight – in 1913 or 1914. Coincidentally this was exactly at the time when, less than a mile from where the young boy was living with his parents, the baby was born (in October 1914) who would become the poet Dylan Thomas.

Both Dylan Thomas and Vernon Watkins belonged to the generation in Wales whose parents were Welsh-speaking but were brought up speaking English. A friend of both Thomas and Watkins, the writer John Prichard, described the mysterious effect of this:
"it is a strange experience to grow up in almost total ignorance of the language one has been accustomed to hear at home and in the streets, one's native language. And it is an experience which possibly tends to develop a peculiar sensitivity to language ... Having been denied our native tongue, the only form of revenge we can take is to turn the other cheek, as the Irish have done, and try to write English better than the English ... the Welsh language's loss may be English literature's gain."[21]

Vernon Watkins also alluded to the connection between the loss of his native language and a heightened sensitivity to the music of the English language: "From the first I was accustomed to hear the Welsh language (from) my parents ... Instead of becoming bilingual, as my parents were, I grew up under the spell of the English poets, who began to influence me when I was six or seven years old."[22]

Incredibly young as this may have been, "there was nothing really precocious about this",[23] and it might rather be said that he retained his early childhood for longer than is usual. He makes this clear in an autobiographical story, where he characterizes his six year-old relationship to the "English poets":

"He could remember even at six years' old hearing someone say that Milton was a very great poet. Then, when he saw his name lettered on a book, it seemed to him to shine like starlight, and with a wonderful, unaltering appearance. But when, one day, he heard someone say that Shakespeare was even greater than Milton, this name when he saw it for the first time appeared more dazzling still, and Milton's now seemed to have a borrowed light."[24]

There is no doubt, however, of the significance for the young boy of these first experiences of poetry and his sister records:

"my mother recalled with regret that when Vernon announced at the age of five that he intended to be a poet, she had laughed. Vernon flushed and turned away. Nothing ever made him change his mind or determination to reach this goal." (True as this was of Vernon's determination, even as a boy, this probably only took place when he was seven or eight and had begun to write poetry.)

Schooldays and the outbreak of the First World War

In September 1913 he was sent to school for the first time, with his younger sister Dorothy, to St. Anne's Kindergarten and Preparatory School at 8, Gwydr Terrace, very near where they lived. This did nothing, as yet, to remove him from the dreamy world of childhood – a classmate recalls how he loved his nature walks: "over Town Hill ... where we picked armfuls of purple vetch" or "higher, to the quarry where we caught tadpoles".[25]

At the moment of the outbreak of the First World War, in August 1914, the family, seemingly in complete unawareness of world events, had gone on holiday to Parame in Brittany, and had been forced, when war broke out, to catch one of the last passenger boats back to Britain. His sister recalled: "I remember before we left St. Malo seeing the first French volunteers marching through the streets to the wild cheering of a not too sober crowd." They saw the famous 'conqueror of Tibet', Sir Francis Younghusband, waiting on the quay, who their father pointed out to them. William Watkins, either before or after this encounter, had read to his children "the story of the 'Stolen Dalai Lama', which printed indelibly on our young minds the mysterious magic of Tibet." Thus Dorothy recalls how she and Vernon "gazed with reverence at the first European to have set foot in the city of Lhasa." The stories of Tibet, the Dalai Llama and the legendary city of Shangri-La certainly worked strongly on Vernon's imagination, so much so that years later he would say that: "walking in Swansea gives me the excitement of walking in a forbidden city", adding that he found Swansea "more extraordinary even than Tibet, which was my favourite country when I was a small boy."[26]

The war also brought many Belgian refugees to Swansea[27], and Vernon's mother busied herself very much on their behalf. A large benefit concert was organized at Swansea's Albert Hall[28], which included "a children's tableau representing the allies." Vernon was obliged by his mother to wear a kilt and "dance some sort of Scottish reel" to represent Scotland.[29] Artificial displays, let alone with any element of propaganda, would always be foreign to him and, comically, he came out on stage at the wrong moment, when India was being represented, and danced "his ... jig to the mournful strains of an Indian dirge"[30]. He was, says his sister, "constantly left with one foot in the air, waiting for the next beat. He never forgot the experience and used to say that it put him off dancing for life."[31]

Meanwhile, at school, it was clear that he stood out from his fellow-pupils in his approach to his learning. He was, said one of them: "somewhat untidy, socks wrinkled and inky fingered, but rather grown up in his deep voice and choice of words. As the only student of Latin, he often sat apart at a small table, deeply concentrating and becoming more and more inky-fingered."[32]

On the one hand being obliged to live within strict parameters at home and at school, he was, on the other, with his mother involved "in all the local war efforts", given plenty of time to himself. He later wrote of his "loitering as a child/ In paving square and field"[33] and of his being "long left with a coin to be good."[34] His sister told how they would "cycle freely through the town and into the wild, beautiful peninsula of Gower".

In these years at the beginning of World War One, aged 8 or 9, in the Uplands of Swansea, he loitered and played in the same places that Dylan Thomas, a baby living a few streets away, would later make famous. He played in Cwmdonkin Park[35]; he was part of the "mob of children ... with collars torn and scattered ties"[36] that "swarmed" every Saturday over the brass railings of the Uplands Cinema, called by Dylan Thomas the "Itch-pit".

In a poem written as an adult, at the outbreak of World War Two, Watkins recalled the experience of himself and others, as children, influenced by and yet unconscious of the horrors of the war that, in Wilfred Owen's words, was killing "half the seed of Europe, one by one." The poem is dedicated to the actress Pearl White, the heroine of most of the heart-stopping adventure-films they watched: "It was wartime, and in our mock street wars she became the centre of many fights and struggles." Speaking of the children sucking liquorice with "round terrified eyes" he writes: "You glittered where the tongue was curled/Around the sweet fear of the world." And again: "From penny rows, when we began to spell,/ We watched you, at the time when Arras fell."[37]

Vernon's own fears, he said, were never merely confined to the "thumbscrewed terrors" within the film, but always also extended to the actress portraying them, believing that her life too was at stake: "I was even more concerned than the rest, as I was more credulous. So, when we all rushed in … I could not for a moment forget Pearl White, who risked her life in the making of the film."[38]

Meanwhile the reading and the writing of poetry took greater and greater hold of him. He was "already writing poems when I was seven or eight", as we have heard, "and between that age and twelve I bought the great English poets one by one"[39]. And so: "by the time I was twelve I had most of the great poets and read them with undiscriminating enthusiasm."[40]

At ten years-old Vernon's foretaste of the world soon to be inhabited by Dylan Thomas continued, when he was sent to the Swansea Grammar School, where Thomas would also go to school and where his father, D.J. Thomas, was already a teacher. Vernon's memories of it were bound up with his relationship to poetry at the time: "I came to the old Swansea Grammar School as a pupil when I was ten. I was already writing poetry and deeply absorbed in it. With pocket money and money from presents I was gradually collecting all the great English poets in beautiful editions." He would give these books as presents to his family, and they "seemed to me … the most precious gifts one could give." "Beautifully bound" as they were, "in leather or suede"[41], their real treasure, of course, was not their covers, nor their narrative content, but *words* and their *music*:

"Words in *cadenced* form, whether in rhyme or not, seemed to have an unrivalled power over the imagination."[42] He was thus, he says, over and over again: "moved to inexplicable tears by a pattern of words which seemed to me unforgettable". And thus: "the hold which poetry had on my sensibility increased, and hardly ever relaxed its grip."[43]

Tyttenhanger Lodge
"the most boring poem on earth"

Vernon Watkins in Tyttenhanger Lodge uniform – aged 11 or 12

In January 1913, aged 11, Vernon's gifts and intelligence, his mother's ambitions and his father's means, all combined to take Vernon for the rest of his education away from Wales and the bay of Swansea and into the traditional world of private English education – "the best education money could buy", for those who could afford it. He was sent as a boarder to Tyttenhanger Lodge preparatory school at Seaford, near Eastbourne, on the South Coast.

Tyttenhanger Lodge School originated near St. Albans, in Tyttenhanger House, which has a history associated with Henry VIII, Cardinal Wolsey and the family of Sir Francis Bacon.[44] George Barker (1913-1991) a poet contemporary with Watkins, later sent his son to Tyttenhanger, who described his arrival at this "large Victorian mausoleum ... set in twenty acres of playing fields ... I was in awe as we clambered off the bus from the station. This was a *school*?" Barker was immediately beaten for the wildness of his behaviour on his journey to the school, which had been reported, after which the Headmaster told him: "I hope that has taught you a lesson about the codes of behaviour we at the Lodge expect of our pupils."[45] Vernon had been at the school 35 years earlier, when its "codes of behaviour" must have been even stricter, but Vernon, whose rebellion was always more of an inner one than an outer one, got by without complaint and even according to his sister, "always spoke of the school with great affection."

The school offered a strong focus on modern languages, daily "religious instruction", "swedish drill" and even "sea bathing (under strict supervision)". Vernon would have found no problem with these, but one thing was no doubt at the source of his good humour, his absorption in poetry, which continued to fill his days and nights and was the only thing he would refer to regarding the school. Not that he ever deluded himself about any precocious flair in his writing. The *length* of a poem was what was most important for him at the time:

"At the age of ten I looked at long poems with admiration. It was the longest that I admired most. When I went to a preparatory school on the South Coast I took with me a large notebook. I began writing in it an epic which was intended to be a line longer than 'The Idylls of the King'. This was still unfinished when I left. If I had managed to finish it it would probably have been the most boring poem on earth."[46]

And again: "my ambition was so shallow that I usually identified the longest poem as the greatest; and at my preparatory school I counted every night the lines of the Arthurian epic I was writing."[47]

His sister described how she missed Vernon terribly when he was sent away. Vernon never described any such feelings, but as Tennyson's *Idylls of the King* were not only based on Welsh Arthurian tales but were even written in Wales, perhaps Vernon's nightly labours over with his "Arthurian epic" were his own particular way of dealing with his homesickness.[48]

The main task the school set itself was to prepare its pupils "to take their place in Public School life" – and in July 1920, aged 14, Vernon passed his entrance exams into Repton College, which he would attend in September.

CHAPTER TWO

Repton (1920–1924)

*"The Chronicles of
The Unconventionals at Repton"*

The village of Repton in Derbyshire, with Repton School in the middle of it, is the site of one of the earliest Christian centres in England. In consequence many a spiritual or cultural battle has been fought out there in English history.

Between the 7th and the 9th Centuries A.D. Repton (Hrepandum) was one of the main homes of the Kings of Mercia. Mercia first welcomed Christianity in 653 A.D. when a Mercian Prince married a princess of Christian Northumbria, who arrived in Hrepandum with four monks from Lindisfarne. Seven years later, in 660, Repton Abbey was founded. A stone pillar outside Repton School marks the place where Christianity was preached for the first time in this whole region of England. Having become an important place of pilgrimage, Repton was sacked by the Danes in the 9th Century. Christianity reasserted itself, however, and in the 12th Century an Augustinian Priory was built there. During the dissolution of the monasteries this Priory was sold to Sir Thomas Cromwell's steward, whose son, Gilbert Thacker, systematically demolished the Priory to ensure that Christian life would not reawaken there. His aim, he said, was to "destroy the nest, for fear the birds should build there again." In 1557, in one of the only buildings of the Priory that remained, Repton School was founded.

As with some of the other earliest Christian places in Britain, such as Iona, Glastonbury or Winchester, one still feels the influence in the fields around Repton of an older Christianity, one that still lived in a mutually transformative relationship with the natural world and the surrounding landscape. At the same time the far more mercenary and utilitarian direction represented by Sir Thomas Cromwell and Gilbert Thacker, which has stood behind Britain's striving for power in the world and has too often spilled over into its cultural life, has, more often than not, dominated the running of the traditional English "Public School", Repton School.

The battle between these two elements had still sporadically flared up at Repton until just before Vernon Watkins went there as a pupil in 1920, and, sensitive as he was, he would be powerfully affected by both of them.

Elephants in the birdcage
"A positive outbreak of 'education'"

In the years of World War One, immediately prior to Watkins's arrival at the school, there had been something like an educational revolution at the school, which went so far that the War Office eventually intervened and put a stop to it, to prevent any further growth among Repton schoolboys of politically free-thinking and even anti-war feelings.

A history teacher at the school – David Somervell – gave a first-hand account of this revolution. Repton School, in its scope of vision and the freedom of thought it inspired in its pupils, was, as he put it, "a birdcage".[1] Twice, however, the school had employed individuals of far greater stature – "elephants" – who had done all they could to burst open the bars of the cage.

The first had been William Temple, a man with a profound and far-reaching spiritual outlook, who had been headmaster of Repton between 1910 and 1914 and had gone on to become Archbishop of Canterbury. Temple had declared from the outset that he would approach the task of headmaster as a "revolutionary", but, says Somervell, though Temple made many of the boys "think about religion and God as they would never otherwise have done … there was no revolution." In 1914, with the outbreak of World War One, and with the school determined to reassert a more conventional stance, Temple was replaced as headmaster by the far stricter Geoffrey Fisher, Churchman and Freemason[2], who would be Vernon Watkins's headmaster. Fisher, like Temple, would also later become Archbishop of Canterbury. In his early years as headmaster, however, Fisher happened to employ the school's second 'elephant', the cultural and political thinker and writer

Victor Gollancz, whose influence on the school was far more radical than William Temple's had been, for Gollancz: "approach(ed) everything as a revolutionary."[3]

Somervell said about the two 'elephants', Temple and Gollancz: "Both were, by Repton standards, giants ... Both were God-intoxicated men ... Both ... (had) an idealistic socialism of their own which was all mixed up with their religious beliefs ... Both adored Plato, Shelley, Blake and Beethoven. Both were spiritual beings encased in delightfully homely exteriors ... Thus they were both of them extraordinarily attractive to boys."[4]

Even though Watkins arrived at the school two years later, he still somehow managed delightedly to drink in there precisely such artistic, religious, "God-intoxicated" idealism, inspired by Plato, Shelley and Blake, yet clothed in homely dress.

As Watkins later on saw Geoffrey Fisher, his headmaster, as the greatest enemy of such idealism, the character of what William Temple and Victor Gollancz brought to the school, as well as the character of all that fought against them, represented primarily by Fisher, provide important clues to the world Watkins now stepped into at Repton.

Gollancz, from the first, had been appalled by Fisher's educational views. Fisher had reprimanded Gollancz for not maintaining the correct distance between teachers and pupils, telling him: "there are two distinct classes: the teachers and the taught." Gollancz wrote about this: "how insensitive, how arrogant, how mechanical ... For in true education there are no teachers and taught. There is an interchange: the master learns as he teaches, the pupil teaches as he learns. Both give, and both receive ... and transform one another."[5]

In a letter to a friend, Gollancz was even more forthright about his differences with Fisher:

"Fisher has come forward with an amazing accusation that I had influenced ... a boy to conceive doubts of the Divinity of Christ! An amazing accusation, without a thread of truth in it (except, perhaps, in so far as I had made the boy *think*) which I made the nasty little man withdraw.

... I found his mind tiny & cold, & his views on education deplorable

… But the boys are a joy – & I'm not going to allow any miserable little pedantic parson of a schoolmaster to make me alter my attitude towards them."[6]

Yet this was merely the beginning. For as Gollancz himself recollected: "without reflecting on consequences, I took my decision. I would talk politics to these boys … day in and day out." And "politics", for Gollancz, "included philosophy, religion and morality."[7] One example of this, therefore, that he discussed openly with the boys was that "he had not believed the Germans to be solely responsible for the outbreak of the war. Most of the blame lay with the 'personal egotism and greed' of all humanity."[8]

Another teacher at the school expressed the British-centred attitude to the war he expected from masters at Repton: "it's our solemn duty to instil into the boys such a hatred of the Hun (the Germans) that for the rest of their lives they'll never speak to one again".[9] Gollancz's Christian socialism stood in radical opposition to this, as he stated to *The Times:* "all my instincts, (are) offended by a hatred of any race whatever – be they Jews or Indians, or even fellow-countrymen of Goethe and Wagner … no one detests Jewish legalism and Prussian imperialism more than I; but towards Jews and Germans let our attitude be a little more consonant with that ideal of brotherly love which is one of the sublimest conceptions of (our) faith."[10]

Gollancz was hugely popular among the boys that he taught and there was great interest in his views about the war. This was hardly surprising, as "the average expectation of life of a subaltern on the Western Front was supposed to be three weeks."[11] Over 350 young ex-Reptonians would be killed in the war. In the words of one Repton boy: "the older you get, the nearer comes the time when you'll have to go over the top and get a bellyful of shrapnel. People don't complain about this, it's taken for granted, but it does make life rather depressing."[12] There was a vast turnout, therefore, when pupils influenced by Gollancz proposed to the School Debating Society a motion about everyone's absolute right to be a Conscientious Objector.[13] The conservatively-minded at the school were incensed, declaring it: "a disgrace to Repton that the motion had been permitted at all".

The last straw came when at the end of the war the Gollancz-inspired alternative Repton magazine, *A Public School Looks at the World*,[14] condemned the Treaty of Versailles and the Prime Minister Lloyd George's part in it and when the magazine, furthermore, was brought out not only in Repton but also in London.[15] The War Office, who had had "a file on Repton ... building up ... for a considerable period", intervened and Fisher removed Gollancz from the school.

Somervell concluded: "Both Temple and Gollancz left an awful mess behind them. Put the elephant in a birdcage and what can you expect?" After they left, said Somervell: "Repton relapsed into the useful insignificance from which it had momentarily emerged. But ... there had been in both episodes a positive outbreak of 'education.'"[16] As we have intimated, however, even two years later when Vernon Watkins went to the school, 'education' was still sometimes capable of breaking out.

First years at Repton

Vernon Watkins was among a fairly remarkable group of pupils arriving at Repton soon after the end of World War One. Seven of these, including Watkins, went on from Repton to Cambridge University. All the central concerns of Watkins's life – literature, Christianity, the desire for human and social transformation and even tennis – shine out from their respective achievements. They were: the writer Christopher Isherwood (b.1904), in the same house as Watkins, though two years older; Isherwood's closest friend at Repton and fellow-writer, Edward Upward (b.1903); Charles Smyth (b.1903), later an outstanding historian of early Christianity, who was also in Watkins's house when he arrived; Michael Ramsey (b.1904), who later became Archbishop of Canterbury[17]; Bunny Austin (b.1906), who would become England's greatest tennis player, but who also bore within him in some way, as did all these individuals, the legacy of William Temple and Victor Gollancz, for he was ostracised by Wimbledon for his Christian pacifism during World War Two; Arnold Cooke (b.1906), the modest but brilliant classical composer; and Vernon Watkins (b.1906).

Nevertheless, English Public Schools in the 1920s, and for decades afterwards, were harsh and brutal places for any remotely sensitive boy arriving at the school. Quite apart from the frequent bullying, the "fagging" system itself, in these models of gentlemanly civilization, had something barbaric about it. The writer Roald Dahl, who attended Repton ten years after Watkins, gave a vivid portrayal of it:

"The rules and rituals of fagging at Repton were so complicated that I could fill a whole book with them ... I spent two long years as a Fag ... Prefects were called Boazers, and they had the power of life and death over us junior boys. They could summon us down in our pyjamas at night-time and thrash us for leaving just one football sock on the floor of the changing-room when it should have been hung up on a peg. A Boazer could thrash us for a hundred and one other piddling little misdemeanours – for burning his toast at tea-time, for failing to dust his study properly, ... for being late at a roll call, for talking in evening Prep ... The list was endless."[18]

Vernon Watkins was subjected to this and was also "like all juniors ... seriously bullied".[19] An immediate effect of this was that for the only time in his life, between the age of 7 or 8 and his death, he stopped writing poetry: "Only when I went to Repton did I stop my writing of poetry for a year."[20] (On another occasion he described this as lasting for 18 months.[21])

During this time Vernon Watkins excelled in his school work, coming top in his form and getting four successive distinction cards for languages, leading Fisher in his report to call him "a very meritorious & good boy" and to say after two years: "we are very pleased with him".[22] Watkins's diligence at his schoolwork was almost certainly, however, his way of compensating for the fact that the main wellspring of his life was currently blocked.

However, when Vernon was about 15½, the event occurred which unblocked it once again: "a lecture on Shelley by one of the masters brought back the irresistible impulse, and I wrote poems again."[23] The dam removed, his poetry burst out with unprecedented force: "I wrote nothing but verse between the ages of 16 and 22, until one or two every night. I was writing verse all the time."[24]

Nor was it just a question of the amount of poetry the teenage Watkins was now writing. Whereas previously he had been reading Browning, Wordsworth, Tennyson, Longfellow, and attempting to

The Watkins family, c.1920
Vernon William Marjorie
Sarah Dorothy
Vernon Watkins is probably 13 or 14, during his first year and a half at Repton

imitate the length of their poems, he was now, inspired by Shelley, launched into whole new realms of idealistic experience. For Shelley: "trod the hills of heaven – proud and free" and "with uplifted wings (...) soared through/ The clouded, blind mist of mortality".[25] Watkins later recalled how at Repton, beside the Trent River, he had often felt the presence of something greater than himself:

> And often by that stream
> I felt a secret power
> Making the passing hour
> A gift of small esteem.
> Verse could for me redeem
> What nature could devour. [26]

In one of his earliest surviving poems from Repton, he describes how one evening, watching the stars emerge, he had an experience of spiritual truth far beyond what the traditional world of the school could show him. The poem ends:

> *I forgot surplices and gown uncouth,*
> *And, for one blissful moment, saw the Truth.*[27]

As a mature poet Vernon Watkins would write: "A poet is born when his ambition is born. A metaphysical poet is born when his ambition dies." As a teenager at Repton, Watkins was now experiencing the first of those births. The poet in him, with the profound ambition to "be numbered among the English poets", was being born. His schoolwork, though still competent, inevitably took second place as he sat up writing poems till "one or two every night" in spontaneous outpourings of inspiration. "In my teens", he said:

> "I identified poetry as spontaneous genius pouring through the poet and requiring no effort from him ... I distrusted in composition what did not come rapidly ... I knew that 'Adonais' had been written in five days, and I saw inspiration as ... the original brilliance which could only be tarnished by the deliberating mind."[28]

What also became clear was that whatever the shock that had stopped him writing poetry during his first year or so at the school, the gap had also marked a definite transition between the innocence of his pre-pubescent days and the romantically-charged idealistic feelings of his adolescent self, into which he now awoke.

It is probably no accident that it was only after Christopher Isherwood left the school, at the end of 1922, that Watkins began to give full voice to his feelings there. Isherwood and Watkins saw a lot of each other, being in the same house, but were also worlds apart. The term after Isherwood left, at Easter 1923, one of Vernon Watkins's closest lifelong friends, Eric Falk (or 'Fig')[29], also left Repton. In Watkins's letters to Falk he gave candid reports of many of his experiences during his last four terms at the school.

Christopher Isherwood – aged 17
photograph by Eric Falk

"A craze for Rupert Brooke"

He signed his very first letter to Falk with a pseudonym – Chas. P. Bryant[30] – announcing, as it were, the departure of a previous personality. The next letter announced the appearance of a new star in his poetic firmament, who the 16 year-old Watkins idolized not just for his poetry, but also for what he could teach him about *life*. "A craze for Rupert Brooke", he told Falk, had been spreading through the school.[31] It is unlikely, however, that any of the boys identified with Brooke as completely as Watkins did:

"As Rupert says, 'I'm writing nothing; I am content to live.'"

In this mood Watkins gave himself exultantly to the bliss of the present moment at Repton: "At present I'm consummately happy … I've given up the future." He pities other boys who are unable to experience this, who can be "glad to go at the end of this time. Poor fools! They don't know, and never shall know, what true happiness is." He signs off, in these high spirits:

"Until Niagara falls I remain

yr faithful secretary

Vernon P Watkins"

In his next letter, on June 24th, 1923, three days before his seventeenth birthday, he writes:

"We've come back from chapel & I can't think of anyone except Rupert Brooke … This place is wonderful; and so, alas, is everybody and everything in it. In a year, I have absolutely changed my attitude to everyone. They're all wonderful now, and I love everybody."[32]

"I'm keen on the whole lot"

Watkins's soaring idealism was indeed interwoven with the intense throes of an erotically-charged, yet highly romanticized love – for the only recipients of it possible in the all-male world of Repton, the beautiful young boys around him.

Isherwood's biographer writes: "According to Upward, 'everyone was homosexual, up to a point, at Repton.' That point was sexual expression, and most boys contented themselves with romantic friendships."[33] This was undeniably true of Watkins, with the difference, perhaps, that as he was also undergoing some kind of spiritual or idealistic awakening, together with his birth as a poet, it was not very easy for him to say *who* he was in love with – and he was certainly not willing to reduce it to the love for one particular boy. He confided in Falk: "I'm not keen on anyone at all – certainly not R.T.V. – or else I'm keen on the whole lot."³⁴

The "inconstancy" of Watkins's behaviour did not go unnoticed by others and Eric Falk received a letter from another boy at the school, Richard Sykes, informing him of what was happening:

"Watkins has got a colossal lust on at the moment – he is keen on: Vaughan – Pavitt – Speight – J. Lees – young Pondie Gaskin (fatherly eye shut). Such inconstancy!" This had gone so far, said Sykes, that it was highly likely that Watkins would be refused the normal privilege of being given an independent study:

"I don't know about Watkins getting a study – I personally rather doubt it. He really is making an awful ass of himself over his tarts – night after night … and all the bosers regard him as being an absolutely irresponsible ass … I don't know if he realizes it – if I could raise the guts I'd tell him to ease off a bit."³⁵

Watkins, however, had no intention whatever of heeding any conventional attempt to limit his soaring, blissful experience during that Summer of 1923. Telling Falk that he was "the most obstinate person in Repton", who "have always had emotions", he declared "Away, logic!" and that "I laugh when I think of studies, after reading Shelley."³⁶

"All this is biblical"

What Watkins was experiencing was in fact more than merely erotic love for another, or for many others, as Sykes presumed. Had Sykes or anyone else at Repton really seen what was going on inside Watkins, they may well have been even more concerned about him than they already were. For the ecstatic sense of bliss Watkins experienced during his last terms at Repton would take on a mythological and even a biblical significance for him, which it would take him years to come to terms with, to accept the loss of and finally to overcome. It is therefore necessary that we look at it more closely.

Looking back on those days at Repton Wordsworth's words would certainly have been true for Watkins: "Bliss was it in that dawn to be alive". The sense of this was created by numerous elements. There were the large numbers of friends, which Vernon had never had before. There was all that they shared and discovered together regarding poetry, culture and their awakened idealism. There were the summer sports of cricket and tennis, tennis above all, which Vernon would always love playing and was very good at. And there was the setting of Repton itself, on the site of one of the earliest Christian centres in Britain, whose surrounding fields still seem imbued with the influence of this. Even Victor Gollancz, the radical Christian socialist, associated his greatest joys at Repton with his Summer afternoons next to the site of the old Priory, by the school cricket field, "The Paddock":

"it merges into a buttercup meadow, and flows on, watered by streams, to the sky. Hitherward rises a slope; and on it I would lie through those long afternoons in the glare of the sun, with the click of a ball in my ears, and a company of friends by my side, and the smell of grass in my nostrils, and the yellow and green out beyond … Much else was of greater importance … but in terms … of a carefree and innocent happiness, the Paddock is my Repton." Gollancz wrote in a letter: "The very thought of next term, with the sun & the grass & the cricket field, makes me feel like a lover about to see his mistress!!!"[37]

Vernon Watkins had a similar sense, effusing in a poem about Repton: "O fields, O fields, lovelier than all these Isles!"[38]

And all of this was joined and heightened, taking it to an almost ecstatic pitch, by Watkins's burgeoning feelings of homosexual, idealized love. It was this culminating element which gradually grew to take on a significance for Watkins far beyond the normal experience of erotic love.

Vernon Watkins's hero at the time, Rupert Brooke, around whom a whole mythology had arisen during World War One, was eulogized for possessing a "perfect symmetry of mind and body".[39] Watkins's blissful experiences at Repton were increasingly filled with exactly this kind of Greek ideal of beauty, where what is spiritual and what is physical appear inseparable from one another.

In a long poem written a few years later, when Watkins had become unable to let go of this experience and attempted to celebrate it to the utmost, he recalled the intensities of love he had felt for one boy in particular, despite his claims to the contrary. The poem begins: "Sing the great birth of Love". Watkins remembers: "those delirious nights/ When

Space was ours, and ours the unspeakable joy." But above all, looking back on his experiences at Repton, he recalls the experience of a world where there was no distinction between inner and outer reality:

> *Each careless movement of your hands*
> *Allures me to the wall*
> *That guards the age-forbidden lands*
> **Where thoughts are physical.** *(XXI)*[40]

Again, declaring he has found the source of his beloved's beauty, not in the physical world but in the "ethereal plane", he states ecstatically:

> *And in that peace and in that light*
> *Your body and my mind are one.* (XIX)

This merging of physical and spiritual he equates with humanity's paradisal experience in the Garden of Eden, and thus in this later poem,

Vernon Watkins at Repton – Summer 1923
(Second from left in the second row. The headmaster, Geoffrey Fisher, is in the front row, third from left.)

speaks of his days at Repton in biblical terms as an experience of 'Eden'.[41]

Such descriptions lay slightly in the future, but even while at Repton Watkins knew that what he was going through was not to be reduced to conventional terms, joking with Falk: "All this is biblical. And the rest of the acts of Vernon, are they not written in the book of the chronicles of the unconventionals at Repton?"[42]

At the end of the summer term 1923, right in the midst of his blissful "summer of love", he was wholly aware of its impermanence and of how swiftly time was passing. Having announced at the beginning of June: "I have given up the future", as his birthday approached, a few weeks later, he wrote: "I cannot get rid of the awful thought that I shall be 17 next week ... there is such a difference between 16 and 17." He was therefore even more determined to enjoy every moment of it, while it lasted.

Autumn 1923

The previous Summer (1922) Vernon had travelled abroad on his own for the first time, to Nuremberg, to improve his German, staying with a Jewish lady, Frau Hechinger, who he would later revisit.[43] This year he spent most of his Summer holidays in France – three weeks in Brittany with his family and "3 in Tours by myself"[44], immersing himself again in a foreign culture and language. While he was there, he made his earliest surviving translation of a poem in another language.[45] The translating of foreign poetry remained a love of his throughout his life.

Returning to Repton in the Autumn his joys there continued – "everyday, the amount of humour I get here is wonderful". He was given his own "fag", David Cochrane, whom he treated humanely and well,[46] which was by no means always the case, and who would become an important friend. There was also, of course, his unfailing commitment to poetry: "I spend most of my Sundays this term writing poetry, at which I am improving considerably." This was all clearly of far greater importance to him than his academic work, for in December he took the entrance exams to Cambridge, but failed to get the scholarship necessary to be able to afford going there. In March 1924 he attempted a scholarship to Oxford instead, but failed again. Oxford and Cambridge's standards were high and not being from the English upper classes Watkins would have had no favours done to him. Tellingly, however, he never even mentioned to Falk that he was trying to get into Oxbridge. His letters were filled with everything else he had been up to.

In December he was involved in a school play – *Hassan* by James Elroy Flecker.[47] In the play, two lovers in 9th Century Baghdad are accused of "Sufic doctrine ... most dangerous to the State".[48] They are given the choice (by the Caliph Haroun al Raschid) either to live long lives but never see each other again, or to enjoy one last blissful day and night together and then die the most horrible of deaths. They ecstatically choose the latter: "I die for love of you ... you are one with the Eternal Lover, the Friend of the entire World ... We are in the service of the World." Watkins, presumably sensing a parallel with his own situation, soon wrote: "I rave over Hassan day and night ... I absolutely let myself go, as I've never done before, and I love the part."[49]

Watkins even trusted himself to speak out at the school Debating Society on the Machiavellian view that "*Lies are Justifiable*". After stating that people were only speaking "from the point of view of the relation which lies have to the present state of the world", he defiantly declared, as he quite certainly believed, that: "the world at present is not justifiable" and that present-day society is merely "an organized hypocrisy." As the school magazine reported it: "Mr. Watkins said that the whole present state of the world was unjustifiable, and that everybody in the room was unjustifiable."[50] His words presumably being ill-received or worse, laughed at, Watkins concluded: "It was a dreadful ordeal, and probably I'll never speak again."

Anonymous poet

The event of by far the greatest significance, however, certainly to him, would have gone almost entirely unnoticed. For the very first time he had two of his poems printed, in the school magazine in December, yet put no name to them. His anonymity was so successful, in fact, that these first published poems of his remained unnoticed until work on the present biography.[51]

For anyone who has only known the mature poetry Watkins later saw fit to publish, his first printed poem may be a shock. For Vernon Watkins, unlike Wordsworth or Traherne or Dylan Thomas, is not known for his "intimations of immortality in early childhood", but rather for his sense of the renewal that may be experienced, even in life, by undergoing an experience of death. It might well be thought, therefore, that experiences such as Wordsworth's or Traherne's were unknown to Watkins. Yet his very first poem – 'The Flower' – tells an utterly different story. It tells of his sense, through and through, of the divinity of childhood – which was the source of all his boyhood joys – and then of the tragedy that this must be lost. The "secret of our life", according to the poem's creation-story, is that the flower of life, that "God once threw/ Upon the sleeping earth", cannot survive into the years of adulthood:

> Woulds't know the tragedy of Life, my friend?
> Life was a seed which fell on stony ground, (...)
> And all we know of Heaven's a little child!

Watkins's second printed poem was called 'As', which we have quoted from earlier.[52]

In the following term, Watkins had another poem printed and this time dared to put his initials underneath: "V.P.W." Despite its borrowed "poetic diction" there is nonetheless something remarkable in the poem's depiction of the seventeen year-old's visionary encounter with the being of poetry and his discovery that, like the child in 'The Flower', it had not been able to survive into the present day:

> I heard the magic voice of Poesy,
> – A mighty voice crying out into the Night,
> – Yet a sad music stilled...
> And (...) saw her lovely head
> – Uplifted for a song... but silent – dead...[53]

Alec Macdonald

Towards the end of 1923 Watkins also struck up a strong friendship with a highly literary and inspiring teacher, Alec Macdonald. Watkins delightedly told Falk about one of their meetings:

"I went out for tea with him yesterday ... 4 hours and 50 minutes solid talking on poetry and Public Schools ... He's read every poem under the sun except about 4 ... He was the editor of the Cambridge Review, and has a consuming passion for Walter de la Mare ... He has peculiar and very impressive deep, blue eyes, which go right through you, and I know he's got a large and somewhat mysterious soul."[54]

In Alec Macdonald Watkins had indeed discovered a teacher who, in Gollancz's spirit, was rightly able to break down the barriers between 'teacher' and 'taught', enabling what David Somervell called true 'education' to take place.[55]

One of Watkins's remarks in particular led Macdonald to dramatically break down the barriers between them, in an attempt to make Watkins change his mind. Watkins, having failed to get a scholarship to Oxbridge, must have accepted his father's demand that he would have to take up work in business or the bank. Macdonald – understandably, it must be said – found it incomprehensible that the highly idealistic young poet in front of him could contemplate this:

"Mr. Mcdonald ... asked me what I was going to do. I said I was going in to business, and he asked me why. I told him – Money – upon which came a magnificent outpouring of literary invective. When it was half subsided, he took a little of the 'filthy lucre' out of his pocket – lying back in his chair all the time, and hurled it across the room ... This morning he came and confessed he found 1/1½d this morning on the floor of his room."

Eighteen years old

The time when Vernon would leave the school and need to answer this question about his future grew ever nearer. On his eighteenth birthday at the end of the Summer term, just as when he had turned seventeen, he was bitterly aware of time passing: "O, as Rupert would say, 'I'm as old as death'. I didn't know it would be quite as terrible as this to be eighteen years old."[56]

Nevertheless, his final Speech Day, in July, was like a glorious culmination for him of his time at Repton. In the midst of a sea of friends, with his mother and older sister present,[57] he was awarded three prizes for his work in Modern Languages as well as the Howe Verse Prize. The theme for this prize was set by the school – which had this year asked for poems about the vast earthquake disaster that had

Headmaster ar Repton, Geoffrey Fisher – (photograph by Vernon Watkins)

recently (September 1923) devastated Japan, causing over 100,000 deaths. Watkins's long poem, called "Japanese Disaster",[58] depicts both in earthly and super-earthly terms the almost unimaginable scale of the Great Kant Earthquake. It is striking not only for the scale of its vision but also for its empathy with a far-off people.

As the headmaster, Geoffrey Fisher, handed Watkins the prize, which also included a cheque, he quipped that Watkins would never again earn so much money per line. As the poem was 84 lines long, it showed what little value Fisher placed in Watkins's poetry and Watkins never forgot the insult. Having long seen Fisher as a Philistine, however, he would certainly not have allowed it to ruin his day.

"I am, of course, dying"

With Speech Day over, and with his needing to make his way from the blissful highs of his days at Repton to the rest of the world in front of him, hardly surprisingly he fell ill: "just after Speech Day, I was visited by the Mumps Angel, & have since been resident at the School Sanatorium, Repton, Derbyshire."[59] Still obsessively identifying himself with Rupert Brooke, he romanticized to his friend Falk the cause of his illness:

"I am, of course, dying. My strength is failing, as I see the end of the term approaching ... I shall miss the people like hell, but I suppose that I'll get over it, and God will be kind – as always ... my beloved Rupert Brooke has taught me all the subtle pangs of leaving in advance, so I shall be prepared, at any rate."

He received three different pieces of advice from friends who had left before him. "Holland cheers me by telling me that I never really leave Repton; Upward by reminding me that I'm shaking off foolish conventions"[60]. Christopher Isherwood provided the necessary, if icy counterblast: "Isherwood cynically tells me that it's all only a beautiful dream, & I'm waking up to disillusionment now."

Once he had recovered from his mumps, he enjoyed his last days to the full – "my last fortnight was a dream; I think I enjoyed myself more than ever before" – and at the same time, like someone facing a death sentence, he carefully observed the process of his own dying:

"Then those last few days – a strange, dazed and thoroughly happy and glorious existence, – very frightened of what was coming, and punctuated by amazing & sudden realizations of everything."

He unhappily said goodbye to his friends and to the boy he had loved above all others – as he happily confided to Falk:

"Going round the beddars was the world's worst ordeal, but I got through it (noone knows how) carefully leaving one beddar to the last."

When it was finally time for him to go: "Leaving Repton was what I had expected it to be; – a ghastly affair which left me in tears before I grew cold and stiff with disillusionment and resignation."

At the last minute, staring down the barrels of his future, he decided he should seek at the very least for a stay of execution and announced: "I'm going to try to get to Cambridge after all."[61]

***

Vernon Watkins, the First World War and Rupert Brooke

Vernon Watkins was to invest his experiences at Repton with such vast significance, before eventually overcoming them, that it is essential we attempt to understand them a little better. A few further characteristics of the particular years he spent at Repton can help us to do this.

Christopher Isherwood, who had gone to Repton in 1918, said of his own age-group:

"we young writers of the 'twenties were all suffering, more or less subconsciously, from a feeling of shame that we hadn't been old enough to take part in the European war ... I denied my all-consuming morbid interest in the idea of "war". I pretended indifference."[62]

Vernon Watkins did not share this standpoint. Firstly, being two years younger than Isherwood, the presence of war was not quite so immediate, and secondly Watkins, being in many ways genuinely naïve, unlike the self-aware Isherwood, could never have "pretended indifference."

These two young writers would therefore have had very different responses to the grand and emotive ceremony that took place on Armistice Day, 1922, to commemorate the 353 ex-Reptonians killed in the war. It was attended by bishops, military officers, previous headmasters, five hundred Old Reptonians and by the whole of the school. The old ruined cloisters of "The Priory" were renewed as a Memorial Garden. One of the schoolboys described his sense of the sacred memory of those who had lost their lives uniting with hallowed places of Repton's past:

"As we stood bidden to silence, there was a splendid outburst of triumphant bird song, which seemed to many of us symbolic. And when the procession made its way to the Headmaster's garden, as we marked the ... surplices and ... hoods of the Bishops' robes, we felt a link with the Priors and Canons who had trodden the ground in procession many years ago, and felt that it was good to offer all Repton's Past as Priory and School to the memory of these our brothers who ... have given their lives for us."[63]

Isherwood, who was right at the end of his time at the school, would have been unlikely to let the ceremoniousness of the event affect him. Watkins, who at 16 was only just emerging from boyhood[64] and had very recently begun writing poetry again, was hardly likely *not* to have been affected. This is not to say that he felt any allegiance to the antiquated traditions of the school for their own sake. The poem he wrote exactly a year later, 'As', perhaps even refers to the outer ceremonial character of the event of 1922, compared with the inner character of his own experience: "I forgot surplices and gown uncouth,/ And, for one blissful moment, saw the Truth."[65] Nevertheless, there was a certain unquestioning and deeply felt relationship to the First World War that he drank in unconsciously.

This is epitomised in his idolizing identification with Rupert Brooke.

In May 1923 Watkins had said there was a "Rupert Brooke craze" running through the school. This must almost certainly have been triggered by the 1922 memorial ceremony to the Repton war dead. For one of the Repton masters killed in the war, each of whom was specially honoured at the memorial, was one of Rupert Brooke's closest friends, Denis Browne.[67] Browne had been with Brooke when he died [68] and had chosen the site of Brooke's grave on the island of Skyros. Browne, who was himself killed six weeks later, was therefore intimately linked to the whole poetic mythology around Brooke's death, which had become almost a national symbol for all the young deaths at the beginning of the war.

That Vernon Watkins, while at Repton, had drunk in this mythology, including the picture of Brooke's beautiful and romantic acceptance of the death he would have to die, is made completely clear in his letters to Falk: "O my belovéd Rupert Brooke has taught me all the subtle pangs of leaving in advance, so I shall be prepared, at any rate."

Watkins seems to have borrowed Brooke's feelings about dying as a soldier and transferred them onto his own feelings about the "death" that leaving Repton would mean for him. He even seems to have borrowed the feelings of the boys who had left Repton in World War One, many of whom really had gone off to their deaths. A Repton

Armistice Day Memorial at Repton – 11th November 1922. Clergyman on left, behind buglers, Headmaster Rev. Geoffrey Fisher. Clergyman immediately to the left of Memorial – Right Rev William Temple (Bishop of Manchester).[66]

tradition is for school-leavers to go round the dormitories (bedders) saying goodbye to the younger boys in their house. Speaking of how this was during the war, one Reptonian wrote: "I can well remember boys who had been … called up … coming round the bedders on their last night … and shaking hands with everyone, knowing, as we also knew, that in the following term, at the … services in Chapel on Friday evenings, we might hear their names read out … in the Old Reptonian casualty list for that week."[69] Watkins's experience was like a strange after-echo of this: "Going round the beddars was the world's worst ordeal, but I got through it (noone knows how)".[70]

The greater problem – which Watkins would eventually have to come to terms with – is that the grounds for Brooke's exalted flight towards death were highly unstable.

Firstly, there had undoubtedly been a propagandist element to the mythologizing of Brooke's death by Winston Churchill and his Private Secretary, Edward Marsh, so well did it heighten the sense of poetic heroism about the hundreds of thousands of young men sacrificing their lives in the war.[71] Even today not everyone is aware that Rupert Brooke did not die some heroic death in battle, but was killed by a mosquito bite.

Secondly, as recent biographers of Brooke have increasingly become aware of, Brooke's motives for seeking his own death were far from being purely selfless and spiritual. They were also bound up with the desire to escape many of the torments associated with his youth, such as his failure to resolve the nature of his own sexuality and homosexuality. One writer, who thinks that had Brooke been able to "live out his hidden desires without guilt" he might have resolved his dilemma, says that after Brooke's early poems, which were "implicitly homosexual and explicitly neo-pagan": "sexual confusion drove him to a nervous breakdown in 1912 and six weeks of psychiatric care … He came to reject Bloomsbury[72] out of shame, and to seek purification through death in war … His '1914' sonnet sequence shows a desire for death as the only resolution to his inner conflict."[73]

Thirdly, these two elements – the propagandist mythologizing of Brooke's death, and the quest for death as a way of purifying his homosexual tendencies – had in fact been merged into one. For the person chiefly responsible for creating Brooke's romantic image was Edward Marsh, (the friend of Brooke and Browne and also of Winston Churchill), who might be termed a rarefied, platonic homosexual.[74] Marsh was the person who authored the greatest single piece of propaganda about Rupert Brooke, Winston Churchill's obituary of him in 'The Times', which speaks of how: *"with classic symmetry of mind and body*, he was all that one would wish England's noblest sons to be in days when no sacrifice but the most precious is acceptable."[75]

All of this has profound echoes with Vernon Watkins's condition while at Repton. It is not hard to see how his identification with Rupert Brooke and his poetry would have interlinked with his own homosexual feelings and the spiritual light in which he viewed these. And as with Brooke, Watkins had in no way yet arrived at any satisfactory resolution of his feelings.[76] It was not the case, for example, as he had first declared, that his feelings of love were entirely universal and did not focus on any particular boy. His grief at saying farewell to his friends was not only that of someone heading to his own doom, but was also the personal grief of someone saying farewell to his beloved: "Going round the beddars was the world's worst ordeal, but I got through it (noone knows how) carefully leaving one beddar to the last … "

Watkins, in other words, was living in an extraordinarily similar state of sexual-spiritual confusion to that of Rupert Brooke. Brooke had ultimately found "release" from the complexity of his condition in his willingness to die a heroic death in battle. This was not a solution that was available to Watkins. Vernon in other words was on a head-on course with some extreme crisis, before he might hope to find a way of resolving the almost impossible tensions with which he was leaving Repton and heading into adult life. It was from this inevitable crisis that he won something like a stay of execution, or at least a little time, through his last-minute decision to go to Cambridge.

Vernon Watkins aged 17 or 18 (photograph by Eric Falk)

CHAPTER THREE

Cambridge (1924–1925)

Through the side-door to Cambridge

In mid-August, Vernon Watkins told Eric Falk: "Since Repton many things have happened. I am going to Cambridge (Magdalene; Heaven knows how it happened.)"[1] What in fact had taken place was a considerable amount of letter-writing and negotiation.

At the beginning of August, on the advice presumably of Alec Macdonald,[2] Watkins had simply written to Magdalene College and asked "whether there are any vacancies … for this next term."

Despite Alec Macdonald's diatribe against "filthy lucre", Watkins clearly if surprisingly stated that his main reason for wishing to go to Cambridge was to gain the qualifications for a career in banking:

"My father is thinking of sending me into the Bank, and I should like, if possible, to choose my course at Cambridge with a view to this career; and although I want to keep up my Modern Languages I feel that a study of Economics would be still more useful for my further career.[3]

"I am afraid I am very late in asking … I know it will mean a great deal of trouble … but if I could possibly get in, I feel that your college would be excellent for me economically as well as intellectually, judging from what I have been told about it."

He also made clear that he was by no means a free agent – that his father, who was unsure if he could afford the fees, would certainly not pay for him unless he studied something "suitable":

"I am still uncertain whether my father will be able to send me to Cambridge; and this will largely depend upon the suitability of the course I should take, and the probable expenditure per year.

Yours very sincerely, V.P. Watkins"[4]

The senior tutor at Magdalene was A.S. Ramsey. Ramsey knew Repton and its headmaster Geoffrey Fisher very well, as his second son, Michael, had recently been at the school. (Michael Ramsey had been at Repton for two years with Watkins, was currently an undergraduate at Magdalene, and would later succeed Geoffrey Fisher as Archbishop of Canterbury.[5]) A.S. Ramsey therefore wrote directly to Fisher, asking for his honest opinion of Watkins, as he had no wish "to add to our numbers unless the applicant really is meritorious and likely to be useful to the college."

Fisher immediately replied, in a letter showing as much about himself and his patronising attitudes towards others, as it does about Vernon Watkins:

"Watkins is a queer little person – full of merit and virtue ... he has any amount of industry and application. He would be pretty certain of a 2nd in the Tripos, though probably he has not enough intellectual powers to get a 1st. Apart from that he is something of a poet – an honest and ambitious soul – and a good companion.

"On the other side there are large gaps in his general knowledge (he is always very poor in his general paper), he is derivative rather than original, and has more of the ivy than the oak in him."

Before concluding, Fisher made clear the Watkins's family situation:

"Finance is a difficulty: it is the mother who wants him to go to the Varsity – one sister is at Oxford and the expense of the two is almost beyond them. If not the Varsity, the boy is to go into the Bank in which his father is.

"He is ... meritorious, deserving, within certain limits capable, in certain favouring circumstances a definite & entertaining personality."

Ramsey was somehow not put off by Fisher's remarks and, a mere six days after Watkins had written his letter, told him: "though you are rather late in applying, as your Headmaster has reported favourably of you, we are prepared to admit you."[6] Ramsey supported Watkins's unrealistic suggestion of what he might study: "you might take the First Part of the Modern Languages Tripos at the end of your Second Year and then take Economics or Law for your third year."

Watkins accepted the offer[7], but asked about the possibility of applying for a scholarship to help with the fees. Ramsey told Watkins's father that only those "placed in Class 1" after their first year were eligible for scholarships, but that a grant for those in difficult circumstances might be available, if Mr. Watkins would provide details of his income and expenditure. William Watkins, somewhat embarrassed, declined the offer,[8] but it was clear that he could barely afford to send Vernon to Cambridge and that Vernon would need to prove the financial worth of going there. Nevertheless, Vernon had won his reprieve and had been accepted to Cambridge and could now happily enjoy the rest of the summer.

Summer and Gower
He spent it in his parents' large house, 'Redcliffe', next to the sea, at the back of the beautiful and windswept Caswell Bay on the Gower Peninsula. At the end of the First World War the family had moved from the Uplands to the Langland Bay Hotel for a few m onths, his mother being in a state of exhaustion and needing to recuperate. They then lived briefly in the Mumbles before buying the large and at that time idyllically situated 'Redcliffe.' From here all the beaches, cliffs, coves and inland places of Gower were immediately accessible to Vernon, who remained incredibly fit all his life, clambering up and down cliffs, walking long distances, swimming whenever and wherever he could, besides cycling and playing sports like hockey and tennis.

Caswell Bay taken from above Redcliffe House

Vernon's most regular companions were his two very different sisters. His older sister, Marjorie, was said by Gwen Watkins to have been the "great spiritual adviser of Vernon's life". Highly gifted at Oxford, she had not pursued her academic studies, but chosen instead to devote herself to social work in Bethnal Green, East London.[9] Introverted and quiet, with a profound interest in Christian mysticism, Vernon wrote of her: "she is such a strange person, & you can't get to know her for years." Vernon's younger sister, Dorothy, was boisterous, extrovert, an indomitable lover of outdoor adventure and exercise, who also committed her life to social work, as far afield as Poland and Australia.[10] Vernon, born between them, somehow united the characteristics of both. Thus in his long days and nights in Gower, he would play tennis, canoe, climb, swim and catch prawns and lobsters, while never ceasing to be deeply absorbed in poetry. Dorothy describes that he would never set out on one of their explorations of Gower without a book of poetry.

Vernon's days at Redcliffe were always happy ones, with his family around him, the whole of Gower accessible from the doorstep, a tennis court, and with plenty of room for his friends to stay – particularly those from Repton. That Summer, therefore, Vernon's teacher and mentor Alec Macdonald came to stay, who wrote in a letter from Redcliffe: "I am staying with a family who walk on average twelve miles a day and who never stop talking."[11] Eric Falk, who must have been going through a troubled period, also came to stay. Watkins offered him all the encouragement he could and exuberantly anticipated their time together: "If you brood you will always stagnate. Read poetry & it will tell you all you need to know & will be your greatest sympathizer. There are more things in heaven and earth … And shall we not shout and leap in September when you come? Let us know … whether you're prepared to swim … and walk 300 miles a day. Ever Thy Hectic Brother & Troll-King, Vernon."[12]

"The Dutchman"
Cornelis van Stolk

Watkins began at Cambridge on October 9th, 1924. Having made such a swift decision to go there, and going there almost straight from Repton, he must have hoped that the joys he had experienced at school could somehow continue at Cambridge. And at first, as he told Falk ("Fig") in a letter, there indeed appeared to be a blissful possibility of this. He had met someone! A fellow-student for whose company he felt once more a soaringly idealistic enthusiasm. As this encounter would soon lead, indirectly, to disastrous consequences, drastically altering Watkins's whole time at Cambridge, we shall quote at some length from his description of it to Falk. In this sole surviving letter of Watkins's from Cambridge it was anyway the only thing he wished to talk about:

"I ought to have written before, but honestly I haven't had a <u>minute</u>; every night I've been up till twelve … So you will excuse me if … *I confine this letter … to one subject.*"

At one 9 a.m. lecture, with only a few people present: "a man with powdered face rolled in & sat in front of me. He asked me to lend him a pencil, & I did so."

Watkins realizes the man is Dutch and cannot help being struck when this Dutchman, instead of doing his French translation, carefully transcribes a poem. "At the end of the hour, I asked him whether it was a French poem that he had been writing out, and he said it was, – a beautiful sonnet of De Musset's. We talked a little (about 5 minutes) on poetry, – French, English & German, comparing them in sound & c. Then he burst out, 'But music is the only thing in the world', & I immediately asked him to lunch … (!)"

When the Dutchman arrived: "I was a bit nervous about the powder (in the light of aestheticism) – but as soon as we started talking seriously I realized what a wonderful man he is. He talked to me about philosophy, poetry & c (apparently he knew the greatest Dutch writer for years, has a very good style & was advised by him to go in for a literary career.) I was amazed at his intellect & enthusiasm."

In Watkins's room were photographs of his Repton friends and his family, and the Dutchman, who Watkins never named, "proceeded to describe the characters of all the photos wonderfully accurately."[13] When the Dutchman then went on to describe his own life, Watkins, whose life had been strictly limited to home and school, clearly felt he had stumbled across another kind of human being entirely, with a life-experience beyond any comparison with his own.

"He then told me about his life – a family of genius's – father a philosopher & writer of sex books – told all about sex at age of 10 – disinherited at 13, because he wouldn't accept his father's philosophy – studied philosophy & religion – wandering from family to family, – Germany, France, England (knows all these languages perfectly) – friendless – associations with whores ,,. came to England – by this time had been 'reinherited' – offered choice of £90,000 a year in father's business, or Varsity Education & not a penny afterwards. Chose the Varsity."

The Dutchman – whose real name was Cornelis van Stolk – clearly held out the promise to Vernon of a vast increase in the range and depth of his understanding and experience and Vernon was delighted by and in awe of his new friend:

"I've seen quite a lot of him since. In his rooms he keeps a lute and white mouse; he sung to Upward[14] & me on the lute – extraordinary.

"He has the most astounding intellect, I think of any man of his age I've ever met in my life. You ought to meet him. In argument he is invincible, in philosophy wonderfully sound."[15]

Cambridge was all he could have hoped it to be. He had even met someone who would publish his poetry: "P.S. I'm going to write for a paper a man in Sidney's bringing out ... Far be it from me to patronize the Granta, or other Cambridge papers." Candide-like, all was for the best in the best of all possible worlds: "P.P.S. Don't be depressed. Life is wonderful. Everybody is wonderful. Talk to Marjorie; only then will you understand."[16]

Isherwood and Upward

In his first weeks at Cambridge Watkins would also have leaned on old friends and acquaintances from Repton who were there – such as Christopher Isherwood and Edward Upward. The latter's younger brother, Mervyn Upward, was one of Watkins's closest friends at

Repton and they had both begun Cambridge at the same time.[17] They saw a lot of each other – (van Stolk had "sung to Upward & me on the lute") – and as Isherwood had been in Watkins's school house there was every possibility that, together with Mervyn Upward, Watkins might also have been welcomed and taken on by Christopher Isherwood and Edward Upward in some form of older brother/younger brother relationship.[18]

At the start this was clearly the case. Isherwood and Upward openly confided in Watkins regarding some of their activities and Watkins too shared completely openly with them. Mainly, of course, this meant telling them about his new Dutch friend.

Isherwood describes this in *Lions and Shadows*, his novel about his years at Repton and Cambridge, where he gave new names to his friends and acquaintances and referred to Watkins appropriately, even if it was intended mockingly, by the name of the innocent holy fool – *Percival*. This, therefore, was how Isherwood characterized Watkins during his first term at Cambridge:

"Percival was an enthusiastic person, always gushing over some newly discovered teacher or master. This term, it was a Dutchman. The Dutchman, whom we never saw, was a rather sinister figure: he read philosophy, was an anthroposophist,[19] and kept white mice. Percival quoted his every word with the utmost admiration and awe: we got very tired of hearing about him."[20]

Wolves in the garden

What happened next, however, completely ended any sense of kinship Isherwood and Upward may have felt with Watkins and, even more categorically, any he may have felt with them.

The novel *Lions and Shadows* is in many ways a description of Isherwood's journey to "adulthood" and to becoming a writer, involving for him the progressive stripping away of whatever he saw as belonging to a naïve or unexamined relationship to the world.[21]

Isherwood is honest about describing the lengths he and Edward Upward sometimes went to in order to prevent themselves falling into unexamined behaviour. At the time Watkins arrived in Cambridge they had invented an unseen companion called 'The Watcher in Spanish', who watched their every move and fiercely judged them when they fell back into old habits:

"We imagined him as a macabre but semi-comic figure, not unlike Guy Fawkes, or a human personification of Poe's watching raven. He appeared to us ... at moments when our behaviour was particularly insincere ... he warned us never to betray ourselves by word or deed. He was our familiar, our imaginary mascot, our guardian spirit. Often, when we were alone together, we spoke to him aloud."

"The Watcher" would always appear when Upward and Isherwood were with someone else. "On the rare occasions when we attempted jointly to entertain, 'the Watcher' immediately put in his appearance; our whole behaviour, when a third party was in the room, became ... strained and falsified." Thus it was a definite mark of their ease with Watkins's company that, far from being "strained and falsified", they had spoken quite openly with him about their invisible companion.

Isherwood and Upward had somehow managed to put up with Watkins's euphoria about the Dutchman. What they found intolerable, however, was when one day "Percival informed us, not without malice, that he had just told the Dutchman about our Watcher in Spanish" and, furthermore: "that the Dutchman had dismissed the whole idea as 'childish and silly'."

Isherwood and Upward were "*furious*" – "with ourselves, chiefly, for having ever confided our 'blagues' to a third person" – and "decided that Percival must be taught a lesson."

In the fictionalized version of *Lions and Shadows* their "lesson" consisted of pretending to Watkins/Percival that they too had met someone as strange and mysterious as the Dutchman: "We, too, would have a sinister, omniscient friend." The "gullible Percival" swallowed their whole story, until they went too far even for him and stated that this new friend "owned a large black serpent which accompanied him on rambles after dark". At this "Percival began to smile reproachfully and murmured, in his deep musical tones: 'Do you know, I believe you're ragging me?'"

In real life, however, Isherwood and Upward's "lesson" was far more severe and would have a devastating effect upon Watkins. Isherwood may have stated later that "we were furious *with ourselves*, chiefly", but their fury was initially solely and savagely directed at Watkins. *They* were the intellectually mature ones, so how dare *he* now declare their most precious secret conceits to be 'childish and silly'? Furious words must have followed, ruthlessly aimed Watkins's greatest weakness, which they were all too aware of, his child-like naïveté and his absurd romanticism about Repton. They plunged a metaphorical knife-blade into his childish heart and the immature dreams it harboured. Watkins staggered away, wounded, and responded in the only way he knew how – through poetry.

Watkins had written to Falk about "the Dutchman" – Cornelis van Stolk – on the 17th November. The disastrous meeting with Isherwood and Upward must have taken place two or three days later.[22] On the 20th November Watkins gave his spontaneous response to it in a poem. It is an immature poem in both style and content and belongs among the juvenilia Watkins would later repudiate. Nevertheless, he could hardly have expressed himself more directly:

> *You led me from the ways of childhood,*
> *From the garden of enchantment.*
> *Into the waste (…)*
> *There you bade me seek, among the grasses,*
> *Not the beauty of the flower,*
> *But the worm that lay hidden beneath it. (…)*
> *And you tell me that you are men! (…)*
> *I say you are wolves,*
> *Preying upon the love*
> *Of one who would still be a child.*
> *But (…) though (…) (y)ou should turn our life to a shadow,*
> *And the flowers of the soul into weeds, (…)*
> *I shall not heed the wickedness of your tongues,*
> *The filth of your deceit (…)*
> *For I shall remember that you are a pack of wolves*
> *Seeking to devour my soul,*
> *And the beauty of life,*
> *And the goodness of man,*
> *And his love which passeth all understanding –*

Then I shall return,
– Return again to the garden of enchantment,
*And walk there, – among the flowers ...*²³

Immature as the poem is, of course, it makes three things abundantly clear. Firstly, there was now a "great gulf fixed" between him and Isherwood and Upward, and with the intellectually ironical world they stood for, in other words with almost the entire intellectual environment at Cambridge. Secondly, Watkins has been *wounded*. Isherwood and Upward's cynicism, and by extension the intellectual atmosphere of Cambridge, has struck him a fatal blow. The result of this, as he fully recognizes, is that he *has now* been shut out from the "garden of enchantment". The third thing the poem makes clear is that Watkins is set on some kind of "collision course". "The most obstinate person in Repton", as he had once called himself, is quite determined that he *will* finally "(r)eturn again to the garden of enchantment", whatever this might mean or cost.

Poems tell the story

From that moment on any hopes he had held out about Cambridge were over. We know next to nothing about the remaining seven months he spent there. There are no further surviving letters to Falk or to anyone else. He must have kept up his friendship with Cornelis van Stolk, for on at least one occasion he met up with him again after Cambridge, but the experience he had had of being cast out of "the garden" also seems to have put an end to the possibility of van Stolk being inspirational in showing him new ways forward. He never referred to van Stolk, Isherwood or Upward again, in writing.²⁴ The only thing that never stopped was his poetry and, though he later destroyed huge amounts of his juvenilia, enough remains for us to clearly chart the inner journey he now went on, even if we know little about the outer one.

By the start of his second term, in January 1925, he already appears to have accepted the bitter lesson he has been taught. He accepts that "Time" never fails to "outwit man and cheat him of his dream"; that death seemingly "steals ... the breath of love/ For ever"; and that it is hard to contradict the cynical claim that: "Life's but a little paragraph of lies". One last thread of hope remains to him – that undergoing death might lead to the renewal of life. The poem, called 'Immortality',[25] ends: "We die to live, e'en as we live to die."

In 'Despair'[26] he also fully accepts that nothing can "bring dead years again." He has no wish to hear about: "flowers, sunrise, forest, early Spring", which "seemed so eternal" and yet, like the beauty of his earlier days, would soon pass. Better to face this honestly and despair: "Despair is dear, despair is recompense." Once he has reached this point, the miracle occurs. Despair keeps growing until even "heaven is black;/ *Then somewhere in the shadows a boy's eyes/ Glitter with love and bring the boy's love back.*"

Watkins, in other words, had found no remedy whatsoever for his grief. For all his bold acceptance that his Edenic world of childhood and Repton has been lost, never to return, his imagined miracle is that this world, despite everything, would suddenly reappear, almost unaltered.

In a poem called 'Stone Love',[27] written in February, he imagined in more detail how he could accomplish this miracle. He does so according to the example of Pygmalion, who fell in love with the stone statue he had created, which miraculously came to life and became his actual belovéd. Watkins, likewise, realizing the pointlessness of hoping the beauty of youth and "the joy/ The lover feels for blue-eyed boy" could ever return, seeks to gaze on a statue of "a Grecian boy, a lover's head", whose beauty can never be touched by death. He will then, in his own way, magically call back to life the *real* object of his love:

> *Show me but this, and I will swear*
> *My model had more perfect hair;*
> *And gaze in ravished, slow surprise,*
> *Knowing his eyes were lovelier eyes.*

Life at Cambridge – I. A. Richards – differences with Isherwood

This hardly suited him, of course, for life at Cambridge. He attended two evenings at the 'Société Francaise' – a lecture about music as "the queen of the arts" and a "soirée poétique"[28] (poetry evening) – but for the most part he found the whole of Cambridge life "cold and dispiriting."[29] Quite how at odds he was with it can be seen by casting a sideways glance at Isherwood and Upward, and seeing how *they* were faring compared to him.

Although Watkins was studying Modern Languages he would no doubt have had some interest in the youngish lecturer at Magdalene responsible for teaching "English Literature and the Moral Sciences", who was rapidly becoming a hugely influential literary critic – I.A. Richards. It is hard to imagine anyone whose approach to literature and poetry Vernon Watkins at 18 (or indeed at any age) would have been more likely to be repelled by than that of I.A. Richards. Here, by contrast, is the experience of Isherwood and Upward (one year later):

"For both of us, the great event of that term was the series of lectures on modern poetry given by Mr. I. A. Richards. Here, at last, was the prophet we had been waiting for ... who announced: 'According to me, it's quite possible that, in fifty years' time, people will have stopped writing poetry altogether' ... Up to this moment, we had been a pair of romantic conservatives ... who refused to read T. S. Eliot ... or the newspapers, or Freud. Now, in a moment, all was changed. Poets, ordered Mr. Richards, were to reflect aspects of the World-Picture. Poetry wasn't a holy flame ... it was a group of interrelated stimuli acting upon the ocular nerves, the semi-circular canals, the brain, the solar plexus, the digestive and sexual organs ... We became behaviourists, materialists, atheists."

Even Isherwood and Upward did not find this easy at first, but the change, once they had made it, was total:

"But if Mr. Richards enormously stimulated us, he plunged us, also, into the profoundest gloom. It seemed to us that everything we had valued would have to be scrapped ... it was no good: we were banished from that world forever: we could only pay it short occasional visits, as mourners visit a cemetery, and then return."[30]

Watkins, in his very first printed poem had mourned the loss of the divinity of childhood and now, in the arid intellectual world of Cambridge, he had experienced that "banishment" in far more bitter terms. He also knew that there was no way *back*. Yet life for him was unimaginable if some way of overcoming this sense of banishment could not eventually be found. Thus Isherwood's way of facing this situation, by simply joining the ranks of the "behaviourists, materialists (and) atheists" and accepting that people will soon "stop ... writing poetry altogether", could never have been Watkins's. He would one day launch, with Dylan Thomas, his own mature revolution against the literary world dominated by Isherwood, Auden and Spender. At present, though, aged 18, he had not even begun to resolve this crisis, and so his poetry and his approach to life, compared to Isherwood's, appear childishly naïve in their innocence. Thus a poem Watkins wrote at Cambridge after "reading some modern verse" ends: *O hollowness! / Better be mute/ Than so pollute/ With borrowed lute/ The poet's love and holiness.*[31]

Such lines as these massively contrast with what had happened to the poetry of Edward Upward. Looking back on their immature days at Repton, Isherwood ironically recalled telling Edward Upward that: "I am certain, absolutely convinced, that he is going to be a really great poet, the greatest of our generation. My voice trembles with excitement."[32] At Cambridge, however, Upward "felt, now, that he would never be a poet ... his thought was tied up in bizarre adjectives, deliberately obscure phrases, conceits." These had been "his final undoing."[33] Watkins, by contrast, stubbornly rejected the intellectual climate around him, preferring to remain "mute", if necessary, and immature, as he undoubtedly was,[34] rather than to lose touch with the springs of his poetry.

The extreme difference between Isherwood and Watkins is also revealed in their relationship to homosexuality. Christopher Isherwood was fully open about his homosexuality from a young age and became an important figure in the movement for gay rights. Any thought that Vernon Watkins's early homosexual feelings might also have come to expression in this way – or that, as has been said of Rupert Brooke,[35] this might even have provided him with a solution to his inner turmoil – falls far short of understanding Watkins's inner state. As so much of his early poetry shows, he had felt something *paradisal* in the childhood world that he experienced the younger boys at Repton still to be living in. Take *that* experience of paradise away from him – as it *had* now been taken away – and nothing would ever be able to compensate for it, other than some true way of regaining that experience.

It would be years before he would find that way, but right now, in the immediate aftermath of his "fall from grace", he was a long way from accepting life after the fall, as Isherwood advocated, and his whole striving was for how he could arrest that fall or, better still, hoist himself back to before it ever happened.

This determined his whole approach to art and to life. *Art* was the only means he knew by which it was possible to stop the flow of time. Thus in 'Stone Love' the only way he can win back his childhood love is via a *statue* of a boy, whose beauty has been preserved from death.

The same was true of his life. The only means he knew by which it was possible not to fall prey to the passing of time was to attain "immortality" through one's art – through which one's "name" lives on after one's death. This was the central focus of Watkins's life, which drew all else behind it – to achieve greatness as a poet and a lasting name: "I wanted, at that early stage, to be 'numbered among the English poets'"[36] and: "I aimed at writing a kind of poetry that would be remembered after my time."[37]

To leave!
Clash with A.C. Benson
As the months went by, Watkins found life at Cambridge not merely unconducive to this, but to be ever more likely to have a devastating effect on himself and on his poetry. The critical and even cynical intellectual attitudes fostered here seemed opposed to everything he cherished and stood for. He found no understanding for the extreme and unusual inner crisis he was suffering from and could certainly see no possibility of finding any remedy here for it. He therefore had no alternative but to leave.

In May, he found the opportunity to talk about this with the Master of the College, A.C. Benson. Benson was a large, colourful and contradictory personality, representative of many of the contradictions at the heart of Cambridge itself. He had been part of an intellectual statement against England joining the First World War[38] and yet was the author of 'Land of Hope and Glory'!

On May 12th, 1924, Benson had some business in London, and was accompanied by a number of undergraduates, including Vernon Watkins. They visited some of the poorer parts of the city, including Crouch End, where Benson maintained there was no real suffering or "lack of prosperity" to be seen. He wrote in his diary: "the big endless city is fine … No signs of dirt or squalor – the children so plump & well dressed." He noted at the same time: "One tiresome banking artistic man, nice with boy & girl." "Tiresome" was a word used frequently by Benson[39], and this 'banking artistic man' was none other than Vernon Watkins. Watkins's attitude to the poor was quite different from Benson's. In a poem called 'An Incident', probably having its origin in this same visit to London, he encounters "three poor little girls", each of them a "slave /Of poverty." He gives one of them a sixpence, hoping to bring her joy, but her only response is "a little, frightened cry", making Watkins realize his inability to enter their world and "stir their secret happiness."[40]

The day also gave Watkins the opportunity to speak with A.C. Benson about his plight and to ask him directly for help. The conversation was a critical one for Watkins and has been described before by others, although it has falsely been presumed to have taken place in Benson's study. Roland Mathias writes, therefore, that Watkins "told A.C. Benson … that he was interested only in writing poetry and that he didn't intend to stay in Cambridge and see it criticised out of him. Benson … retorted that if becoming a poet was his aim, he would curse the day he had been born. Vernon, … hot with anger, muttered that he had cursed it many times already and slammed the door as he went out."[41]

The conversation in fact took place away from Cambridge, and Benson's utter rejection of Watkins's calling as a poet came after Watkins had asked Benson to find him a job where he could devote himself unreservedly to his poetry. Mathias is correct, though, that Watkins began the conversation by stating that Cambridge had nothing to offer him as a poet and that he would therefore be leaving. Benson left a terse record of their conversation in his diary:

"Watkins a tiresome undergrad, with an overweening belief in his own poetry, came for a voice. He wanted me to find him a well paid post with little to do & that interesting & giving time to do his own work. I found it difficult to persuade him that such posts are not common."[42]

It was a strange clash between the two men – Watkins at the very beginning and Benson at the very end of his working life. Exactly five weeks after declaring that Watkins would "curse the day he had been born" A.C. Benson died of a heart attack.[43]

For Watkins, this was the third time that someone had tried to dissuade him from being a poet. His mother had laughed at him as a boy; Geoffrey Fisher had said his poetry would never earn him any money; and Benson had even now tried to pour derision on his whole calling as a poet. He became, if anything, only more determined on each occasion. If Watkins in fact did not slam any physical door, he most certainly slammed a metaphorical one. He firmly and finally turned his back on Cambridge. He would finish the term, but would never return.

"The German Romantic Movement"
Vernon Watkins and Monty Python

On a more humorous note, the earliest surviving example of Vernon Watkins's light and comic verse is from these final months of his at Cambridge. For all the sufferings he experienced at Cambridge, he would at least have been grateful for his closer knowledge of French and German poetry, which he would frequently translate. His German course would almost certainly have given him his first major exposure to the range and profundity of the German Romantic Movement. He penned his own comic homage to it – ('The German Romantic Movement – as seen by an undergraduate and a fan') – based on finding English rhymes for every German name. Thus:

> *Goethe*
> *Was a terrible flirter.*
> *"He started at nine!"*
> *Said Charlotte von Stein.*

Or:

> *When Mrs. Schlegel*
> *Tried to inveigle*
> *Fichte*
> *He kichte*

Six years after Watkins's death the Monty Python team (who had also been at Cambridge) created their own comic sketch rhyming with many of the great philosophers – 'The Philosophers' Drinking Song'. Although it is unlikely they knew Watkins's poem, they used exactly the same rhymes as him for Kant and Nietzsche. Watkins: "*When Schleiermacher/ Saw a fly attack an/ Ant/ He told Kant.*" Monty Python: "Immanuel Kant was a real piss-ant/ Who was very rarely stable." Monty Python: "There's nothing Nietzsche/ Couldn't teach ya/ 'Bout the raising of the wrist." Watkins: "*Uhland/ was no fuhl, and/ Nietzsche/ No tietzsche.*"

Watkins made his final version of this poem 42 years later, in May 1967.[44] Only one stanza in it remains unchanged from the version he had written at Cambridge:

> *Schiller*
> *Grew iller and iller*
> *Till in eighteen-five*
> *He wasn't alive.*

Watkins was not only highly aware of number, but also constantly saw reflections of his own life in events and circumstances outside him. Particularly as 'eighteen-five' is an odd way of referring to this date, it is possible that the 18 year-old Watkins was drawing a humorous parallel between himself and Schiller, who in 1805 died young from an inexplicable illness. Eighty years later, in 1925, Vernon Watkins might perhaps be seen to have been suffering from the same fate. He might well have been saying, with a certain tragic-comic genius, that during this last year at Cambridge he too had been growing "iller and iller/Till in 'twenty-five/He wasn't alive."

Exams, leaving, letters from home

Watkins did take the exams at the end of the summer term, but scored marks as low as 13 out of 50 in French composition; 38 out of 100 in French literature; 22 out of 50 in German translation and 57 out of 100 in German literature and history.[45] He informed the College that he would almost certainly *not* be returning, which would be confirmed in writing after discussion with his parents, then packed his things and left.

Once back home, Vernon announced his decision to his parents, to his mother's great disappointment, for she still apparently harboured completely unrealistic hopes that her son would enter the diplomatic service. Soon afterwards a letter arrived from the senior tutor at Magdalene, A.S. Ramsey, asking that the college be given a final decision about Vernon's future: "I shall be glad to know definitely whether you propose to return into residence or not."[46] Ramsey's letter also informed the family that Vernon's exam results were not good enough for him to be able to apply for a scholarship, but that if he did choose to return, the "College Benefaction Fund" could make a grant of £5 a year to help with the family's finances.

Intense discussions followed, with Watkins's parents urging him not to throw away the career prospects Cambridge offered. When Vernon remained adamant, his father, presumably at his mother's insistence, offered to pay for some other training, like teaching, which could lead to a profession. But Vernon already had a full-time profession – his poetry – and the last thing he wanted was a demanding career which might compete with it. He had already told A.C. Benson quite clearly the kind of job he was looking for. In that case, stated Vernon's father, he must simply join the bank and the start at the bottom as a clerk. Without regard for the consequences, and banking having anyway always been his 'default' option, the work, so he hoped, that would place least demand on him, he accepted.[47]

Vernon replied to Ramsey, with perfect courtesy, though not quite with perfect honesty, as he made no mention of his own part in the decision:

"Dear Mr. Ramsay,
I must apologize for my delay in answering your kind letter. I was very glad to learn that I had been awarded the Language Prize[48], and I am extremely grateful to you for all your interest and generosity during my year at Magdalene – from which I have certainly derived much enjoyment and benefit.

Unfortunately, I am afraid I shall be unable to return into residence in October, as my father has now definitely decided for me to go into the Bank in the Autumn. I think he will write to you to confirm why this is necessary or desirable, as I do not know all the 'facts of the case'.

We are both very much indebted to you for your help; and if, in a few years' time, I find myself in a position to study for a degree, I shall be very glad to return to Magdalene.

Very sincerely yours,
Vernon P Watkins.

P.S. Is it possible to take my other two years for a degree at a later date, or must the 3 years' residence be consecutive?"

Reading this, together with the correspondence before Vernon went up to Cambridge regarding William Watkins's difficulties affording the fees, one might presume that Vernon's decision to leave had been made solely by his father. This would fail to understand, however, that this was exactly what Vernon wanted Ramsey to think. Despite the strength of his inner rebellion and his uncompromising commitment to poetry, he was young for his age and still in no way independent. Regarding actual administrative arrangements with Cambridge he would quite certainly have been happy to hide behind the voice of his father, as he does in this letter.

Moreover, before Vernon had started at Cambridge Ramsey had informed William Watkins that if he provided evidence of his financial difficulties Vernon might be able to receive extra financial help. When William Watkins declined this offer, Ramsey had told him: "If at any future time there should be need to do so we should be glad to consider your son's case sympathetically." There is no mention of this now, however, either from the Watkins's or from Ramsey, for William Watkins's finances were *not* the main reason for Vernon's sudden departure, which he had already announced to the College before travelling home. It would in fact have been Vernon's father who attempted to ensure that Vernon did *not* close the door completely on Cambridge and made him ask if it might be possible to complete his degree later on. Despite his words to the contrary, Vernon was actually the only one who fully knew the 'facts of the case', and who had made the firm decision to 'burn his boats' and leave Cambridge.

Farewell ritual
'On the Passing of June'
He wrote his 'farewell letter' to Cambridge on June 28th. He could at last let the death-like experience of Cambridge slip from his shoulders. In Gower, in the summer, before starting in the bank, he could reconnect to life again and commit himself, from now on, wholly to his poetry. It is possible that he even performed, in nature, a small and silent ritual to celebrate the event and to mark his new beginning. He certainly announces his intention to do so in a poem written in the days immediately after sending his letter, called 'On the passing of June'.

In a sacred ritual, performed in nature, he will forget the death-world of Cambridge and create for himself a new reality:

> *I shall forget Death's awful trysting-place*
> *Of wild surmising;*
>
> *And build there a fresh altar*
> *Of dreams new-gathered* [49]

At this altar, a memorial too to the heavenly beauty of youth now gone, if he cannot halt the destruction time brings, he will at least be free from the pain of this:

> *Before the white shrine kneeling*
> *– Dead Youth's memorial –*
> *I shall not hear Time's fingers nailing*
> *My bier for burial.*

Vernon Watkins at Cambridge

CHAPTER FOUR
Cardiff (1925–1928)

*'Three Years Long Lasted My War
With Time'*

On September 1st, 1925, Vernon took up employment as a junior clerk in Lloyds Bank at the Roath Park branch, Cardiff. He lived in a rented room nearby at 73 Connaught Road. His impracticality at the job was apparent from the start: "On my third or fourth day in the bank, in trying to seal a packet of bank notes, I quite unintentionally set fire to them."[1] Such incidents would later lead to many jokes and stories about Vernon Watkins, but initially the life-choice he had just made and the daily work in the bank were no laughing matter. The burning banknotes, as he tells us, "were saved, and so was I, for the time being." But only for the time being. For there now began in earnest his "war with time", which he would wage with increasing intensity throughout his next three years in Cardiff, culminating in the greatest crisis of his life.

For after all the exalted experiences of his childhood and youth, either surrounded by friends or in the beauties of nature or immersed in culture and poetry, he had now consigned himself to a life devoid of any of these, to routine clerical work in a bank, in an ugly and uninspiring suburb of Cardiff, where he had no friends.[2]

1st Year – 1926
The first effect on Vernon, plunged into this alien environment, was that of an inner withdrawal from the world around him. His sister described that when he went to Cardiff: "His early shyness ... developed into a deep reserve".[3] He himself wrote, looking back on this time: "First felt I like an exile from my kind".[4] These are both understatements regarding what was actually taking place within him, which, as usual, he would

only reveal within his poetry. Five months after arriving in Cardiff he wrote one of the strangest poems ever seriously meant by a 19 year-old. The previous June, in Gower, he had hoped to create a protected shrine in nature where he might stave off destruction, even for a while. In his bedsit room in Connaught Road, alone at night, this possibility no longer exists and he enacts a very different ritual, a kind of dance of death:

> *Watch me move across the room*
> *As one who studies his own doom;*
> *And read in movement lithe and fresh*
> *The slow corruption of my flesh …*
>
> *Feel the fingers gently pressed*
> *Against your shoulder, arm or breast*
> *Mortally; and hear my breath*
> *Sighing like the wind of Death.*
>
> *But question not the apocalypse*
> *Shaped by the utterance of these lips …*

Only by thoroughly embracing death in this way, the poem concludes, will "true lovers" find any grounds for "immortal hope".[5]

As is not difficult to imagine, he was wholly alone with these experiences. A poem written a month later reveals the only company he enjoyed as he sat night after night, after the day at the bank, writing poetry and observing "his own doom". The poem is called 'Company':

> *O Angel invisible! …*
>
> *My spirit feels thee; … //*
> *Here in this chamber*
> *At night thou dwellest,*
> *And the mystery tellest*
> *That I scarce remember.*[6]

It was a very odd, schizophrenic existence. He obeyed all the strict working-practices of the bank and worked a 5 ½ day week, finishing at lunch-time on Saturday. He would usually then make his way back to Gower, telling Falk: "I go home most weekends now & see practically no one." He was very fit, walking everywhere and playing tennis when he could.[7] He therefore led an outwardly 'normal' and healthy life, with little time in it seemingly for much else. Yet his inner life left him no rest, and neither did his poetry, which he mentioned to no one, yet which never ceased to pour through him. As he once recalled: "Repton and Cambridge – continuous writing of poetry. Joined a bank. *Wrote more than ever: told nobody.*"[8]

"My grandfather dying"
On Monday November 1st, 1926, after Vernon had been in Cardiff for over a year, his beloved grandfather James Phillips died aged 86. He had been living, since becoming ill, in the house of Vernon's parents. Vernon spent that weekend there and stayed for as long as possible. He therefore caught the early Monday morning train to Cardiff, saying goodbye to his grandfather before he did so: "I left you after dawn ... at sundown you were dead."

In the strange state in which Vernon was, being slightly more than "half in love with easeful death", and feeling anyway a close kinship with his grandfather,[9] he identified so strongly with the old man's experience that in a poem called *My Grandfather Dying* one can sometimes wonder if he was describing his grandfather or himself:

> On that white bed you seemed less man than boy ...
> So young, so strange your conflict was, but oh
> So pitiful, for there seemed no hope of rest
> Except in loss.[10]

True as this might be of James Phillips, that he could only win peace from his death-throes after death, it was less clear what this might mean for the "so young" Vernon Watkins, and what "loss" or death *he* might need to go through to win any "hope of rest".

The following Saturday Vernon returned to Gower and walking back to his parents' house, his grandfather strongly in his mind,[11] he was once again lifted into an experience closer to the dead than to the living. After sensing the "wild sweet odours" of the fields in winter, "(t)he air grew thin and rare" and then: *"The sky was filled with voices, voices of death./ Dear voices!"* He felt, in a *"moment's ecstasy"*, united with his grandfather and attuned once more with himself and his poetic calling, so that the experience granted him *"some certain footing"*.[12]

However unstable such a "footing" might ultimately prove to be, it is nonetheless easy to imagine Vernon feeling it, walking in the beautiful Gower landscape and sensing the presence of his beloved grandfather. Once he was back in Cardiff, though, the gap grew rapidly ever wider between the world of his inner experience and the daily world around him.

Byron Street

Several of the streets near Watkins's lodgings, which he often walked through, were named after great English poets – Shakespeare Court, Wordsworth Avenue, Shelley Gardens, Milton Street and Byron Street.[13] Oddly, at this time, Watkins was so immersed in the visionary worlds of some of these poets that he would barely even register the ordinary world around him, except through their eyes: *"At the age of twenty-one the poems and letters of Keats, and the poetry of Shelley, Milton and Blake so governed me that the everyday world hardly existed for me except as a touchstone for protest and indignation."*[14]

A month after his grandfather died, walking through Byron Street in such an extreme condition, he was struck by the extreme poverty of the children playing there, and the miserable conditions of their lives became precisely such a "touchstone for protest and indignation." It led to a long, visionary poem called 'Byron Street', which clearly shows how almost dangerously unhinged he was becoming from reality.

The poem begins with a dream Watkins had – either actually or in imagination – of Byron Street and its children reappearing in some parallel reality, a Grecian idyll, perhaps inspired by thoughts of Lord Byron in Greece, but equally by Watkins's own childhood romantic fantasies:

"O Byron Street! I dreamed there was a road" where, as well as *"lovely*

dancing girls", *"naked boys ... played around a fountain of white marble"* and where there were *"brave men ... of Ancient Greece"*.

Aware that this is *not* the present-day reality, Watkins leaves this idyll and embarks on a five page, megalomaniac exhortation, addressing not just the poverty-stricken children he has seen but the whole sleeping populace around:

> *Awake, awake, people of Byron Street!*
> *You are God's children, you the sons of light,*
> *Not less, but mightier than your lords and kings.*

He desires to show them what he has been fortunate enough to experience – the wonders of nature and the blessings of death, where they will be free from earthly injustices – before he realizes that these can never answer the real cause of both their and his suffering – that the beauties and joys of childhood have no hope of surviving, are crushed and even murdered – and with this his own massive, unhealed wound opens up again:

> *But there are bodies,*
> *Young and innocent, laughing, light foot bodies*
> *Of love impetuous ...*
>
> *O men will bind those limbs*
> *And bow those beautiful heads, put out those eyes*
> *Even in the noon of childhood.*
> *Who'll do this?*
> *I tell you all will ...*
> *Men's hands are red with unacknowledged murders ...*
> *This is the unforgiveable sin.*

The only solution is that the people of Byron Street join with him in creating a parallel world where childhood never suffers such destruction: *"A world not unlike ours ... / But filled with all the music of child-laughter,/ For naked there your children shall be free."*

Deep in the night as he writes, he feels that this world has miraculously already come about: *"yours it is in this mysterious hour"*. He hears the proclamation ringing out in his dream that a whole new day of light is indeed dawning for them, which he calls on them to be aware of:

> *O Byron Street! I dreamed there was a cry,*
> *'Hellas of Beggars dawns!'*

The poem ends with Watkins awakening from his visionary dream. One may well ask, though, how Watkins, after sitting up into the early hours dreaming and writing such visions, in stark opposition to the existing world around him, would then have experienced his work at the bank. For all his attempts to escape this world through his poetry, he was in fact at this time, as he later described, "more miserable than I like to remember".[15]

The cry of 'Hellas' at the end of 'Byron Street' links with the dream at the start transferring all the children of Byron Street to Ancient Greece. It also links with Shelley's poem *Hellas*, which Watkins would have known, about the revolutionary struggles in modern Greece, in which Byron had fought and died. Hardly surprisingly, therefore, the thought soon took root in Watkins that maybe in the South, in Greece or Italy – where Shelley and Keats had both lived – he might find some way of curing his misery.

He wrote 'Byron Street' during December and January 1926. During this time, at Christmas, he wrote Eric Falk the briefest of notes, making clear that all was far from well and showing too that Italy was on his mind:

Dear Fig,

  Aren't the evenings closing in, Mrs. Fisher? We're approaching the last signpost of detachment, mon ami ...

  Buona notte – Vernon.[16]

2nd Year – 1927

In March, 1927, Vernon had two weeks holiday and seized the opportunity to go to Italy and Rome.

He looked all around Rome, visiting among other places the Vatican[17] and the Coliseum. In the catacombs, imagining the early Christians who had lived there, he sensed the presence of the dead around him: "when the footstep dies/ Out of the dust they rise,/ Out of the walls they come".[18]

But above all he was drawn unavoidably to one place – to the Protestant Cemetery where Shelley and Keats were buried. Looking back on this visit years later, it was only this that remained in his mind:

"I went to Rome in 1927, when I was twenty, and saw the graves of Keats and Shelley. I was … very much under the influence of Shelley; I should say really very unhappy at the time."[19]

Shelley and Keats had also both been drawn to Italy, seeking for the realization of their hopes, as had been not been possible for them in Britain. And both had died there – Keats at 26 and Shelley at 30. And with their deaths, English Romantic poetry itself may be said to have come to an end.[20]

Already in Vernon's third poem in 'The Reptonian' he had briefly heard "the magic voice of Poesy", only then to realize that it was now "silent – dead". And the ultimate symbol or expression of this was the *young deaths* in Italy of Shelley and Keats. So Vernon, making his pilgrimage to their graves, was on the one hand arriving at the place of his greatest hopes, and on the other at the place symbolizing the destruction of those hopes and the impossibility of their being realized.

Watkins went first to the grave of Shelley, who had inspired him to start writing poetry again at 15, and who was his predominant influence at the time. But it was the grave of Keats, which he went to next, which made by far the greater impression on him. Watkins was never self-centredly focussed on himself and his own actions, but instead frequently found himself reflected in realitics he observed around him. In his extreme inner state, walking across the cemetery, he was "stopped in his tracks" seeing a grave which bore no name, but only the words in large letters: YOUNG ENGLISH POET. He then read the whole inscription:

> **This Grave**
> contains all that was Mortal,
> of a
> **YOUNG ENGLISH POET**
> Who,
> on his Death Bed,
> in the Bitterness of his Heart,
> at the Malicious Power of his Enemies,
> Desired
> these Words to be engraven on his Tomb Stone
> **Here lies One**
> **Whose Name was writ in Water**
> Feb 24th 1821

Above it there is a harp engraved into the stone.

In Watkins's life all that he "loved and treasured most" seemed "irreparably lost".[21] The young deaths of Keats and Shelley also spoke to him of "youth cut off".[22] He wrote a poem where he saw Keats's grave as the whole world – or the whole world as being Keats' grave: "Here I come to find you, stone/ … All the world shall be your tomb,/ A violet-covered catacomb."[23]

He spent his final afternoon, March 21st, wandering through the Borghese Gardens, with its many fountains and lakes surrounded by sculptures of deities and youths. In the afternoon, watching some young children playing, "(t)heir bodies loosened and light,"[24] there re-awoke in him his seemingly unquenchable desire for all the lost joys of his youth.

He stayed in the gardens until very late and, in the awareness that he had to leave Rome the following day, his inner state intensified to the point of mania. Wandering among the statues under an almost full moon he wrote in his increasingly smudged and rain-spattered

John Keats's grave in the Protestant Cemetery, Rome

notebook, giving spontaneous expression in poetry to what was happening inside him.

He expresses his present state: "How came you to this great loneliness/ This final devastation of all your days". He then, however, in "this great garden infinite in forms," swings rapidly high up in the opposite direction, feeling "joy to the point of madness."

A wall broke down within him somewhere and he again felt no separation between this world and the world inhabited by the dead, leading him to proclaim, in Blakean manner, to the whole of humanity:

> *Be comforted, be comforted, O ye millions of mortals, there is no*
> *Death! Ye are all eternal, this I know*
> *For it is breathed within me. Your raiments fall away*
> *Your bodies live in joy. Know ye the way*
> *Back to the gardens naméd Life? Have ye the key*
> *To that eternal door?*

His justified sense of the possibility of life continuing after death had almost immediately changed into the quite *un*justified wish to find himself back in the days of his childhood ("Know ye the way/Back..?"). And so from addressing all the "millions of mortals" he turns suddenly to the single individual who remained the central focus of his attention, his boyhood love from Repton. Here amidst the ruins of Rome, might not the impossible happen, and his lover return to him and they both miraculously find themselves again in "the gardens naméd Life?" –

> *… so beautiful and light,*
> *Running between the ruins, come,*
> *Give me your arms, but come tonight*
> *Out of the years that are no more*
> *Come to me softly, here I'll wait*
> **And find your Repton in my Rome …** [25]

He recognizes in the end that he is unable to "stop the footstep of the hour" and so can only "smile, because you're far". But Watkins had given voice to the full extremity of his condition and had come nowhere near resolving it.

Vernon travelled from Rome to Menton in France, where both his sisters were staying, and joined them in time for Dorothy's birthday on March 23rd.[26]

One day, as Dorothy described, they "climbed the hot, dusty hill to Roquebrune, then a little-visited jewel of a place, where some modern troubadours were playing on very old instruments and singing 14th century French songs. It was a magical occasion."[27] Twelve years later W.B. Yeats would die in Roquebrune, which Vernon called: "a lovely place with rocky walls, cobbled streets, a hill and narrow passages, exciting as it grew dark."[28]

It was, however, another event, in the present-day, which had a much greater impact on him. Watkins had stayed in touch with his most significant friend at Cambridge, "the Dutchman", Cornelis van Stolk, and van Stolk now joined Watkins and his sisters in France – briefly, anyway, before being arrested and put in prison for the night, and then returning to tell the tale:

"A Cambridge friend [29] ... came to Menton with Vernon and proved to be quite as vague and absent-minded as our brother. He went missing for a couple of days, only to return as suddenly as he had left, with a bunch of violets which he presented to Marjorie, saying that he had picked them from his prison walls ... on one of his walks he had inadvertently crossed the border into Italy, where he was promptly arrested and kept under guard for the night as he was not carrying his passport."[30]

Cornelis van Stolk was possibly the one person, both at Cambridge and now, who had a genuine affinity with Vernon and who was potentially able to understand his condition. (Except perhaps for Marjorie, with whom van Stolk had immediately felt a connection on seeing her photograph: "Marjorie he was tremendously struck with, and is frightfully anxious to meet her."[31]) That van Stolk should have been thrown into prison for trying to enter *Italy*, and had then found *violets* on his cell-walls, which Vernon had seen on the tomb of Keats, leading

> Be comforted, be comforted, O ye millions of mortals,
> Death! Ye are all eternal, this I know there is no
> For it is breathed within me. Your raiments fall away,
> Your bodies live in joy. Know ye the way
> Back to the garden named Life? Have ye the key
> To that eternal door?

Come to me through the other door,
But come, so beautiful ~~radiant~~ and light,
Running ~~between~~ the ruins, come,
Give me your arms, but come to-night

Out of the years that are no more
Come to me softly; here I'd ~~die~~ wait
And find your Repton in my Rome,
~~———————————~~
Pillars of Hercules and Love

~~————————~~
Come to me through the other gate.
O lightest, if I had the power
To pull the moon down while you move
And ~~catch the~~ stop the footstep of the hour

I'd laugh to see you come, but now
~~I smile, because you're fair,~~ and still
The moon goes on from bough to bough
And drops behind the ruined hill
                                    Rome.

From Vernon Watkins's Rome Notebook – 1927

him to call the whole world a "violet-covered catacomb", had a powerful effect on Vernon's imagination.

Writing in the same notebook he had been using in Italy, he started a poem for voices called 'Chorus of the Prisoners'. This quickly transformed into 'The Prisoners' in a new notebook, whose opening clearly sprang from the experience of Italy and of van Stolk being thrown into prison:

> O cobbled Rome, O Greece, O Italy!
> Can walls enclose the imaginative brain?
> Can the wide soul be curled, …
> Or paralysed in one dark dungeon-room?

Next to the title, as the poem's motto, Watkins put Wordsworth's words: "*Shades of the prison-house/ Begin to close/ Upon the growing boy*".[32] Three months earlier Watkins had already put this in his own words to Falk: "*Aren't the nights closing in, Mrs. Fisher?*"

'The Prisoners' then bitterly examines the imprisonment we suffer simply by leaving childhood. Wordsworth's 'Intimations of Immortality' appears optimistically positive by comparison. As Watkins now sees it, the very enjoyment of poetry itself – which had started for him aged 7 or 8 – is already the first sign that we have begun falling from our earliest unbounded experience of *life*:

> Life ends
> When first we feel the energy of rhyme, …
> And we go down to death

After that, memory, puberty and thought imprison us ever more deeply within our bodies:

> *When memory takes possession of our breath,*
> *When falls*
> *Bosom and voice; when first we close our eyes*
> *Not upon sleep but thought …*
> *'Tis then/ The body rushes up into the brain, …*
> *(T)his is the moment when the creature dies,*
> *The moment when the tiger sees the bars.*

Watkins fervently seeks in the poem for states of exaltation enabling him to burst out of the prison-bars, but these always merely exacerbate the miserable experience of "imprisonment" he would then be plunged back into afterwards. Exactly this now happened in his life, in the most extreme way, when after two weeks in Italy and France he was obliged to return to his cramped lodgings in Cardiff and the relentless tedium of his work at the bank.

Incarceration

Despite or even because of all he had been suffering, there had been no let-up in his poetry since leaving Cambridge, either in its profusion or its technique or the visionary intensity of its themes. He *knew* things about Keats, Shelley and even Blake which no one else and no other contemporary poet knew. He knew himself to be, in a very real sense, their *heir*. It is important to understand this about Vernon Watkins as a young poet. There was no doubt in his mind that he would eventually be one of the great names of English poetry. Looking back later at his visit to Rome, he described himself as having been "Confident that he would be/ Remembered by posterity."[33]

The thought therefore occurred to him that *if* he could get back to Italy and live there, within a year he would be able to make a living as a poet, picking up, as it were, from where Keats and Shelley had left off. His father had offered to pay for any professional training Vernon wished to undertake. He thus asked his father if he would consider funding him for a year in Italy[34] – as his own particular professional training – after which he he would, he hoped, be able to live from his writing. His father's reply was a firm and categorical "no". From this moment on Vernon really did experience his life in Cardiff as an incarceration.

Soon after returning to Cardiff, he wrote a long letter to Falk, expressing what he was going through:

"Everything here is inferior, except a little park near here, perhaps, and a little wood not far off, so I simply pull down the blinds and ignore it. It seems to me that after 19 we must choose one of two things, either to drift with the current of time, or to resist it and sink. But if you can see under water ...?

"My love, this is a tedious place they've pushed us into and I wish I could suggest some way out of it ... we <u>knew</u> this was going to come ... we saw it all ... & we laughed at those hollow prisons which were inevitably waiting to receive us not many years later ... I can't believe that this after-life is more than the fulfilment of that ridiculous nightmare. <u>But we need poetry, poetry always, to see that</u>. Without music we should all be lost."

When Watkins says "I simply pull down the blinds and ignore it" he is, according to Gwen Watkins, not revealing his full reason for doing so. He would, she says, frequently dance around his room naked, declaiming Blake. When neighbours complained, his landlady asked him if he would at least shut the blinds.[35] Watkins claimed he was behaving like William and Catherine Blake, who had walked in their garden naked, like Adam and Eve.[36] Knowing Watkins's many references to the Garden of Eden and to "(y)oung and innocent, laughing, light foot bodies", this is wholly credible. Particularly as he now, in his own words, read Blake "all the time"[37] and was wholly "absorbed in Blake's ... tremendous visions".[38] He told the American writer Nelson Bentley that at the time he had "thought (Blake's) prophetic books literally true."[39]

Keats's tombstone in Rome told how he had died "at the malicious power of his enemies", which would undoubtedly have made Watkins think of his own literary enemies, above all Christopher Isherwood, a close friend of Falk's. Watkins's letter therefore continued:

"*Ask Isherwood why he hates me so excessively*. This is only curiosity, because I suppose it doesn't matter much; but wish him luck with the novel he's writing".

Towards the end of the letter, the extent of Watkins's illusions and his inability to abandon the impossible dream that his Repton days might somehow miraculously return, becomes ever more shockingly clear. He begins by wondering about the fact that boys who had been "fags" during his final year at Repton were now "heads of the house":

"Whatever can be done about it? But soon they will leave, I suppose, & then they will immediately become fags again. Even now I can't think of them as anything else – *The real Repton doesn't change.*

"I've been reading *Alice in Wonderland* & *Through the Looking Glass*, easily the greatest prose-books. Every page is immortal. If only we could escape to a cave with certain chosen, and read aloud & tear our hair & go raving mad for an indefinite length of time without ever growing older or wiser or stronger. *Then perhaps we could <u>physically</u> live Repton –* "

He signs off:

"When you are a great barrister & when Pavlova comes again to London, we will set up the tables of the law and play the Eventual game of ping-pong

    Before that time many things must happen.

    Yours ever Vernon."[40]

In June he turned 21. Not long afterwards, in the second half of 1927, as a kind of coming-of-age present, he had a significant dream in which he was addressed by a voice of 'judgement':

"I continued to write poems at increasing pressure until I was twenty or twenty-one. Then, suddenly, I became dissatisfied with them. It was not a critic's judgement which turned me from the course my poetry was taking, but a judgement which I heard in a dream. This judgement was: '*Your poetry is only appreciation.*' It was a true judgement, and it influenced me profoundly."[41]

Had he stayed at Cambridge, he would by now have completed his degree. So too, on the different course he had chosen, he was also asked to "graduate" and make his way forward without his teachers. He was forced to recognize that the "hold on my imagination" of the poets he loved "was much stronger than I supposed.[42] My own writing suffered from an inability to separate what I wanted to say from those great poets."⁴³

This would eventually be an important step on the path to finding his own genuine poetic voice. For now, though, it undoubtedly accelerated his inner crisis. Prior to this, he had at least had the imaginative worlds of Blake or Milton or Shelley to hold onto, unstable as they might appear to some. To let these go and rely solely upon himself was the equivalent of throwing off his moorings and heading out to sea alone, on a highly uncertain voyage.

3rd Year – 1928

For the next nine months or so we hear, ominously, nothing at all about Watkins. He probably destroyed his first attempts at poetry after this dream. He would also have tumbled, quietly, further into crisis.

In 1928, in the week after Easter, on Thursday 12th April, the event occurred which severed, at one blow, the threads connecting him in any 'normal' way to the daily world around him.

In 1927 Watkins had moved to the Cardiff docks branch of Lloyds Bank at 1 Montstuart Square, about a thirty minute walk from where he lived. That evening, he took his usual way home after work, from the docks to Newport Road, which he would walk down for half a mile or so, before turning off for his lodgings.

Right next to him on Newport Road, as he walked along it, the sidecar of a motorcycle accidentally smashed into the car in front of it, spinning the motorcycle and sidecar upside down and hurling out both rider and passenger onto the road. Not only did Watkins witness the whole dreadful accident, but the sidecar passenger was thrown out very near him. The driver of the motorcycle, a policeman, P.C. Charles Davies, lay dying in the road and later died in hospital. His passenger, George Davies, covered in blood, staggered towards Watkins and desperately reached out to him for help. He survived, despite 'multiple injuries' but Watkins, who was already in a highly unstable condition, was shattered by the experience. It triggered what in psychiatric terms must be called psychosis, but for which the more fitting term, in his case, is a 'spiritual emergency', which now moved inexorably to its conclusion.⁴⁴

The following day, which was Friday 13th, Vernon would have read the report of the accident on the front page of the South Wales News. As he did so, his attention would undoubtedly also have been caught by the headline underneath it – 'A MAESTEG EPIC'. On the same day, in another accident, in Vernon's birthplace, a miner had been "entombed" by a falling roof. Rescuers had struggled to reach him for five hours, "and it was with great difficulty that the victim was eventually recovered." With a certain grim humour the report concluded: "Unfortunately, he was dead."

"I walked in a sacred darkness"

These two events usher in the third and final year of Watkins's strange three-year journey, of which he once said: *'I walked in a sacred darkness three long years'.*[45] However unusual it may sound, it must be seen in many ways as an ever-intensifying journey into death. This was no longer something mysteriously uplifting, as when his grandfather had died in 1926, or something he felt a profound and tragic resonance with, as at the graves of Keats and Shelley in 1927, but was now, through the injured motorcycle passenger, something that had almost literally walked up and grabbed him.

The catalytic effect this had on his inner life is seen in a 77-page long poem he began writing soon afterwards called 'Poeta Caecus' – meaning 'Invisible Poet' or perhaps 'Poet of the Invisible'. Urged also by his dream to free himself from the influences of others, he now set out to explore the character of his own particular vision, describing along the way many of his previous visionary experiences

The "sacred darkness" he has now been plunged into has enabled him to *see*, he says, for the first time:

> *Surely I was blind ... till sight was lost*
> *And Night's refracting prism the image tossed.*[46]

SOUTH WALES NEWS, FRIDAY, APRIL 13, 1928.

OF REAR-ADMIRAL C

CONSTABLE KILLED.

NEWPORT ROAD FATALITY.

SIDECAR CRASH WITH MOTOR-CAR.

A MOTOR-CYCLE accident, with fatal consequences, occurred on the Cardiff-Newport road last night, when Police-constable Charles Davies, of the Cardiff City Police, received injuries, from which he died in the Cardiff Royal Infirmary.

P.C. Davies was riding a motor-cycle combination in the direction of Cardiff, and was accompanied in the sidecar by Mr George Davies.

Proceeding in front of him was a motor-car, driven by Mr E. Powell, a greengrocer, of Crichton-street, Cardiff, and by some means the wheel of the sidecar collided with the mudguard of the motor-car. The impact caused the combination to turn over, and P.C. Davies and the passenger were thrown out. They were attended to by passers-by, and later by Police-sergeant Taylor, St. Mellons, and were afterwards conveyed to the Cardiff City Police Infirmary, where P.C. Davies, who resided at Ordell-street, Splott, Cardiff, died.

His companion, Mr George Davies, of 7, Kerrycroy-street, received multiple injuries, but he is not in a serious condition.

POPULAR OFFICER.

The deceased was well known in the Splott district, and his loss will be felt by very many members of the Cardiff City Police Force, of which he had been a member for some years.

He leaves a widow (who is very ill), and a grown-up family.

NEWPORT'S CHOICE.

FIRST LABOUR ALDERMAN.

MAN WHO ONCE SLEPT ON EMBANKMENT.

COUNCILLOR PETER WRIGHT, J.P., who will to-day be elected as Newport's first Labour alderman, is one of the most interesting personalities in South Wales local government.

As a sailor he has formerly travelled in many climes, and has slept on the Thames Embankment, been kicked off hotel steps in New York, assisted in running a blockade in China, and more than once has rounded Cape Horn.

This varied career brought him in touch with men of all beliefs, and after he retired from

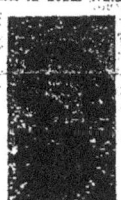

PREMIER'S OFFER.

MISTAKEN FOR A CIRCULAR!

STORY BY THE DEAN OF NORWICH.

AT a service in Norwich Cathedral yesterday the Rev. Dr. Grensge was installed Dean of Norwich.

Previously, at a luncheon in the Bishop's Palace, he related an amusing story of how he became aware of the appointment. He had been in America for three months, he said, and came back on the evening of November 21st.

An old servant, who opened the house, said, "I have put your letters on table in the writing room. There are several circulars you would not care to be troubled with."

Having had a rough passage and a tiring journey, he went straight down to dinner. Just before going to bed, however, he thought he would examine the "circulars." He turned them over, and saw one with the name of the Prime Minister at the bottom. He thought perhaps it was an appeal for the Armenians. (Laughter.)

It bore no ordinary stamp, and in the letter the envelope contained the Prime Minister offered to nominate him to the King for the Deanery of Norwich. One could not venture to think of a more delightful and surprising way of being made aware of the appointment than that. (Laughter and applause.)

SPILLERS.

As will be seen in our Reports and Dividends column on Page 12, the directors of Spillers Limited, have decided to recommend a dividend of 5 per cent. on the Ordinary shares in respect of the year to January 31st, 1928.

A MAESTEG EPIC.

FIVE HOURS UNDER A "FALL."

HEROIC RESCUE EFFORTS

FOR nearly five hours yesterday workmen and officials at the Maesteg Deep Colliery, Maesteg, were engaged in a heroic effort to rescue an entombed miner, Mr David John Morgan, aged 36, single, residing with his parents at Llwydarth-road, Maesteg, who was buried by a fall of roof.

The rescuers were greatly handicapped in their work owing to falling debris, and it was with great difficulty that the victim was eventually recovered. Unfortunately, he was dead.

Dr. Bell Thomas descended the mine immediately after the fall, and remained there until the recovery of the body.

"GUNM LETTE

MINING SEN

THREE LE THREATE

A SENSATIONAL made at a meeting yesterday of the Notts Political Union. It was stated had been received lives of Mr G. A. Spence (of the Union), Mr R. secretary), and Mr J. C treasurer), who was agent to the Notts Min

The letter, addressed to dated April 4th, and read
"To all Concerned,—
"Owing to your treach of the workers of the world to go against you if you treacherous actions and be causing millions to suffer.

"We give you time to the event of your failing power which we have at ou carry out the slogan 'B die than millions to suffer.

"Therefore, do not tre tempt and fool you are as Sir Henry Wilson's death,

"We advise you to wa ates, because we give the strike at them as the resp "We address this notice secretary," warning G. A. G. Hancock and R. Gasco "(Signed), THE GUNMEN

The meeting decided th be taken by Non-Politica in the ballot suggested by Congress to determine wh organisations in Nottingham of pitworkers were desirou

ATLANTIC

GERMAN STAR

LINERS' W

The German monoplane donnel (Ireland) yesterday to attempt to fly to New Captain Kohl, with Baro and Commandant Fitzmau

South Wales News – Friday 13th April, 1928

After exploring the philosophical grounds for this, as far as he is able to, he moves to his visionary experiences themselves, which frequently involve his perception of previous times in history. When this occurs, he is first plunged into a state where the day-lit world is blotted out. Finding himself still conscious, however, he asks if he is permitted to explore what he can now see:

> *Should the eyes*
> *Close on the vision? Should not they explore*
> *The caverns of the new-discovered skies?*

One is reminded of his question to Eric Falk, after stating that if one refused to "drift with the current of time" one could only "resist it and sink": "*But if you can see under water...?*"

The first image that appeared to him when "buried mystery calls back my thought", was that of a slave chained to an oar at sea:

> *Above an ocean mountainous and vast*
> *My midnight dream is caught*
> *To a white galleon. From her trembling mast*
> *I see below, chained to a Spanish oar,*
> *One slave, who never ... heard*
> *The voice of friend or bird.*[47]

> *A series of other images follow:*
> *(I)n a monastery that since has sunk*
> *In desolation, I have seen ... some pale, hooded monk,*
> *... and through the pregnant air/ I have seen his lips ...*
> *Move in the dim light to breathe a prayer.*

> *And I have watched a mourner at the tomb*
> *Of Tutankhamen ...*

> *And I have seen the prison of the doomed*
> *Who for their faith once prophesied and fell.*

This is a mere fraction of the poem's ecstatic outpouring, which finally proclaims that all the "prophets" of the past, from different cultures, are now returning and that their modes of vision are again becoming possible:

> *Draw near, O prophets of the West and East, …*
> *You dreamer of the Pharaohs come, and you,*
> *Dark son of Buddha, you, o Jewish priest;*
> *And you with sacred lilies on your brow,*
> *Pale poet wandering by the grey sea-shore (.)*

All of these prophets, together with Watkins himself, who must surely be linked with the "pale poet", then cry out to everyone who can hear:

> *Be of good cheer. Jesus of Nazareth,*
> *Shelley, and Blake, and Michelangelo,*
> *Dante, Raffaello, Milton and the rest*
> *Have overcome the world.*

Quite how Vernon managed to keep going at all in the bank during the months that followed is unclear. If his setting fire to a wad of bank notes in his first week had been smiled on, his superiors by now must have had serious concerns about him. Somehow, though, he managed to carry on for almost the whole of the rest of 1928, during which his poetry was published for the first time publically[48] and he discovered the later work of W.B. Yeats, reading 'The Tower' when it was published that year.[49] Watkins saw in Yeats a model for how to link Blakean vision with individual, personal experience: "I was absorbed in Blake's Prophetic Books, but those tremendous visions … lacked personal statement, and this appeared in the new poems of Yeats with piercing clarity." [50]

'Repton: An Epic'

In September he therefore turned to the place of his own most intense personal experience, his unhealed wound which remained at the root of his whole "war with Time" – *Repton* and all it continued to mean for him.

He set out to write a poem on an epic scale to immortalize his years at Repton and his experiences there of 'Eden'. He called it simply – *Repton: An Epic* – and wrote more than ninety sections of it. 'Poeta Caecus', complex and visionary as it is, may even to some people appear healthy and sane compared with what Watkins set out to achieve in *Repton: An Epic*.

Two events occasioned the writing of it. Firstly, Watkins had decided to revisit Repton in December and attend an old boys' reunion there. This created the desire to "immortalize" the blissful memory of his boyhood loves in their prepubescence, *before* this might be contradicted by meeting these same boys aged 17 or 18. Secondly, since the accident he had witnessed, he had repeatedly been having a strange experience. He had a photograph in his room of the greatest of his boyhood loves.[51] What had been happening was that when he closed his eyes at night or when he slept, this image of the boy, in his mind, seemed to burst into life:[52]

> *I sleep ...*
> *And then your shining photograph*
> *Takes life within my brain.*
>
> *Soon as I shut my eyes, I see*
> *The statue on my shelf*
> *Leap to a living ecstasy*
> *And be your marvellous self.*

There is nothing accidental about Watkins referring to the photograph as a *'statue'* that then sprang into life. Watkins was again linking to the myth of Pygmalion, on whom Aphrodite, the Goddess of Love, took pity and magically brought to life the statue he had made of his beloved. With his night-time experiences of the boy's image springing to life, Watkins felt he had at last found the key to realizing the mystery of Pygmalion. With this key he also felt he might now achieve his greatest dream of all, the conquering of Time, and thus might find his way back into the Garden of Eden and Childhood. And *this* magical accomplishment he would reveal to the world in his Epic.

Though this might well appear a form of madness – which Watkins would soon have to face the consequences of – the young poet was in deadly earnest. Through stanza after stanza he develops the analogy with Pygmalion and the statue, and its strange meanings for him, longing for his lover to: *"leap into flesh from a haunting statue/ Closer than my shadow, in this room".*

The uncomfortable fact Watkins has to face, however, is that when he visits Repton and meets the boy as he now is, he will possess none of the beauty and innocence of the "statue" living in Watkins's mind:

> *I'll see your face when a year is over,*
> *But will it be still your own, your own?*
> *I'll touch your wrist with the hand of a lover*
> *But shall I attain that passionate stone?*

Before he encounters the boy as a young man, therefore, at the end of the year, Watkins must have completed his act of Pygmalion-like artistic magic, making the boy ever-young through his Epic, and thus defying Time:

> *The voice will have broken, the light will have set in*
> *The mind that was music, the eye that was flame.*
>
> *You, like a star, will be flung from heaven;*
> *But still for a year you are fixed and mine;*
> *And when it has ended,* **will you not be graven**
> **For ever and ever, a body divine?**

If this can be achieved, it would not even matter were his lover an old man, Watkins would always be able to re-experience him as a young boy:

> *I'd press your withered hand and feel*
> *That smaller hand beneath;*
> *And your dead eyes would still reveal*
> *Those eyes too deep for death.*

And Watkins really did believe this was possible for him – that even if we have tasted of the apple, expelling us from Eden, he had found the way back to it:

> … *the apple has ripened,*
> *And fallen, and withered,* ***and buds there still****:*
> *Since I left Repton nothing has happened*
> *Stranger than this, and nothing will.*

He has, he feels, broken back in to the "*the age-forbidden lands/ Where thoughts are physical*", to the world of childhood or "Eden", where spiritual and physical are merged, and where his lover will therefore have "*a body divine*".

The problem is that this was a form of madness. Watkins wanted something back *physically* that had long since disappeared in space and time. Despite his belief that he was magically resolving all he had been suffering since leaving Repton, he was wanting above all, Peter Pan-like, to return to the idyllic world of childhood:

> *Have you heard for us what the old have planned? …*
> *Come, let's escape! We'll save Youth still …*
> *Still knowing all things, you and I.*

He had in fact moved far beyond the point of no return down the path he had set out to Falk: "If only we could … go raving mad for an indefinite length of time without ever growing older or wiser or stronger. *Then perhaps we could <u>physically</u> live Repton*".

It was impossible for him to bring his "Epic" to any kind of conclusion, despite his huge hopes for it[53], and his desire to finish it before going to Repton in December.[54] But he had also gone far too deeply and uncompromisingly down the path he had taken to be able now to find any way back or to free himself from his condition.

He somehow managed to continue at the bank in this state until the end of November, then packed a few things and headed off by train for his impossible "reunion" at Repton. Had he thought at all realistically about what might happen when two contradictory realities met, his paradisal inner world named "Repton" and the boys' boarding school of the same name, he might have given the bank some warning and might not have committed the almost unforgivable crime in their eyes of leaving his bank-keys in his room. For his three nightmarish years at the bank in Cardiff were over and he would never return.

Repton

During the Old Boys' weekend Watkins must have spun deliriously backwards and forwards between his images of Repton and his friends as they were now, in 1928, and as they inhabited his inner world, "before the Fall". It is not known how his former friends experienced his desire to transport them all back to the Edenic world of their childhood. What is known is that by the time the weekend was over, having at last arrived at the goal of his dreams, it was impossible for him to imagine returning to Cardiff. He therefore decided to stay on for a few days at Repton with his friend Tom Shapley, who was now a young master at the school.[55] The longer he stayed, he must have plunged ever deeper into the imaginary "Repton" of his inner world and his grip on the outer everyday world, which already in Cardiff "hardly existed for me"[56], must have grown ever weaker.

On Wednesday December 5th, the Headmaster Geoffrey Fisher encountered Watkins on the school grounds and they had some kind of conversation together. Almost immediately afterwards Fisher wrote to his wife: "V.P. Watkins is here staying with Tom – and I *really* think is *genuinely* dotty. I met him just now in the School Yard and his conversation was *really* not that of one not in his right mind. I am worried about it and must see Tom."[57]

Whatever Tom Shapley told him must only have increased Fisher's worries and must also have made him realize that Watkins had no intention of leaving Repton for the time being. Fisher, it seems, therefore decided to have Watkins forcibly removed from the school and returned to Wales. A near contemporary of Watkins at Repton, who had also been at the Old Boys' Reunion, briefly described what happened to him next:

"On our return to the school for an Old Boys gathering he showed great reluctance to return to the hard outside world. Eventually the

School marshal was instructed to take him to Willington station and put him on the train. The story went that as Watkins left the school yard on a taxi he was seen throwing clothes out through the window."[58]

As Watkins did *not* get on any train back to Cardiff, the school marshal must have soon seen that this young man, stripping his clothes off in protest and hurling them out of the window, was in no fit state to go anywhere and probably took him straight to Geoffrey Fisher in his study.

Geoffrey Fisher and Vernon Watkins

There followed the final "showdown" between two spiritual opposites – the raving youth who would later become the "best religious poet in England"[59] and the fiercely disciplinarian headmaster and Freemason[60] who would later become the Archbishop of Canterbury.

Their conversation presumably consisted of Watkins deliriously describing his own vision of "Repton" and Fisher firmly telling him that he was mad and would be removed from the school as soon as it could be arranged. Fisher may very well even have attempted to restrain Watkins physically.

Watkins's mind by now was travelling at lightning speed. He described that in the gaps in their conversation, while waiting for Fisher to reply, he would "read eleven pages of the book of Job which he had taken with him."[61] Inwardly racing, he suddenly perceived Fisher with crystalline clarity as the great Anti-Spirit of Repton, the ultimate Philistine, the destroyer of all that he held most sacred, who was now attempting to evict him from Eden. Watkins fought back, hitting out and yelling at Fisher, denouncing him as a Satanic "destroyer of youth"[62] and part of the evil principle at work in the world.

Watkins was clearly on the verge of insanity, but it is interesting that Roald Dahl, who went to Repton nine months later, devoted a whole chapter to Fisher in his memoir '*Boy*' and had a very similar picture of him to Watkins. After alluding to the clear workings of power politics in Fisher's career[63] and describing the savage beatings he inflicted on his pupils, Dahl writes: "I would sit ... and listen to him preaching about the Lamb of God and about Mercy and Forgiveness and all the rest of it and my young mind would become utterly confused. I knew very well that only the night before this preacher had shown neither Forgiveness nor Mercy in flogging some small boy who had broken the rules. So what was it all about? I used to ask myself. Did they preach one thing and practise another, these men of God?"[64]

Be that as it may, Watkins's assault against Fisher was clearly ineffective. He was easily restrained and made to sit and wait while Fisher telephoned the nearest psychiatric institutions and Watkins's parents. When the latter arrived they readily agreed to sign the papers certifying Vernon as insane and took advice on where he might best be cared for. He was soon taken to a "private nursing home" in Derby – a euphemism, presumably, for a small-scale psychiatric clinic.

Vernon's sister Dorothy briefly described these events from the Watkins family's perspective. Throughout his three years in Cardiff Vernon apparently "hid his deep unhappiness from his family." It was therefore: "an appalling shock to us all when … he had a complete mental breakdown. The first our parents knew of this was when they were alerted by Repton School that Vernon had arrived there and was obviously ill. They travelled up at once and immediately arranged his admission to a private nursing home in Derbyshire. He remained there for several months."[65]

'Beyond Time's Chain'

When I count the poets I love, each has a moment of terror. The rest of his life is a fiction.[66]

The following weeks in the nursing home would lead to the single most important event in Vernon Watkins's life, the "pivotal moment" around which he would eventually completely *reorientate* himself, his poetry and his life. It was a moment "out of time", of which there can be no question of any physical record, but from the little Watkins said about it and the three poems[67] he wrote addressing it, we can nonetheless attempt to reconstruct the unfolding of this event.

Initially, he was clearly in a raving and intoxicated condition, his inner state having grown more and more extreme since the motorcycle crash he had witnessed, before reaching its highest pitch at Repton. His mind was still racing at speeds far beyond the ordinary. He would barely sleep and would keep others awake too with his long declamations of Blake or of his own writings. A male psychiatric nurse was in charge of him, for whom, one imagines, Watkins was a wild but genial and endearing patient.

At some point, perhaps around Christmas and New Year, three to four weeks after he had been admitted, something began to change in his experience. The intoxicated state in which he had arrived would have begun wearing off. His forced eviction from Repton and delivery to a psychiatric unit signalled the end of his whole desperate attempt to break back in, Peter Pan-like, to the years of his childhood. This had been revealed to be quite without foundation. As the world of his former days and his obsessive relationship with it fell away he entered into ever stranger and more terrifying realms of experience. The physical world and his own body lost their weight and substance for him. He felt at one point that were he to hurl himself from an upstairs window no harm would come to him, that he would be borne up and gently carried to the ground. He told his wife that had he done so people would have completely mistakenly viewed it as suicide.

The fact that he was thinking of physically jumping shows that, even if only by a thin thread, his experiences still had some relationship to the outer, physical world. Soon after this, however, this ceased to be the case. He was thrown in his consciousness into a realm beyond time – *"pitched by utmost thought/ Beyond time's chain"* – and beyond space and the transient world of nature: *"Pitched beyond reclaim/ Of things that seemed to bear the brand of doom/The flowers, the birds, my brothers in farewell".* Outside the realm inhabited by his physical body he entered a non-physical, spiritual and initially terrifying realm of inner experience. The nearest parallels to what he now went through are possibly in so-called "near-death experiences", where people have returned to life sometimes even several minutes after being pronounced dead, and have described their experiences during this "time".[68]

His first experience "there" was of himself falling towards the edge of a vast abyss – in which, if one should fall into it, one would be lost beyond all hope of redemption – an abyss, in other words, recognizable as "hell", though not as a traditional picture but as immediate experience. Nor was this hell separate from him, but was linked with his failings and desires and fallen nature. It was also, therefore, his own hell. Slipping ever deeper towards it he heard, he said, at the very edge of the abyss, the horrendous reality the Bible speaks of as "the wailing and gnashing of teeth"[69] – he wrote therefore of "the trough of groans". At this abyss, "in the black hour that cast salvation out", he describes undergoing "more terrors than the sea has waves".

Having experienced this to the utmost, at the very point where it seemed he might indeed slip into the abyss, he felt himself gently and miraculously held back[70] and redeemed from the abyss by the one being capable of doing so, a being of infinite love, light and compassion, who Watkins, in whatever form he beheld or experienced Him, recognized as the being of Christ.

As this happened, he also heard words spoken, which one of his poems about this event renders: *'Your life is come'.*[71]

Watkins depicted in a poetic image how he himself had responded in this inner event: *"I drew my strength up like a proud deep wave/ And cast myself upon the feet of life."*[72] The image echoes the description of St. John, who "was in the Spirit … and heard behind me a great voice … saying, I am

Alpha and Omega, the first and the last ... And I turned to see who spake with me ... *And when I saw him, I fell at his feet as dead."*[73]

Watkins was also 'as dead', wholly and willingly *dying* to his previous existence – and in so doing, *renewed life* was given to him. This did not have only to do with himself but with the possible transformation of the relationships between people:

> *I ... woke to naves*
> *Of daybreak; there men walked in brotherhood,*
> *Mutual forgiveness, love; their speech was good ...*

Having "walked in a sacred darkness three long years", this whole experience was his moment of "initiation". Although he never used this word to describe it, he nonetheless always accorded it this degree of significance in his life. He spoke about: "*a moment of change, a pivotal crisis in time that renews him*"[74] and wrote:

"I had read Blake's words:

> 'Each man is in his Spectre's power
> Until the arrival of that hour
> When his Humanity awake
> And cast his Spectre into the lake;'

and the Eternity of which Blake spoke suddenly seemed to me more accessible than time itself."[75]

On the few occasions when he referred to this experience he only did so in the most sparing of ways. Only once did he attempt to depict it directly, in a poem he never published:

> to lives healthy and well
> I lift no gratitude in the course of days,
> But to Him only who in a night could raise
> Miraculous life from miracle-murdering hell.
> For I have seen, ...
> In the black hour that cast salvation out,
> Love snatch me, a miracle, from the trough of groans
> To the infinite, suffering love of my great Redeemer.[76]

At some point, after the enormity of these inner events, he returned to his 'normal' experience of himself and of the world around him – and found himself back in his room in the 'nursing home' in Derby, on a cold morning in early 1929:

> *Frost-flowers upon the window, deep blue sky.*
> *Life surged through me, that ancient alphabet,*
> *More clear, more true than it had ever been.*
> *Life glowed to me, its falsehood all cast out.*[77]

Filled with this new experience of *life*, Vernon was completely healed of his previous psychotic condition, from which he would never suffer again.[78] He was, however, still in a highly sensitive and delicate condition and would need many months to recuperate fully, before he could even consider working again. He would return to the Gower Peninsula to undergo this convalescence and to begin to take in what he had been through.

CHAPTER FIVE

'Pivotal Crisis in Time' (1929)

There is nearly always, in any serious poet, a moment of change, a pivotal crisis in time that renews him.

Such is the significance of Vernon Watkins's inner experience of early 1929 that he may almost be said to have two biographies – a first life that ends with this experience and a second life that begins with it. He himself saw it in this way: *"The state in which I found myself when I had experienced my metaphysical change was very much like a rebirth. I had died the death of ambition, and found that death was only a beginning."*[1]

We shall therefore pause briefly, as he did for a year, to see some of the characteristics of his 'moment of change' – to see, that is, how his second life will be different from the first.

TIME

"Time would have no power over my work"

The first great change was in relation to *time*. His desperate and almost insane longings to 'stop time' were over. He had undergone an experience tantamount to dying and would never again *resist* time in this way. Furthermore, he had, been granted an experience of a realm "beyond time", which was not subject to the natural cycle of birth, growth, ageing and death against which he had fought. In the light of this he recognized the immaturity of all the poetry he had written:

"I was twenty-two when my poetry underwent its most violent change. Up to that age all my poems, and there must have been a thousand, were written out an oppressive urgency in conflict with time. After that age I knew that whatever happened to me, time would have no power over my work."[2]

AMBITION
"I had died the death of ambition"

His second great change, linked with the first, was with regard to "ambition". During his "war with time" his whole ambition had been to *outlast time* by achieving 'immortal fame' as a poet. This too he now saw as immature if not irrelevant. The only thing of importance to him now was to be true to the *reality* he had experienced, irrespective of whether he would be remembered for it or not:

"I also aimed at writing a kind of poetry that would be remembered after my time. Life seemed to me terribly short, and the men who gave it meaning were those whose works lived on in succeeding generations.

"This is only to say that I composed in the shadow of time. The act of writing itself was an heroic act, a protest against the tyranny of time. So it went on until my twenty-third year."

Having used Blake's words to describe what then took place,[3] he continues: "I experienced an upheaval which made my work hitherto worthless, a complete revolution of sensibility. *It no longer seemed to me interesting that a poem should be remembered; its sole interest was that it should be valid.*"[4] As he put it elsewhere: "*Fame ceased to be interesting to me, and the validity of a poem from then on was to depend on something else.*"[5]

This led to his own way of characterizing the two different poets he had been – the 'poet' Vernon P. Watkins, who had aimed "to be numbered among the English poets", whose life had now come to an end; and the 'metaphysical poet' Vernon Watkins, whose life was just beginning, whose only aim was that his poetry "should be valid":

"*A poet is born when his ambition is born; but he is born a metaphysical poet when his ambition dies.*"[6]

PUBLICATION
"I set myself against publishing"

The above quotations were written later, with hindsight, when the second poet had become fully established. In 1929 he was only beginning to discover his new approaches to poetry and to life. What, for example, after this "death of ambition", should be his attitude to publication? In March 1929 he wrote two poems on the same sheet of paper, giving opposite answers to this question. In the first, he will: "keep my songs in cellars like old wine". He will, in other words, keep his poetry hidden from the world until it is found long after his death. In the second poem, 'The Auction': "My songs are all for sale" and he intends to become free of the past by giving away his "old words", his "scraps".[7]

The latter point of view clearly made him decide to submit some of his early poems for publication. Thus in May 1929 the prestigious literary journal 'The London Mercury'[8] published his poem 'True Lovers'. He must then have found it a difficult and even embarrassing experience to see a poem of his appearing so publicly which he now "repudiated" as "worthless". He therefore made the firm decision never to publish again: "I … set myself against publishing, and against sending poems away to a magazine".[9]

NATURE AND GOWER
"I witness here in a vision the landscape to which I was born."
(*'Taliesin in Gower'*)

Vernon's respectable parents obviously felt there would be considerable social stigma if people knew that their gifted son had suffered a severe "mental breakdown". Dorothy Watkins makes clear how unmentionable what had happened to Vernon was: "in the 1920's a mental breakdown was hardly more respectable than a prison sentence. Vernon's illness was never alluded to outside the family." This also shows that Vernon did not confide in his family – with the probable exception of his older sister Marjorie – the deeper aspects of what he had been through. The question of social stigma, however, would have been of no concern to Vernon, whose behaviour may well have added to it. For an essential part of his return to health was that during the months that followed, in the open and highly sensitive state he was in, he was free to wander the Gower peninsula, immersing himself in all he found there.[10]

Almost every aspect of the Gower peninsula would eventually be depicted, imaginatively transformed, in Watkins's work. After his death his close friend Ceri Richards, the painter, would write: "*The sea and surrounding landscape, which he celebrated, were his by spiritual and observational right.*"[11] What Ceri Richards is referring to owes its origin to this time[12] when, in the immediate aftermath of his "death and rebirth" experience, Watkins had been able to wander the length and breadth of Gower, almost uniting himself with it.

This is not mere Romantic terminology. The earliest poems of mainland Britain are the old Welsh poems of Taliesin[13], who unites himself with nature and speaks with its voice. ("I have been a drop in the air,/ A shining bright star,/ In water, in foam ... / There is nothing of which/ I have not been part."[14]) Vernon Watkins would later give voice to his own experience of nature by casting himself as Taliesin in many poems. Though he *wrote* these poems later, their profound immersion in the landscape of Gower occurred at this time. Watkins described how he never knew when his experiences of landscape would appear in his poetry: "one day, when his intention to write a poem has been abandoned, the place will return by accident, and a poem about it will be written."[15]

When the poems were eventually written they had a poetic maturity beyond what he now possessed. But one of the earliest drafts of one of his Taliesin poems enables us to glimpse the strangeness of his wanderings in 1929. A raven spies him emerging from a cave and calls to his fellow-ravens:

> Look down,
> Taliesin is there
> Gorged with visions; he is catching in his hands our shadows ...
> Escape to the upper light ...
> Let him stand there alone, and reconcile Time with time.[16]

STYLE
"It took several years for my style to catch up with this experience"

'Taliesin in Gower', depicting the entire landscape of Gower through Watkins's newfound vision, is perhaps the greatest of the Taliesin poems owing their origin to this time. At its end he breaks off his celebration of the landscape, saying: "But first I must cut the wood,/ Exactly measure the strings".[17]

This too was his clear experience in 1929 – that although his *vision* may have been renewed, he did not yet possess the poetic *instrument* capable of expressing it: "I could not translate my transfigured vision of the world into language."[18] Having said: "In my twenty-third year I suddenly experienced a complete revolution of sensibility" he therefore states: "*It took several years for my style to catch up with this experience*".[19] Elsewhere he was more exact: "It took me perhaps six or seven years to catch up with this experience in my writing."[20]

This was less a question of content than of *style*. It had little to do with speaking *about* what he had gone through, but rather with developing a poetic music or style attuned to his new-found relationship to the world – or with creating a poetic *instrument* on which the music of his own particular vision could be played.

BACK TO WORK
"A poet can do any work in the world"

Around the age of 23, having written about a thousand poems, all of which he now "repudiated"[21], Watkins was finally beginning, therefore, his true poetic apprenticeship. Since his "moment of change" he stood in a wholly different relationship to everything in his life. His healing had been consolidated by immersing himself in the landscape of Gower. He had given up any idea of publishing. He was happy to go on writing, unknown to the world, until perhaps, like Gerard Manley Hopkins, his poetry would be discovered after his death.

In this new state of composure, after about nine months at home, he decided he could now happily go back to work. He had no thoughts of earning money as a poet and the bank was as good an option as any. He found figures very easy, being able, apparently, to look down a column of numbers, in pounds, shillings and pence, and to have the sum appear fully formed in his mind.[22] On the condition that he was never promoted to a position whose responsibilities might compete with his poetry, the bank, by solving the problem of how to earn a living, might paradoxically enable him to be completely uncompromising in his approach to his poetry. Gwen Watkins remarks that he could happily have swept the streets, if he had to, for a living. He himself said: "a poet can do any work in the world and not lose by it, provided that he is a poet first."[23]

The question therefore, was not whether he was prepared to go back to the bank, but whether the bank was prepared to take him on again. This was no foregone conclusion, not only because of his 'mental breakdown' and his simply disappearing one day, never to return, but worst of all because, in doing so, he had left the keys to the bank lying around in his lodgings, which, for the bank, was an almost unpardonable offence.[24] Clearly influenced, however, by Vernon's father – "no doubt in consideration of my father's long years of service" (Dorothy Watkins[25]) – Lloyds Bank agreed to take him back, and found him a position, moreover, in Swansea. This meant that he could go on living on the Gower peninsula, in the Watkins's large house overlooking Caswell Bay, taking the bus to and from work every day. Thus on November 1st 1929, he began again as a clerk at Lloyds Bank, in the St. Helen's Road Branch, Swansea, where he would remain for the next 37 years.

Not that the work itself had become any different. Dorothy comments that he "accepted his return to banking, if not with elation, at least with determination and resignation". But he successfully avoided achieving promotion[26] and once the work had become habitual, it clearly proved of no hindrance to his poetry, for as he said, he had: "lines … running through my head all the time – even when I work in the bank"[27]. That his poetry was sometimes a hindrance to the bank was another matter and many humorous tales would circulate about this particular cashier's absent-mindedness. A friend who banked at his branch commented that on some days he would be present enough, but on others he was clearly "composing", and there was then no chance of engaging with him.[28] One of his colleagues at the bank echoed this: "When he was in the middle of a poem he just wasn't with you. You could tease, but he didn't hear so it didn't make any difference."[29] Almost a year after his breakdown Vernon Watkins began again, therefore, both at his poetry and at what he did for a living – setting out upon his life, as it were, for the second time.

CHAPTER SIX

Second Apprenticeship (1930–1934)

'Am I Not Then By Right The Muses' Son?'

For all this Vernon Watkins was still a very young man, aged 23, just setting out on his life – albeit for the second time. There was therefore still an immaturity in his work, which he would only outgrow through the years of his 'true apprenticeship' which now followed.

Through his experience of "rebirth", however, he could also be said to have *regained* his youth. For years after leaving Repton his life had been, in his own words, "forfeit to regret". He had ceaselessly hankered after and tried to recapture a childhood that was gone. Through his "death-experience" this striving had completely died out in him. But he had then been graced with a new and super-abundant experience of *life*:

> *"Life surged through me …*
> *More clear, more true than it had ever been."*
> *('Document of a Live Poet')*

It might also be said that his sense of nostalgia and regret had been so extreme precisely because, earlier, he had had an equally extreme experience of the innocent joy of childhood, which time had robbed him of. No longer bound down by grief or nostalgia, his deep delight in the world flooded back to him, initially in a great outburst of joy and exuberance.

As he would soon write:

> *Who but the unafraid of time can sing*
> *Out of sheer joy, the novelty of day?* [1]

There were released in him a whole spate of comic, often zany poems and even, for the only time in his life,[2] prose stories and 'fairy tales', rediscovering his love of the childlike. They have such titles as: *Ool of the River-People, Bakkakak the Witch, Garden of Chimaera (For a Fairy Comic Opera), Pan and the Wind, Brobno* and a *Galloping Song* that begins: "*James, James, his hairs on flames*".

The sequence of poems and stories grew rapidly and Vernon soon hatched the plan of an illustrated children's book. He did so with James Thornton (who had been at Cambridge with Watkins and was now a reader at Dent's)[3] and Thornton's girlfriend, Jackie, who created the illustrations. This was, of course, in immediate and blatant contradiction of Watkins's decision no longer to publish anything. Though he later said this had not applied to his light verse,[4] he clearly could not go back on his word completely and so took the only available option – to use a pseudonym! He would write under the name "John Barleycorn".[5]

Thornton and Watkins submitted the book by "John Barleycorn" to Dent's, who rejected it. They probably saw that behind the pseudonym there was a young author still struggling to free himself from some of the ghosts of his own past, albeit humorously. In one of the stories, 'The Visitors', a strange young man lives at the top of a large house. Passers-by wonder what had made him so strange: "Some said he had been to sea, others that he drank ... Was he disappointed in love?" He alone knows the cause of his condition: "His own idea was that he was a great artist."

This is not a question of arrogance on the part of Watkins, writing in 1929 and 1930. The story depicts a person who *suffers* under this idea and is humorously mocked as he attempts to break free from it.

"He would be famous soon and he hated himself for it ... 'They will come', he said, under his breath ... Black, hooded men would come ... and seize him and carry him away to the cold frozen North, to the Aurora Borealis of the famous. Then he would be a glittering name, he would be something not himself. He would be that other."

The black figures *do* come, in the form of three vast jackdaws and take him away. He manages to escape, but a mole of "enormous size" arrives at his door.

"'I shall bury my books, and burn everything I've written,' he said …
'Who then will say I am better than anyone else?' …
"Just then he was caught up into a great furry darkness. He was aware that he was hurrying down a tremendously long passage … Huge, powerful arms were dragging him on, through an ever-winding tunnel.
"He suddenly got the illusion that he was back in Egypt, listening to the guide. 'This is the tomb of Rameses' …
"He was wrestling with the furry darkness, but the darkness was too strong.
'There's no way out,' said the Mole.
'Have they gone?' he said.
'Go to sleep,' said the Mole, 'you are famous now.'"

Such "John Barleycorn" humour was a constant part of Watkins's daily persona in life – his zany wit and charm were always attested to by those who knew him. The poet Hugo Williams, for example, would say of him: "Like Don Quixote, he was a cock-eyed optimist, lovable and rare."[6] With his life now given back to him, Vernon would always continue to scribble such light comic verses, almost like doodles down the side of the pages on which his true lyric poetry was written.[7]

Death on Parnassus

An event of 1931 was not only impossible for Vernon to treat lightly but also powerfully underlined that, for all the new life he had been granted, the path back to his childhood and his schooldays was permanently barred.

Shortly after Easter, Watkins's 'fag' from Repton, David Cochrane, currently a Classics undergraduate at Oxford, fell to his death in Greece from a high point on 'Cochrane Mountain', which looks across at Delphi and up at Mount Parnassus. He had been alone at the time and it was months before his body was found.[8]

Watkins had remained in touch with Cochrane and not only felt genuine affection for him but held him in the highest regard: "Although he was slightly deformed by infantile paralysis, his mind was brilliant and he struck me as the most original boy at my school."[9]

On Easter Sunday (April 12th, 1931), just before he had set out for Parnassus, Cochrane had written a postcard to Watkins, depicting the

Postcard to VW from David Cochrane from Greece, Easter Sunday, 1931.[10]

Temple of Nike (Victory) in Athens. Watkins kept the postcard throughout his life.

Watkins was deeply struck, as a friend, by Cochrane's death, but this was greatly intensified by Cochrane's dying beneath Mount Parnassus. At Repton Watkins had been deeply interested in the Parnassian poets[11] and his whole immature Romantic striving connected with Repton might be described as his attempt to scale 'Mount Parnassus'.

In 1929 this Grecian or Parnassian striving had 'died' in him, leading to his 'rebirth' or resurrection into a greater reality. David Cochrane's dying on Parnassus, and his Easter Sunday postcard to Watkins, resounded so strongly with what he himself had gone through that in the poem he wrote years later about Cochrane's death he mistakenly believed Cochrane to have died not in 1931 but in 1929, in other words at the same time as his own "death and rebirth" experience. The poem is called: '*Arakhova and the Daemon* – for David Cochrane, killed on Parnassus 1929'. Even the statement 'killed on Parnassus' is not wholly correct, as the place from where David Cocharane fell, now named 'Cochrane's Point', *overlooks* Parnassus. Such errors are surprisingly rare in Watkins's work. 'Killed on Parnassus 1929' may be inaccurate in relation to David Cochrane, it is, however, completely accurate regarding the significance of the event for Vernon Watkins. Watkins also linked W.B. Yeats with this matrix of experiences. He described Yeats, who continued to be his greatest living poetic example, as: "never in any sense a Parnassian"[12]. He also described Yeats as having gone through a "death and rebirth" experience at exactly the same time as his own: "After a long illness in the Spring of 1929 … life returned as an impression of the uncontrollable energy and daring of the great creators."[13]

Nuremberg 1931

In June 1931, Vernon Watkins went to Germany for his holidays, travelling through Belgium then on to Heidelberg and then Nürnberg.

Throughout his life Watkins retained a deep love and appreciation for the true spiritual and cultural life of Germany. It would be of significance in this regard that now – in the years just *after* his 'pivotal' transformative experience and just *before* Nazism came to power in the country – he could drink in, deeply and naively, the culture and landscape of Germany.

His diary gives a good picture both of his love of being alone in nature and of his fitness and health. On 5th June, he walked in the early morning to Neckargemünd on the river Neckar: "I kept close to the woods and went in lagging fashion over most gorgeous slopes. A day of rare beauty. So on to the road and out again into a path through the wood where I, already having thrown off my coat, found it necessary to throw off my shirt as well. I saw a big snake disappear with a crack and a rustle of grasses. Glorious acacias of sweet scent, rich trees, a little precipitous path and every manner of wild flower." He swam three times en route, once "swimming 3 times each way across the river" against "a strong current", before jumping on a steamer to Heidelberg, "where I bathed again."

His most significant experiences of Germany, though, were in Nürnberg, where he stayed with the Jewish lady, Frau Hechinger, who he had stayed with before, while at Repton. On June 9th he spent the day wandering through the town, walking through its "ancient courts and very old crooked streets", spending time in the old market-place, visiting Dürer's house and the two great churches, the Frauenkirche and the Lorenzkirche. "How I love this place", he told his diary.

That evening he had an experience which seven years later would grow into the poem which opened his mature published work. He went to the opera, where he "sat on honest wood" and watched first a melodramatic opera by Puccini, with "a picturesque Belgian setting", stating: "I didn't like it much."

The second opera, the *Josephslegende* by Strauss, "was very different ... a work of immortal beauty and most wonderfully portrayed. It is a work of really high symbolism and shows the pagan rule of tyranny, savagery, lust & monarchical pride penetrated by the subtle spirit of free untamed aesthetic beauty, evolved from innocent childhood in the figure of Joseph."[14]

By 1931 the annual Nazi rallies in Nürnberg were already taking place. There is a photograph of Hitler in 1928 at the head of an aggressive crowd in front of the Frauenkirche. Vernon Watkins knew none of this, or if he did, was naïve in his relation to it.[15]

His poetic sensibility *did*, however, respond to this. His experience in the opera of what he called: "the pagan rule of tyranny, savagery, lust & monarchical pride" and of that which he hoped might ultimately prove able to transform this, represented in the character of Joseph, was the closest he had come so far to the themes and qualities of the mature poetry he would soon begin writing.

In the autobiographical poem which opens his first book, Watkins as 'The Collier' identifies himself with Joseph: "*A coloured coat I was given to wear ... They dipped my coat in the blood of a kid/ And they cast me down a pit*". Remarkably, therefore, the poem, set amidst the Welsh hills of Watkins's birth, was also partly born in Nürnberg in 1931.

Watkins wrote after seeing Strauss's opera: "The piece leaves in the imagination a feeling of wonderful radiance. A truly great work." The whole of the following day was suffused by this experience. He walked through the town with his Jewish hostess, Frau Hechinger and wrote: "A perfect day ... No end to the marvels of Nürnberg."[16] In the Lorenzkirche, particularly, he had a sense of "truth" and "love" underneath the 'Angelic Salutation' suspended above the choir.[17]

Interior of the Lorenzkirche, Nuremberg

After the Second World War Watkins would return to Nürnberg and the Lorenzkirche and looking back to what he had experienced there in 1931, he joined his memories of Germany, at the time it entered its worst historical trials, with his own experience of descending into hell followed by his rebirth:

> ... *every moment of life, however trivial,*
> *Is pursued by the snake-headed girls, and acclaimed by legions of angels.*
>   *... marvellous music of silence;*
> *In the Lorenzkirche the suspended flight of angels;*
>
> *When I count the poets I love, each has a moment of terror ...*
> *To have heard the terrible cymbals, to have been in that presence*
> *Once, was sufficient to blast time out.*[18]

For all that, Watkins was in a surprisingly patriotic mood when he returned: "Harwich. England again ... Hyde Park and a boat on the Serpentine. I sit beneath the trees on the grass & pay twopence. God bless England. Das Betreten is not verboten any longer. And how splendid the children are. How natural. How simple."[19]

In 1932, the middle point of the years of his "true apprenticeship" between 1929 and 1935, there are far fewer surviving poems than in other years.[20] It was the year perhaps when his old style ended and his new one had not yet begun. As we have seen, the only early writing he still valued was his light verse, but this year saw the end of any serious consideration of it. He completed his "John Barleycorn" book, which was now offered to Dent's for publication, who rejected it and Watkins never referred to it again. Strangely, he also wrote the earliest poem which ever found its way into one of his published books. But for now this was far off in an unforeseeable future. It would be 27 years before the poem, 'Loiterers',[21] was published.

Germany 1933
Heinrich Heine and May 10th bookburnings
Harz Mountains

In 1933 Vernon chose to return to Germany at the end of May and the beginning of June, this time with his sister Dorothy. They visited Hamelin on the river Weser, known to them since childhood through the "Pied Piper". In the neighbouring landscape he drafted the second poem that eventually appeared in one of his published books – 'Swallows over the Weser'.[22]

They did not, however, escape exposure to the increasing horrors of the political situation in Germany in the year when Hitler came to power. In May and June thousands of books by Jewish and Communist authors were burnt in large-scale public "book-burnings" throughout Germany. The works of Heinrich Heine were among those that were burned, and Heine's words were frequently quoted by opponents of what was happening: "wherever they burn books, they will also burn people in the end."[23] Vernon Watkins witnessed one of these book-burnings and Gwen Watkins describes how the public vilification of Heine was more than he could stand:

"Vernon told me that two German friends had taken him to a Nazi gathering (in which town I don't know) and they discovered Nazi officers lighting a bonfire and people were bringing books and laughing and cheering. The Nazis shouted out the names of the authors as they threw the books. The friends wanted to leave, but Vernon heard the name of Heine shouted out, and began to try to push to the front to save the books. The two friends rapidly took his arms and rushed him away in spite of his struggles. He would say jokingly that if the officers had caught him I would probably have had to find someone else to marry."[24]

Dorothy Watkins wrote: "This introduction to Fascism had a profound effect upon us both." This would never show itself in Vernon in any great outer political awareness, but rather in the strength and depth of his inner response to the crisis the world was plunging into.

Above all they spent their days walking and travelling in the Harz Mountains. In the heartland of Germany they were of great significance

Nazi book-burning, Hamburg, May 1933

in the life and work of Goethe[25] and also of Heinrich Heine.[26] Vernon Watkins would make many translations of both Goethe and Heine and now, in May 1933, at this crucial moment in Europe's history, at exactly the same age as Heine had been, 26, he made his own 'Harzreise'.[27]

As someone who had once clung so desperately to the past, he had come a long way in being able to give himself to his *present experience*. Acknowledging that: "the beauty of these mountains defies successful interpretation" he states: "I am content to fail and to be as birds are that sing for pleasure and do not bequeath their song to other ages." [28]

Confirming the mutually fruitful interchange he felt between England and Germany, he made a German translation of German Shelley's poem 'Tomorrow'[29], whose real theme is *today* and the present moment.

Dorothy Watkins describes in her own way the sense of youthful carefreeness and naïveté about the holiday:

"we took off with rucksacks to climb in the Harz Mountains ... and quickly joined up with a couple of delightful young Bavarians known to us as Heini and Toni ... we had a hilarious time, with a charming old man we met on the way, who described himself as the spirit of the Brocken ... All too soon it was time for us to leave for home. Vernon explained to our friends that our free time was over. I remember Heini deploring this and declaring: "We have forever." None of us realized how soon the hated Nazi regime would engulf them ... We never heard of them again."[30]

But Vernon's newfound relationship to the present moment and the world around him had nothing to do with mere youthfulness or with the folly of thinking that *time* might last 'forever'. A sonnet he wrote there about himself makes this very clear:

"Youth will not serve the present consolation ...
He is not of to-day. He knows no station
Within the walls of time."

This is the secret of the new life invigorating him. The sonnet ends:
"And through his limbs the slender fire returns
Which shows of history he is not the sum." [31]

This sonnet, where he suddenly speaks of himself for the first time in a style close to that of his mature poetry, is the real fruit of his visit to the Harz Mountains in 1933, rather than his "failed" attempts to describe their natural beauty.

The workshop of W.B. Yeats

It is perhaps truer to speak of the years 1929 to 1935 as Watkins's "journeyman" years – according to the tradition whereby a craftsman, having served his apprenticeship, journeys from place to place, gaining experience and learning from different "Masters" on the way to attaining his own individual mastery.

In 1933, when W.B. Yeats' book *The Winding Stair* was published, Yeats became for Watkins the living 'Master' in whose workshop he could make the needed changes to his "style" in order to fashion it into the poetic "instrument" suited to his own particular vision and music.

Above all else Yeats showed Vernon Watkins what that no other poet had been able to show him: "*how a lyric poet should grow old.*"[32] Apart from Blake and Goethe very few poets had continued in the full powers of their genius until their deaths. Wordsworth and Coleridge had written their greatest poetry before the age of thirty-five and Shelley and Keats had died young. Victorian poetry had either not aspired to a similar intensity of inspiration or had been written out of the painful acceptance that this had been lost.[33] Thomas Hardy and A.E. Housman continued to lament what is lost with the passing of time. Vernon Watkins, through his transformational experience, had overcome in himself this nostalgic relationship to time and his struggle since then had been how to: "translate my transfigured vision of the world into language."[34] Yeats alone gave Watkins an example of how to do this.

Watkins had already been struck by this on reading Yeats's book *The Tower*, published in 1928:

"I remember the excitement this book gave me when I first opened it ... . I had expected something so different ... quieter poems from the ageing poet, perhaps a mood of resignation. When I came to the poem 'The Tower' itself I was overwhelmed by its beauty and passionate violence. What poet had ever written before in this way about old age?"[35]

When *The Winding Stair* came out in 1933, with the poems Yeats had written since 1929, Watkins was overwhelmed by the Yeats's *poetic* mastery and music.[36] The first poem of *The Winding Stair* contains the lines:

> *The innocent and the beautiful*
> *Have no enemy but time;*
> *Arise and bid me strike a match*
> *And strike another till time catch (.)*

Watkins had already heard Yeats read this poem on the radio and: "the intensity of his reading of those lines had left a permanent impression. I could still hear his voice as I read through the poem."

Watkins recalled his puzzlement and wonder over the secret of Yeats' accomplishment: "What was it? And what is it still that makes that excitement as fresh now as it was then, and even more vivid?... What ... was the secret of this poetry which, as the poet aged, still 'moved towards the dayspring of his youth'?"[37]

"Be dispossessed"
"The airman in the cellar"

Part of the process of learning from Yeats involved a paring down of his style, a continued stripping away of extraneous borrowings.

In October Watkins wrote a poem called 'The Lease'. Having "leased" his house to other people's words, which have filled his rooms and cupboards, he at last drives them all away:

> *Crying, I would sit*
> *Without you awhile*
> *And let silence write*
> *In his own style.*[38]

The poem was almost certainly also occasioned by the fact that Vernon's father William Watkins retired in 1933 when he turned 60, and no longer able to afford their large house at Caswell, Redcliffe, moved to a much smaller house, Heatherslade, on the cliffs at Pennard. Vernon moved with them, and though his sister Dorothy describes finding it hard to leave her childhood home, not only did Vernon love the new setting on the cliffs, where he would have his own small writing room, but the downsizing itself and the stripping away of possessions fitted with his wish, as a poet, to strip himself of clutter: *"There is no law/ Saying possession is sweet. Be dispossessed"*.[39]

And now Watkins at last began to discover his own strength and together with it the beginnings of his own voice and vision. In the garden at Caswell, before leaving, his attention was struck by a jasmine tree whose trunk had been hacked away to nothing, but which had miraculously sprung to life again, "finding a root in air". It resounded strongly with what he himself had gone through and he wrote a poem about it, which he published a revised version of fifteen years later. It ends:

> *Learn from this fable:*
> *Stronger the seed than pain.*
> *Though shock and violence rive,*
> *Black life will shoot again*
> *And quickly will revive*
> *If it have wind and rain.*[40]

Sensing in himself, too, the abundance of new life surging through him after undergoing the seeming loss of all he had loved, he exultantly celebrated the arrival of his true character as a poet:

> *Few there are that share my spirit's daring*
> *And few who have the courage to be sad.*[41]

> *I have a proud laugh life has not yet won*
> *A strength of limb Earth has not called to use …*
> **Am I not then by right the Muses' son?**

> *I am the explorer in the little room*
> **The airman in the cellar …**
> *… the great deserter from the tomb*
> *The spy of life.*[42]

Corsica and Gower

Hardly surprisingly, with Vernon being in such spirits, his holiday in Corsica that summer was, according to Dorothy, of all the trips they made together, "really the best of all." She describes how: "Vernon, who was at the height of his passion for Yeats' poetry, was never without one of his books and would read and recite it until I, too, often knew the poems by heart." They swam – "the sea was brilliantly blue and clear; we would bask on hot, flat rocks to watch the fish swimming lazily below us" – and walked great distances, once "over thirty-five miles through difficult mountainous country". They waded through rivers, walked in thunderstorms and even, after hitching a lift, found themselves caught up in a car chase on thin mountain roads: "Vernon was quiet and when I asked him why, he said he was praying to be killed outright when the crash came, and not just maimed."

Her descriptions give a good picture of Vernon's boundless love of the outdoors, his irrepressible energy and physical fitness – the opposite from what might expect of a bank clerk who sat writing poetry every evening. This was also attested to by Vernon's new neighbour at Pennard, who soon became a close friend, Wyn Lewis. He described what he saw as an outstanding characteristic of Vernon's, that whenever they were together, even if sitting inside, he always had the feeling that Vernon was outdoors. Wyn Lewis also gave a good description of the outdoor life he and Vernon enjoyed together at Pennard: "We played tennis, at which he was brilliant, and croquet which he loved and could more than hold his own at ... Sometimes on moonlit nights we would play croquet till past midnight with the aid of storm lanterns and even car headlights. But above all we walked the cliffs and bathed in the bays of Gower by day and by night in all kinds of weather, and we talked and talked and talked."[43]

"I am prepared"
He was more than fully returned to health; he had arrived onto the cliffs at Pennard which would continue to be his home for almost the whole of the rest of his life; and after his years of apprenticeship he now had a sure sense of his true direction as a poet, speaking of himself as "*by right the Muses' son*". In this state, on June 27th, he turned 28.

His apprenticeship at last was nearing its end – and his style "catching up" with his "experience". He drafted the first two poems, 'Thames Forest' and 'After Sunset', which he would include a few years later in his first book. In 'After Sunset' he is able to let go of his absorption in the past through the intensity of his immediate experience of the stars:

> *Lift up your eyelids.*
> *Leave the broken column,*
> *The crumbled Parthenon, the pyramids ...*

> *Leave where the bats dwell*
> *And the dark bird of night ...*
> *Look up to stars milkwhite ...*
>
> *O life, my mistress,*
> *This moment reclaims you*

The years of his solitary apprenticeship over, he felt ready as 1934 ended to set out on the true adventure of life awaiting him. Feeling all the excitement of an unknown future, he declared his intention: *"to salute the daring of day ... to cut the mooring-rope, to push away"*[44] and announced: *"I am prepared"*.

CHAPTER SEVEN

Swansea's Other Poet (1935–1936)

Two poets

Unbeknown to Vernon Watkins Swansea had simultaneously been home to another young poet, 8 years younger than him, and so who was now, at the end of 1934, just 20. But whereas Watkins, having given up his first life as a poet, had only written 4 or 5 poems, in early drafts, that he would one day publish, this other 20 year-old poet had not only already written more than a third of his eventual *Collected Poems* but had also just published his first book of poems.

These two young poets from the same town – despite an inner affinity between them – were in many other ways too almost the exact opposite of one another. Vernon Watkins, despite the uncompromisingness of his inner revolution against the world, was in outer life modest, gentlemanly and accepting of whatever life brought towards him. Still living in the house of his parents by the sea, he had trodden until now a solitary poetic path. With his large ears he was gifted with a unique ability to *listen*.

This other young poet, with his large lips and mouth, gifted with a unique power of voice was, despite his great inner discipline with regard to his poetry, wild and anarchic and enjoyed living near the eye of the storm of social life. At 20 he had already moved to London in a wish to kick off the trappings of home and live a life beyond the merely provincial. He had also kicked off, far more quickly than Watkins, any extraneous influences on his own poetry and had forged out a style for himself that, even at 20, was startlingly and unmistakably his own. Nor did he have any of Watkins's renunciatory views about publication and fame. Quite the opposite. He had launched himself on a meteoric path to extraordinary fame both as a poet and for the life he led. At 17 he had written: "the most attractive figures in literature are always those around whom a world of lies and legends has been woven, those half mythical artists ... half wild, half human."[1] He indisputably became one of those figures.

This younger poet's name was Dylan Thomas. His first book, which was appeared in December 1934, was called *18 Poems* – consisting of the poems he had written aged 18 and 19.

In a newspaper interview he had given about the book, Dylan Thomas had said, when asked about the notoriously wild life he was already leading: *"I'd give much to be a bank clerk in a safe job."*[2] It is a very strange remark, considering he had never even heard of Vernon Watkins, with whom he would soon strike up a lifelong friendship.

Morgan and Higgs Bookshop

18 Poems was very prominently displayed in Swansea's main bookshop, Morgan and Higgs, frequented by Watkins since his childhood and to which he still often wandered during his lunch-hour.

One day therefore in February 1935, looking at the window-display, he was confronted with the shock of discovering that he – surely the only true poet in Swansea – was not alone. Not only this, but this other young poet, not even 21, had already leaped in front of him into the literary limelight. Watkins may have recently renounced or transformed his desire for this kind of fame, but it was nevertheless a strange and unsettling experience to learn suddenly of this other poet who had sprung up, unnoticed, almost next door.

Jealousy or no jealousy, he felt an extreme reluctance to accept that this *other* could have any genuine claims, as he did, to be viewed as "the Muses' son". When he did finally pick up the book, he did so: "with a curiosity mixed with a *determination not to buy it.*" As he freely admitted, the *last thing* he wanted at this moment was to take on board the presence of another *living* poet besides himself: *"I was completely absorbed in writing poetry myself, so the last thing I wanted ... was a book by another living poet of my generation."*[3] Be that as it may, the book was "finally bought *against my will* and installed, rather uncomfortably, in my room."[4]

"Uncomfortable" it must unquestionably have been, as Thomas's subject-matter was shockingly different from his own: *"Freudian symbols – sexual imagery – birth – adolescence – manhood – death – physical emphasis on organic growth and decay"*. (As Watkins once listed Thomas's early themes.[5])

Nevertheless, there was also something strikingly similar in the intense character of both poets:

Dylan Thomas:	"*Before I knocked and flesh let enter*"
Vernon Watkins:	"*question not the apocalypse*
	Shaped by the utterance of these lips".
Dylan Thomas:	"*Unless I learn the night I shall go mad.*
	It is night's terrors I must learn to love"
Vernon Watkins:	"*my eyes … saw not clear till sight was lost*
	And Night's refracting prism the image tossed."[6]

It was also quite impossible for Vernon Watkins not to recognize the achievement evident in these *18 Poems.* As Watkins wrote later: "It was at once realized by discerning readers … that this poet had … disturbed the roots of our language in an organic way and given it a new vitality. There was nothing stale or imitative in the book."[7]

By merely buying the book Watkins already opened himself to the 'uncomfortable' presence of Dylan Thomas in his life, and events quickly brought about their actual meeting.

Vernon Watkins had been taken as a child by his parents to the Paraclete Congregational Church in Mumbles, where the minister, David Rees, was Dylan Thomas's uncle. David Rees appears to have been mostly appalled by what he heard about the behaviour of his young nephew. Dylan Thomas, in return, wrote a poem about his uncle, renaming Rees the 'Reverend Crap'.

Vernon would probably have heard from his parents about Rees's connection to Dylan Thomas. Vernon happened to bump into Rees in Swansea and of course asked him about Dylan. Rees, presumably feeling much more positively about Vernon than he did about his nephew, gave Vernon the Thomas family's address and encouraged him to visit Dylan. It was the 'Reverend Crap', therefore, who provided the link between the different worlds of Dylan Thomas and Vernon Watkins.

Portrait of Vernon Watkins by Alfred Janes (1947).

Dylan Thomas by Alfred Janes (1934).

First meeting – Pennard Cliffs

Soon afterwards Watkins climbed for the first time to the top of Cwmdonkin Drive, where the Thomas family lived. Dylan was in London, but his mother welcomed Vernon and promised to ask Dylan to contact him. Dylan rang Vernon and arranged to come and see him in Pennard the day after he returned, on a Saturday afternoon.[8]

The strength of Dylan's poetry had obviously led Vernon to expect someone of greater physical stature, for when Dylan stepped off the bus Vernon found him "shorter than I expected". It is clear, in fact, that Vernon was immediately disarmed. Far from whatever threatening figure he had imagined, the young poet in front of him was: *"slight, shorter than I expected, shy and eager in manner, deep-voiced, restless, humorous, with large, wondering, yet acutely intelligent eyes, gold curls, and under these the face of a cherub."*[9]

Watkins's romantic homosexual feelings from his schooldays had died out in him during his 'death and rebirth' experience.[10] Nonetheless, perhaps no one was more predisposed than Watkins to respond to youthful Adonis-like beauty. In exalted mood, no doubt, Watkins set off walking with Thomas over the Gower cliffs, only then to encounter his next shock. For as they started talking Thomas immediately began challenging many of Watkins's long-held and even sacred views about poetry:

"I quickly realized ... that this cherub took nothing for granted. In thought and words he was anarchic, challenging, with the certainty of that instinct that knows its own freshly discovered truth."

Watkins of course told Thomas about his own poetry and their exhilarating walk over, in Watkins' writing room, Vernon now read Dylan some of his poems. Dylan asked if Vernon had any more, Vernon left the room and returned dragging a huge old leather trunk, stuffed with the vast number of poems he had written until then. ("I read him three or four, and, when he asked if I had more, he was very much amused when I lugged a trunk into the room."[11]) It is indeed easy to imagine Dylan's delight at seeing this most unusual 'bank clerk' opening up his great treasure-chest of poems and revealing that down the road from him, in Gower, here was another, like himself, whose life since childhood had been held in thrall to the love of reading and writing poetry.

The "anarchic, challenging" Dylan, though, had matured much faster as a poet than Vernon and hearing Vernon's early poetry he immediately set to work distinguishing the true from the false. Dylan liked two poems Vernon had been working on ('After Sunset' and 'Thames Forest') but ruthlessly pruned much of the rest: He "quickly showed me what was fresh in my work, and what was stale and derived from other poets, not really belonging to myself."[12]

A letter to Vernon three years later gives a direct taste of the kind of criticisms meted out by Dylan:

"All the words are lovely, but they seem so chosen, not struck out ... The whole poem seems to have come out of the nostalgia of literature ... I don't ask for vulgarity, though I miss it; I think I ask for a little creative destruction, destructive creation."[13]

Vernon had once had a powerful dream where a "true voice" had told him "*your poetry is only appreciation*". Whatever Vernon's initial discomfort, he was far too committed to poetry not to recognize Dylan's criticisms as a further message along the same lines, and he would always acknowledge the "great debt"[14] he owed Dylan for this help that he had given him.[15]

Before long, it led Vernon to have a huge and ceremonious burning of great mounds of his juvenilia. He "made a bonfire of nearly all his early work",[16] as he wrote about Wilfred Owen a year later, in words which were more true about himself.[17] When Vernon Watkins recreated this event for a television programme in 1966 he imitated it a little too exactly, throwing new poetic manuscripts of his onto the fire, to the horror of the filmmaker, John Ormond.[18]

Second meeting – Cwmdonkin Drive

They arranged to meet again soon, this time at Dylan's house. A week or so later, therefore, the roles were reversed. Vernon now climbed Cwmdonkin Drive and the stairs of the house up to Dylan's room and it was Dylan's turn to pull out his secret store of unseen writings, and read from them: "He unfolded a large file, marked in block letters POMES."

However the meeting with the other had resounded in each of them during the intervening days, both must have sensed that the meeting with this strange other, if they pursued their friendship, would be of huge consequence in their lives. Did this bode good or ill? The first poem Dylan chose to read – 'Ears in the turrets hear'[19] – confronted Vernon directly with this question:

> *Ears in the turrets hear ...*
> *The fingers at the locks.*
> *Shall I unbolt or stay*
> *Alone ... ?*
> *Shall I let in the stranger ... ?*

Three times, at the end of each stanza, Dylan challenged Vernon:

> *Hands of the stranger ...*
> **Hold you poison or grapes?**

Dylan went on to read several more poems before finishing with the first seven sonnets of the sequence 'Altar-wise by owl-light'. These progressively build on one another, plunging ever deeper into the partly religious, partly visceral world of Dylan Thomas's imagination, with each word weighed and charged for its rhythmical, incantatory, almost explosive effect.

Watkins had already been struck by Dylan's unique gift when reading *18 Poems*. Their first meeting had worked on powerfully in him. With 'Ears in the Turrets Hear' Dylan had launched them into an intense poetic dialogue with one another. And now, with these newly written sonnets, Dylan took Vernon into the farthest reaches, to date, of the strange, controlled and yet almost unconscious mystery of his genius.

To Vernon's ears, so sensitively attuned to poetry, the poem must have been almost giddying in its relationship to language and on account of its sheer consonantal power and playfulness.

The ink of this of sonnet-sequence was still almost wet on the page. It had been started in the month that Dylan and Vernon met and was still growing. Much in fact that had consciously or unconsciously resounded between them during their first meeting was to be found in these sonnets. When Dylan, for example, had asked Vernon what he mainly wanted to write about, Vernon had replied: "grief and time". And now, in the last poem Dylan read that evening, Dylan touched on the very themes closest to Vernon's vision:

> "Who sucks the bell-voiced Adam out of magic,
> Time, milk and magic, from the world beginning.
> Time is the tune my ladies lend their heartbreak".

With Vernon's poetic senses heightened beyond themselves, Dylan, this "young cherub" with the lamplight shining through his hair, now "looked up on reading the last line: '*On rose and icicle the ringing handprint.*'"[20]

It was without doubt a moment of epiphany for Vernon. "I was aware that I was in the presence of a poet of extraordinary genius", he later wrote.[21] But it was not merely a *poetic* epiphany, such as he had had before when reading great poetry. For *this* experience also depended on the living presence of this other looking up at him as the poem finished.

Touch
Death and Life

"So began a relationship for which it would be difficult to find a name", wrote Gwen Watkins. "a meeting with Dylan held the same excitement for Vernon to their last meeting … What was it in Dylan or himself that made him all his life … a giver of unconditional love to this 'young Apollo' who cared nothing whether he was loved or not?"[22]

Despite the difficulties mentioned by Gwen Watkins we must try nevertheless to "find a name" for the relationship between Dylan Thomas and Vernon Watkins, to find, that is, a way to describe what it was about this relationship that made it of such central significance in Vernon Watkins's biography.

Apart from his years at Repton, Vernon Watkins had lived a very solitary existence until now. Furthermore, most of the poetry he had written could well be described as '*death-haunted*' – filled with his inner experiences and frequently by the spirits of the dead, but, like the old leather trunk in which he kept it, badly in need of being *opened up* and exposed to the light and life of day.

Dylan Thomas, by contrast, as we have seen, would concern himself increasingly more with the *social* than with the solitary; his preoccupations were more with childhood, sex and *birth* than with Watkins's themes of time, *death* and resurrection; and it was the *living* rather than the dead who peopled Thomas's writing. Gwen Watkins describes Dylan Thomas being, for Watkins, a 'young Apollo', whereas it was Watkins who was the more 'Apollonian', while Dylan Thomas had much more of the young *Dionysus* or *Bacchus* about him, with his all too often riotous connection to *life*.

Vernon Watkins would always be extremely aware of these differences between them. "*For the dead live and I am of their kind*" ('Gravestones') he would say of himself, and: "*I toil to set the dead at rest*" ('Crowds'). In clear contrast, he never ceased referring to the sheer exuberance of *life* in Dylan:

"The variety of *life in its abundance* sang in his veins. He was born to praise it."[23]

"Dylan ... did not wait particularly for the Muse to catch him. *He was absorbed in life and in people.* He did not know where his next poem would come from, and he did not care."[24]

"I remember him remarking to me with great emphasis that he would ... now write about *real people*; his verse would move in the direction of the *living voice*. He had broken the shell of symbolic time and come out into *real time*."[25]

"I think that *the private figure, 'the proud man apart', was the opposite of the figure (Dylan) sought to cultivate ... He had the faculty of immediacy, of making everything present,* and of becoming a part of people's lives almost before he knew them."[26]

"All Dylan Thomas's works are the product of an innocent vision. His way of looking at the world was to see it as *freshly created* ... His reperception of childhood was easy for him, for he had never really abandoned it."[27]

It was not only these *differences,* however, that made Vernon Watkins's connection with Dylan Thomas of such unparalleled significance in his life but the even greater mystery, in his eyes, of all that was made possible when these two *met*.

Almost immediately after their first two meetings, Vernon began work on a poetic drama – a "Masque" – which he would long consider the central poetic parable of his life – and the key to much of his work – "my Faust" as he would later describe it to T.S. Eliot. It was called *The Influences* and Vernon completed the first draft of it in the months after his first meetings with Dylan in 1935.[28]

Its theme is the meeting of two people who are *polar opposites* of one another. If one thinks of Vernon Watkins toiling, alone, to "set the dead at rest", and of Dylan Thomas with his "innocent vision", who "had never really abandoned ... childhood", it is not hard to recognize the opposites they represent in the two main characters of the *Masque*:

"The first is an Old Man, who has spent the best part of a century toiling with abstract thought, reading, writing and studying; a casual observer might say that he has not lived, but rather prepared all his life for another existence. The second character is a Girl, fresh and young, who enters his room."

These are the two different *influences* which are eventually able to meet and in so doing are transformed by one another:

"*The Old Man may be called 'the life beyond time'; she is the moment of time. Of these two art is born ... These two influences answer each other until the moment of touch which transfigures both.*"[29]

There could therefore be no question, any more, for Vernon, of merely being transported beyond death and time and remaining there. The appearance of Dylan Thomas in his life now demanded that he also fully plunge back into life again.

Friendship and life – 1935–1936

"We became close friends almost immediately", says Watkins, writing of their first meeting. The "almost" points perhaps to Vernon's initial uncertainty facing Dylan's anarchic and challenging character. Any doubts or fears Vernon had, however, were quickly dispelled: "my first impression of a rooted obstinacy ... was really a rooted innocence" and this "was reinforced whenever we met. We met often, either at his house or mine."[30] Dylan Thomas, too, if his reading of 'Ears in the Turrets Hear' revealed any doubts about Vernon, also abandoned these.

And so, after that transformative moment at the end of Dylan's reading – *"the moment of touch which transfigures both" – life* and *colour* broke back in to Vernon's world and nothing thereafter would be the same again.

Vernon rushed out that night into the house of his friend Wyn Lewis and declared: "I have spent the evening with a genius. You must meet him too."[31] Even to say this was to break down the barriers he usually maintained between the private world of his poetry and the public world of his work and social life.

One of the great positives about the bank, for Vernon, was that as no one there knew anything about poetry they could never interfere with his poetic world. He clearly described this hidden blessing about working in an inartistic environment: "Possibly he has met people whose wrong-headed interest in poetry seemed ... more repugnant than indifference ... Anything is better than the false."[32]

His social life, similarly, with his family and local friends or playing tennis and hockey, was congenial, but was a separate world from his poetry. His connection with Dylan Thomas changed all this, for in Dylan there was no such strict division between private and public worlds.

The Kardomah

The painter Alfred Janes, a close friend of both Dylan Thomas and Vernon Watkins[33], echoed Vernon's views on Dylan's relationship to life:

"Dylan was an intensely *human* human. To a fantastic degree. What human beings did interested him; every aspect of their behaviour ... This comes out constantly in his personality, his tremendous sympathy with other people ... Dylan's deal was being alive. Dylan was intensely, as near a hundred per cent alive as a human being could be, and ... death was to him the opposite of this. The calamity."[34]

Fred Janes was one of a group of artists, writers and friends who met every Wednesday and Saturday lunchtime in the Kardomah Café in Swansea. This was on two floors, with a smarter seating area upstairs and a simpler one downstairs – or where, as Watkins put it: "*Swansea's rich artists and poverty-stricken business men used to meet, on separate floors, to discuss shares and pictures.*"[35] Through Dylan Vernon immediately began coming along whenever he could, which was often only during his Wednesday lunch-hour as on Saturdays he usually had to work till 2 p.m. at the bank. As well as Dylan Thomas and Fred Janes, those who attended regularly were the musician Tom Warner, the writer John Prichard and the journalist Charlie Fisher.[36] Dylan Thomas in his radio script 'Return Journey' recalled the wild variety of their conversation: "they talked about Augustus John, Dracula, trial marriage, the Welsh sea, King Kong, anarchy, darts, T.S. Eliot and girls."[37]

The kind of creative involvement with others Vernon had only enjoyed as a schoolboy at Repton was now given back to him as an adult, among working artists and writers. The creative companionship and friendship, particularly when Dylan and Fred were both there, was all that Vernon would have wished for, socially, and Swansea itself suddenly became during these years a rare crucible of living artistic life. In 'Return Journey' Dylan recalled the exuberant mood of these young artists and friends as they looked towards the futures: "How Dan Jones was going to compose the most prodigious symphony, Fred Janes paint the most miraculously meticulous picture, … Vernon Watkins and young Thomas write the most boiling poems, how they would ring the bells of London and paint it like a tart."[38] Vernon himself, speaking of these pre-war years in Swansea, told of "an era and an excitement which cannot be repeated."[39]

Friendship with Dylan Thomas

Vernon's greatest friendship, of course, was with Dylan Thomas. Dylan returned to Swansea in October 1935, having been away for six months and he and Vernon would then, as well as the Kardomah meetings, meet as often as possible either at Cwmdonkin Drive or Heatherslade. Vernon told Yeats that he and Dylan, in these early days of their friendship, saw each other "three times a week revising each other's poems".[40] According to

Gwen Watkins: "socially, Vernon drew Dylan into his own orbit; psychologically, he was drawn into Dylan's." This was certainly true in Pennard where they would walk on the cliffs and swim (or Vernon would) and play croquet and have tea and share their poetry. After Dylan had to cancel one of their meetings he wrote: "I missed you and the unwonted walk and the toasted things for tea and the poetry after it, and I hope … that you missed your hearty, Britain-chested, cliff-striding companion as much as I did."[41] At Cwmdonkin Drive Dylan read Vernon not only his poetry but also his stories. How novel this exposure to the world of prose must have been for Vernon is made clear by the following anecdote of his: "We were having tea once with his parents in Bishopston when his father turned to me and said, 'Dylan is so narrow in his reading. There are so many books that he won't read.' 'Narrow!' Dylan said. '*Me* narrow? Why, *he* stops as soon as the words go to the end of the page.'"[42]

Dylan would also tell Vernon of his encounters with the contemporary literary world and often, as a contrast to Vernon's quiet "Apollonian" genius, Dylan felt almost obliged to play the opposite "Dionysian" role. Thus in his first surviving letter to Watkins Dylan describes the week he has just spent in London: "I … fully lived up to the conventions of Life No. 13: promiscuity, booze, coloured shirts, too much talk, too little work" and tells Vernon about his visit to "Pope Eliot".[43]

Dylan's close friends, particularly those from Swansea, always made clear how very different Dylan was from the outer Bacchic mask he often wore. Mervyn Levy said: "Dylan didn't really drink as much as people like to think he did or as much as he likes you to think he did … I think that had people not inveigled him as much as they did into drinking, his friends, who didn't drink much, could have kept him away from the bottle."[44] Fred Janes described Dylan as: "an absolutely and deliberate and conscientious worker" and added: "drink … didn't seem to be important to Dylan intrinsically at any time … it was the people who interested him."[45] Vernon Watkins remarked that Dylan, in his rejection of any intellectual or 'highbrow' attitude, often: "wanted to emphasise the opposite … and to appear more disreputable than he was. That is the kind of mask he put on with a lot of people, and strangers were totally deceived by this mask. His intimate friends, of course, were not taken in at all. He never changed really … *The poetry was the simple thing; he worked terribly hard at it and the older and surer he became, the harder he worked.*"[46] This commitment and devotion to poetry, which Dylan and Vernon shared with one another, lay at the heart of their friendship.

The poetic lives, however, of Dylan Thomas and Vernon Watkins, are so different – the one so famous and the other so unknown – that it has often been assumed that Vernon Watkins must have been a 'satellite' around the greater light of Dylan Thomas; and not that it was a working partnership between two poetic equals, completely different from one another. To understand this it is necessary, before we return to the story of their lives, to examine their poetic connection a little more deeply.

Affinity

Vernon Watkins often spoke of the profound *affinity* between himself and Dylan Thomas, though he also made clear what a surprise it was to discover this: "I did not expect, when I turned the pages of this book (*18 Poems*), that I should find in their author an affinity so much deeper than anything I can describe."[47]

It can also be surprising, knowing Vernon's profound link with Yeats' poetry, to realize that this was mainly a stylistic one, but imaginatively and spiritually he in fact felt far closer to Dylan: "there was a deep metaphysical bond between me and Dylan Thomas ... ; *his Welsh imagination was closer to mine than Yeats' Irish one*; but stylistically I felt a much closer bond with Yeats".[48]

This affinity is in fact not hard to recognize in Dylan's poetry. Though claims have sometimes been made for Dylan's political interests, these were of no real significance for his poetry. Dylan's whole view of the role of poetry, of its non-political nature, of its relationship to time and the natural world, and its ultimately redemptive character, were at odds with the prevailing fashion of the time, represented by of Auden, Spender, Isherwood and others. As Vernon wrote of Dylan: "He disliked the sociological poetry of the thirties. *My own themes were really closer to his*; we were both religious poets, and neither of us had any aptitude for political reform."[49]

Elsewhere he elaborated: "We were both Welsh, both Christian poets, we both preferred the sea to politics and hated nationalism, and we both believed that a good poem was one that could never be fashionable. We admired the same thing in poetry, the ancient thing which is never archaic, but always fresh; but our affinity was closest in metaphysical ideas, in that part of imagination which bears witness to religious truth."[50]

This affinity was central to their friendship, and was the source, beyond any differences between them, of their fundamental relationship to poetry:

"We became close friends almost immediately, from an affinity which I think we both recognized at once. *That affinity was particularly clear when we talked about poetry or read it aloud.*"[51]

Thomas Taig, a theatre producer in Swansea, witnessed Thomas and Watkins working together and the affinity between them and immediately experienced the intensity of their friendship:

"It was only when I ... heard them repeating fragments of their latest poems that I began to understand the basis of their close friendship and their high esteem for each other both personally and professionally ... there was never any talk ... about aesthetic theories, philosophies or literary movements ... the real interest lay in detailed discussion of the value of a particular syllable in a particular line and whether some word should be changed or deleted. There was no need to argue, for both moved freely in what I have called the inner world and both understood the arduous business of craftsmanship."[52]

Complementary poets
Sculpture and music

The real riddle of their poetry, however, lies not in their similarity but in their *differences* – for as poets they were the *opposites* of one another. In Vernon Watkins's words: "*Our poetic methods were as unlike as possible ... Although we had great affinity of theme our work was complementary.*"[53]

What were these two different approaches to poetry of Dylan Thomas and Vernon Watkins? And how are they complementary?

The difference is in the two directions in which language and poetry can be intensified – on the one hand towards an ever more tangible experience of sculptural substance and on the other towards the sphere of music. It was the difference, in fact, between the two landscapes the two poets chose to live in. Dylan Thomas on the shoreline of the muddy

Vernon Watkins on the Gower Cliffs.

Dylan Thomas overlooking the estuary in Laugharne

estuary in Laugharne, where the winding, tidal river moves great mounds of sand and silt, and the water birds wade, as it pushes its way to the sea. Vernon Watkins inhabited the cliff tops of Gower, open to the sky and the stars, keeping company with the seagulls, with breathtaking views to the sea beneath, to which he would often clamber down and swim.

It is the difference between the powerfully alliterative, consonantal poetry of the North – of the Edda, the Kalevala and Beowulf; and the musical, metrical poetry of the South – Homer, for example – often recited to a lyre. Two of its greatest representatives in English poetry are, oddly, a Welshman and an Irishman – the explosively consonantal Gerard Manley Hopkins and the musically attuned William Butler Yeats.

This fundamental poetic polarity reappears now, in startling manner, in these two friends, Dylan Thomas and Vernon Watkins, as Watkins exactly described:

"our poetic methods were as unlike as possible, he beginning with a ball of phrases which he moulded into a symmetrical shape, and I with a musical cadence, almost out of earshot, to which I slowly gave substance."[54] And again:

"He began with a core of meaning, with a piece of clay which he moulded in his hands. The music of the poem came later ... He certainly did not let it govern what he wanted to say. My own verse composition began with music and arrived, most laboriously, at texture."[55]

On one occasion, Watkins expanded on this contrast to include how they lived their lives:

"Our approach to (poetry) and our way of working presented a complete contrast. Dylan worked upon a symmetrical abstract with tactile delicacy; out of a lump of texture or nest of phrases he created music, testing everything by physical feeling, working from the concrete image outwards. I worked from music and cadence towards the density of physical shape. I worked at night, he in the day, usually in the afternoon, but never in the evening which he regarded as the social time of the day."[56]

Dylan Thomas, too, was completely aware of this contrast, having written (to Pamela Hansford-Johnson) a few months before meeting Watkins:

"Have I ever told you of the theory of how all writers either work towards or away from words? Even if I have, I'll tell it to you again because it's true. Any poet or novelist you like to think of – he either works out of words or in the direction of them."⁵⁷

But Thomas, the day-time poet, was also, at the moment, 'having his day'. Unlike Watkins, therefore, who discerned two complementary methods, Dylan Thomas was firmly convinced that only his own method would do. Thus in 1935, the year he met Watkins, he criticizes John Clare:

"because he worked towards (words), not out of them, describing and cataloguing the objects that met his eyes. In the beginning was the object, not the word. He could not realise, and consequently his expression suffered, that the word is the object."⁵⁸

This was Thomas's "freshly discovered truth": "When I experience anything I experience it as a thing and a word at the same time, both equally amazing."⁵⁹

It is, in fact, fitting that Dylan could not share Vernon's measured recognition of the validity of both approaches,⁶⁰ for they are also an expression of the Dionysian and Apollonian tendencies, and the *Dionysian*, particularly in its youth, could hardly be expected to acknowledge the other to be of equal value to itself. It is also the case that whereas Dylan Thomas matured very young as a poet and wrote less and less poetry as he grew older, Vernon Watkins matured as a poet later, after which he wrote ever more and ever greater poetry. Thus although Thomas would call Watkins "the most profound and greatly accomplished Welshman writing poems in English",⁶¹ and on seeing Watkins's third book of poetry would exclaim: "How good you really are!",⁶² he was unable to gain a full sense of his friend's work, dying before much of Watkins's greatest poetry had been written.

There has as yet been far too little recognition that the poetic friendship between Dylan Thomas and Vernon Watkins, as with that between Wordsworth and Coleridge or Goethe and Schiller, was a connection between two extraordinary, complementary geniuses. As in these other cases, it was their very *differences* that made their co-working so fruitful:

"Partly because our work was so unlike, we did not mind suggesting changes in it to each other where a word struck us as odd, or out of place."[63]

"There was, then, great friendship and no rivalry between us. I recognized at once that he was doing what I could not do, and I had faith in his genius. I realised that he was a true poet of a different kind."[64]

"I ... recognized in Dylan Thomas a genius of a quite different kind which could do with words everything I couldn't do with them; his writing was, I understood from the first, the exact complement of mine."[65]

"The one happy person I know"
Vernon's help to Dylan

Let us now look at the details of this creative working relationship and the effect it had on them both – beginning with Dylan Thomas.

They had first met in March 1935. In October Dylan returned to Swansea for six months, during which time the intensity of their regular meetings and working together began. Despite the positive reception of Dylan Thomas's first book it had had very modest sales and Dylan was eager for his poetry to be publically known. In October he therefore sent his second book (later called *Twenty-Five Poems*) to Dent's. In December he had received a reply from Richard Church, on behalf of Dent's, refusing to accept the volume as it was. Many of the poems appeared obscure or, worse, surrealistic, making the poetry in danger of appearing "a private eccentricity."

Dylan had rejected Church's criticisms, but to no avail, and so Dylan set to work over the next two months to strengthen the book as much as he could. Each time they met, Dylan tried and tested on Vernon many of the individual poems and the form of the book as a whole. The clearest example of the help this gave Dylan was with 'And Death Shall Have No Dominion', which Vernon helped nurse into its final form, thus ensuring its inclusion in the book: "When I called at Cwmdonkin Drive one evening he said that he had almost decided to leave (it) out ... (and) certainly ... would ... unless he altered it. He read it aloud many times, and I said how necessary it was to the book and how much I admired it, especially its impulsive rhythm. He made a number of small changes that evening, and when I left my head was full of the excitement of the finished poem."[66]

In the light of Church's negative criticisms, Vernon tried to persuade Dylan not to include two poems[67] which he felt had an "unwarrantable obscurity". Dylan, despite admitting that one of them "so far as he knew ... had no meaning at all", laughed at the suggestion: "When I said that reviewers would be likely to pick these out ... he smiled and said, 'Give them a bone.'"

After six months Dylan re-submitted the book to Dent's. He boldly told Church that if the book was still unacceptable he would have to approach another publisher, but he also made clear that he still very much hoped that Dent's would accept the book. If not – as he joked but also perhaps partly believed – he might never find a way forward as a serious writer: "I hope ... that you will be able to publish them: if not, the day *may* come when none of my poems will be indecently obscure or fashionably difficult."[68] Church remained unchanged in his opinion and did not reply, leading Dylan to write back to him far more uncertainly: "Have you come to any decision as to the fate of my poems? I do apologize for my delay in writing".[69]

For despite all Dylan's previous bravado ("Give them a bone!"), there *was* a valid charge of obscurity regarding his writing, and hearing no word from Dent's Dylan was forced to face up to it. It was to Vernon that he turned for help, writing on April 20th:

"perhaps, as you said once, I should stop writing altogether for some time; ... (I) can't, for the life or the death of me, get any real liberation, any diffusion or dilution or anything, into the churning bulk of the words ... You might, and would, I know, if you could, help me by talking to me. I don't fear – we talked about it, do you remember – any sudden cessation or drying-up ...; *what I do fear is an ingrowing, the impulse growing like a toenail into the artifice.* Talk to me about it, will you – it's probably a terrible task I'm trying to drag you into – in any way, any words."[70]

It is a pity we do not know how Vernon replied. Vernon had occasionally suggested Dylan use a few more "weak" words in his poems to get "dilution ... into the churning bulk of the words", but Dylan had not wanted to hear of it: "I've always disliked the weak line. I admit that readers of complicated poetry do need a breather every now and then, but I don't think that poetry should give it to them. When they want one, they should take it and then go on."⁷¹ Thus Dylan was *not* merely seeking for Vernon's technical advice.

There was a greater reason that was making Dylan specifically turn to Vernon at this moment. That Dylan was failing to find any way forward and seemingly only plunging his poetry ever deeper into obscurity was not merely a poetic issue, but also an existential one. He was therefore turning to Vernon not just as a poet but also for the completely trustworthy inner ground he stood on:

"I don't really know why I should be unloading any of this on you (…) *But you are – even if only momentarily – the one happy person I know,* the one who, contrary to facts and, in a certain way, to circumstances, seems to be almost entirely uncomplicated: not, either, the uncomplication of a beginning person, but that of a person who has worked through all the beginnings and finds himself a new beginning in the middle – I hope, for your today's happiness, – a beginning at the end."

Vernon's "happiness" was indeed not just naïve, but as we have seen had undergone a death and a rebirth – and this clearly resounded in Dylan with the true source of his own vision and poetry. As Vernon wrote: "there was a deep metaphysical bond between me and Dylan Thomas; we only had to catch each other's eye to recognize each other's meaning". There was no one else with whom Dylan shared this inner affinity and so it was hardly surprising that, feeling himself inwardly blocked, it was to Vernon he turned for help. Dylan was needing to reorientate himself in some way in relation to his poetic vision. And Vernon makes clear that their poetic work together involved precisely such wrestling through to the true grounds of their imagination:

"*if we disagreed it was on a metaphysical issue, for natural observation in poetry meant nothing to us without the support of metaphysical truth.*"⁷²

Dylan Thomas *did* manage to come through this particular knot in which he was in danger of becoming entangled in 1936 – the knot which revealed itself in writing which became ever denser and more "symbol-charged."⁷³ He came through in his prose by moving ever more "in the direction of the living voice" and emerging from "symbolic time

… into real time."[74] Dylan came through in his poetry too, in a different way, to a much more direct and transparent relationship to the world, as would eventually become evident in his third book, *The Map of Love*, published in 1939.[75] There is no doubt that the joyful and profound friendship and co-working with Vernon over the next few years was of huge help to Dylan in bringing this about.

"Of this Moment art is born"
Dylan's help to Vernon

The intense and inspiring 6 months working so closely with Dylan also had a catalysing effect on Vernon's own very different genius and when Dylan left Swansea for Cornwall in April (1936) Vernon at last began receiving the "luck" his poetry needed. In March or April he wrote two poems in one evening, both of which he immediately recognized as finished poems. Even years later he would look back at the extreme rarity of this: "I have been lucky enough to write two poems in the same evening, only one line of which, belonging to the first poem, I wanted later to change."[76]

Nor is there any accident in the *themes* of the two poems. Each poem addresses *one* of the two 'influences' in Vernon's *Masque*. The first poem is called 'Empty Hands' and teaches the young and carefree Dylan-like character (in this case the "spendthrift lover") not to overlook the 'Old Man', for "*he, too, knows delight has empty hands.*"

In the second poem 'Indolence'– it is the Vernon-like 'Old Man' who is addressed:

> Come. You have taken tribute from the dead.
> Your tribute to the quick must now be paid.

'Indolence' had a specific meaning for Vernon. It did not mean 'laziness', but rather the opposite of 'ambition', with which one pushes oneself into the world. With 'indolence', by contrast, one opens oneself to the world around one and allows it into oneself.[77] This is all that is demanded of the 'Old Man'. The poem ends:

> *What lovelier tribute than to rest your head*
> *Beneath this birch tree which is bound to fade?*
> *And watch the branches quivering by a thread*
> *Beyond interpretation of the shade.*

With these two poems, dropping in through inspiration, Vernon had not only found the opening for his 'Masque'[78], but had also written the first two completed poems of his first book. His true voice was letting itself be known.

Vernon must have gone to bed in exalted spirits. The following day, as on every other working day, he would have taken the early bus into Swansea and the bank. According to Vernon: "Lines are running through my head all the time – even when I work in the bank … If you are a lyric poet, this is the way things go."[79] Sometimes, however, the distracting demands of his poetry were even greater than usual. Talking about Yeats, he once said: "The first time I read 'Lapis Lazuli', I got the figures wrong all day at the bank."[80] If this took place simply reading someone else's poetry, one can only imagine this was even more the case on days like this one, after making important breakthroughs in his own poetry.

In April, Vernon had his penultimate holiday with his sister, Dorothy, to Spain – visiting Seville, Madrid and Cadiz. According to her: "from the start nothing went right". These holidays had always been a respite for Vernon from the dreariness of the bank. Now, with so much happening for him in Swansea, they began to fade in significance.

He was, however, in Spain, able to reflect on the changes he was going through – and on the fact that he was at last approaching maturity as a poet. He did so in some poems that must be seen as among the last of his juvenilia.[81] In one of them he thanks the trials he has had to go through before finding his own voice, and even the stark, materialistic world of his work, which forced him to win the strength needed for his poetry:

> *A poet should be reared materialistic,*
> *Callous, indifferent. Every seer or mystic*
> *Must know at length: the poet's first necessity is strength.*
> *That tenderness dies young which is not born*
> *Of tough root guarded by protective thorn.*

His waiting time over, he is at last ready, and the poem ends:

> *who is better fitted to work in stone, than you the hard light*
> *waited so long to call its own.*
> *Coming so late, and with so pure a song,*
> *Who is so gentle, or, indeed, so strong?* [82]

In this mood, the poet who a few years previously had determined not to publish began to make serious attempts at getting his poetry known. As soon as he was back from his holidays he visited Faber's in London and to spoke with Richard de la Mare's secretary, Anne Bradby.[83] This in itself was a fortuitous meeting, as Bradby, a close friend of Charles Williams, who became the poet Anne Ridler, would have had much in common with Vernon Watkins. He gave her one of his translations of a German poem to show to T.S. Eliot and, more importantly, asked her to ask T.S. Eliot if he would be interested to see Vernon's Masque. Eliot said he would be and so on June 1st (1936) Watkins himself wrote to T.S. Eliot, sending him the Masque. He had, he said, been thinking of "publishing it anonymously", and, though he didn't spell it out in so many words, clearly asked if Eliot and Faber's would be willing to publish it: "in this, particularly, if you thought it worth while, I thought you might possibly help me."

Watkins was quick to add:

"But I feel that I must thank you for reading it at all as I have no qualification to show it to you, except perhaps a certain amount of impudence. But I should like your advice."[84]

Once back in Swansea, his poetry picked up from where he had left off and again took huge strides forward. In June he wrote another finished and masterly short poem: 'Old Triton Time'. It no longer sets the opposites of youth and age against each other, but sings of that which unites both:

> *Old Triton Time responds to every mood:*
> *He's the newborn who's older than the flood.*
> *He babbles water from a dull stone tongue.*
> *He's old and cold, and yet the water's young.*
> *To gain him is to lose him. I have seen*
> *Loss bind him up with lichens: he grew green.*
> *But if my fingers touch the water cold,*
> *He suddenly seems young, the water old.*

The poem is a small and early jewel of Watkins's lyric poetry – free from anything 'stale' or 'derivative' and fresh as the water it tells of. It unites the opposites of 'age' and 'youth' not only in its theme but also in how it is written, having both music and sound-substance.

The following month, shortly after his 30th birthday, walking along the Pennard cliffs toward's Hunt's Bay – the strange "moon-pocked" bay of gnarled and sea-eroded stone – he *heard* a full-length poem spoken as if by the landscape itself. The poem would be called 'Griefs of the Sea' – "which I *heard* coming out of the grasses of the cliffs of Pennard and Hunt's Bay".[85]

The event was the inner equivalent of being struck by lightning – of an inspirational not an electrical kind – but which Vernon was prepared for and was able to receive and to write down in perfect health. Some years later he told a younger poet (Peter Hellings): "It takes ages to find a tongue"[86] and this *hearing* of 'Griefs of the Sea' has in many ways to be seen as the birth-moment of that "tongue" or voice.

Dylan Thomas once criticized a poem of Vernon's for not having: "the strong, inevitable pulling that makes a poem an event, a happening, an action". This could never be said of 'Griefs of the Sea', although it *happens* quite differently from the way Dylan Thomas's poems happen. The whole genesis of 'Griefs of the Sea' could hardly make clearer the difference Vernon described between the two poets: "*He moulded his poems. I heard mine.*"[87]

As an example of what Vernon heard, the following lines are from the middle of the poem:

> *It is a horrible sound, the low wind's whistle*
> *Across the seaweeds on the beach at night ...*
>
> *In spite of that wicked sound ...*
> *It is fitting on the curved cliff to remember the drowned,*
> *To imagine them clearly for whom the sea no longer cares (.)*

A couple of months after writing 'Griefs of the Sea' Vernon recited it to his friend Wyn Lewis on the Gower cliffs and Wyn Lewis's description underlines the significance of the poem in relation to Vernon's poetic genius:
"It may seem odd, but when I first knew him I did not regard Vernon as an exceptional person ... In the shallow way in which one tends to judge people by their occupations, I think I regarded him as primarily a bank clerk who was somewhat over-addicted to the practice of versification – essentially an amateur with absurd aspirations to eternal fame! ... I can clearly remember the turning-point in our relationship which convinced me once and for all that his claims were not to be so lightly dismissed.

One September evening I went to call for him as usual, bathing costume and towel in hand ...

It was one of those miraculously calm evenings that you sometimes get in late summer ... and I was impatient to get to the beach ... But as soon as we had turned the corner onto the cliffs Vernon began reciting poetry, on this occasion ... Housman's 'Shropshire Lad' ... and by the time he had finished intoning the fifth or sixth poem I had had enough. So I stopped and said: "Vernon, will you shut up about Housman, or I'll not come another step. I think he's just a poetaster and a bore ... " And it was on the tip of my tongue to add: "And you're another one!", but I think he must have sensed what I was going to say, for he suddenly turned on me, his eyes blazing and his jaw set, and his fist raised as if to strike me. I backed away hastily, and he let his arm fall. Then he said: "You may have a talent for invective, Wyn, but you're not a genius." "I don't claim to be a genius," I replied. "Are you supposed to be a genius, may I ask?" He did not reply at once but just looked at me and smiled a curious glittering smile. Then he said very quietly but with absolute certainty: "I am a genius"; and on seeing my incredulous expression he added: "If you don't believe me, then listen to this ... " And he began to recite 'Griefs of the Sea'. It was the first time that he had let me hear one of his own poems. I listened astounded, awestruck. The last stanza contained some of the most moving and beautiful lines I had ever heard. When he finished I could only ask him to repeat it, still hardly able to believe my ears. When he had finished once more, I managed to say: "But that's wonderful, infinitely better than anything Housman wrote or ever would be capable of writing." He smiled again, that daemonic glittering smile ... Then he turned on his heel and said: "Come on! Can't you hear that surf?"

From that moment on I never doubted his genius and he became for me the living embodiment of poetry."[88]

In 'Griefs of the Sea', not only was Vernon's mature poetry being born, but the landscape of Gower, to which he had so deeply united himself, was also beginning to speak through him. As the years went on, more and more would the ever-varying landscape of Gower be refound, transfigured, within his poetry, intricately interwoven with the inner events the poems describe.

Wyn Lewis was also the person who said that wherever Vernon was one always had the impression that he was outside.[89] Life in the bank never seemed to make any difference to this. He thought nothing of swimming out great distances and lugging large pieces of driftwood back to shore. He found it impossible to believe, according to Gwen Watkins, "that any human being could be near the sea and not want to plunge in".[90] And the same poet who danced around his room in Cardiff naked, reciting Blake, also loved to swim naked: "because it's incomparably better than bathing with clothes on ... In the morning there's no need to wear anything because noone is about."[91] It is *this* individual who speaks in the second stanza of 'Griefs of the Sea':

> *It is fitting to fling off clothing,*
> *To enter the sea with plunge of seawraiths white*
> *Broken by limbs that love the waters, fear the stars (.)*

Watkins also now found himself able to write different *kinds* of poems than he had written before. In 1936, he suddenly began writing ballads, often with dark and disturbing themes, with haunting rhythms echoing the pulse of the blood. Vernon's more purely musical lyrics may have been diametrically opposed to Dylan Thomas's more Dionysian, consonantal poetry, but Vernon recognized the need for both sides of the scales and in these ballads found his own access to a darker, more Dionysian inspiration.

He said of them:

> "The ballad ... will not be led ... It is a poem which writes itself ... My own ballads ... are all rhythmical and intended to be read aloud ... These ballads are elemental and they belong to myth, but they do not belong to history."[92]

He wrote the first of them, 'Ballad of the Rough Sea', in 1936. Like 'Griefs of the Sea' the all-powerful undercurrent of the sea and its dangers dominate the poem. Set in the English Channel, the ballad: "shows fishermen in danger of drowning, and they have two witnesses, a dead witness who emerges from the middle of the chalk cliff, and a living witness standing on the cliff-top".

In the final stanza the fishermen finally "refuse to be magnetized"[93] by the power of these two "witnesses", who would drag them to their deaths:

> *Go back to your rock, go back to your room.*
> *We are men of the heart, not men of the tomb ...*
> *Go back to the crevice, back to the creek.*
> *Go back for we must not speak.*

On seeing this ballad in print three years later Dylan Thomas wrote to Watkins: "Your *Rough Sea* looked splendid. I read it aloud again & woke the baby."[94] Not surprisingly, Dylan could not help preferring Vernon's ballads to the poems that were more characteristic of him: "I've always liked your ballads very much, & so far – inevitably – the ballads & lyrics mean more to me than the long & complicated poems."[95]

***

The floodgates of his mature poetry were opened – not that he wrote *more* than he had previously, but his newly discovered voice would not now be stopped.

He wrote another poem that year called 'Two Decisions'. In the first of its two stanzas the poet decides to break sharply with all he has known, to leave home and begin again elsewhere:

> *I must go back to Winter*
> *   … break fellowship*
> *Leave the ten-windowed house*
> *And merely remark,*
> *The ivy grew too close:*
> *That house was dark.*

In the second, he decides the exact opposite:
> *I shall not go,*
> *I shall wait here …*
> *Let me be nowhere*
> *A melodramatic guest (.)*

The 'two decisions' are not unlike the two different life choices made by Dylan Thomas and Vernon Watkins – the former breaking away, rebelliously, in search of his inspiration; the latter staying where he is and compelling inspiration to serve him there. (*'Winter must come to me.'*)

But the poem does *not* only present two equally valid opposites. Vernon's own poetic genius is speaking, which is sure of its own

direction – and by the end of the poem it firmly rejects, for itself, the first decision:
> Though distant things entreat
> The afraid, the fanciful,
> The near is faithful:
> Do not deny it.

***

Just at this time, ever in need of notebooks, he bought a red school exercise book, with spaces at the front for pupils to write their name and that of their school. *"On the cover of this book I wrote against Name – Vernon Watkins, and against School – Romantic."*[96] He always kept this book, which in a certain way announced his renaming of himself as a poet. (The poems he had previously published he had either done anonymously or had signed: 'V.P.W.' or 'V.P. Watkins' or 'Vernon P. Watkins'.) But the word 'Romantic' had a wholly different meaning for him now than in the days when, by the graves of Shelley and Keats, he had longed for a golden 'Romantic era' that had passed:

> "The word 'Romantic' meant for me a refusal to sacrifice the sacredness of the moment and of individual experience to a general pattern."[97]

What he meant, therefore, by referring to himself as "Romantic" was that he could *refind* in the present moment and in the life around him the same intensity and 'sacredness' of 'experience' that he had previously felt could only be found in childhood and youth.

What had happened to Vernon Watkins since 'Griefs of the Sea' was that he had at last become able to fashion his poetry into a vessel capable of bearing his particular vision – or, in his own terms, into an 'instrument' on which the *music* of this vision could be played. His poetry, that is, had at last *caught up* with the inner experience he had gone through in early 1929.

Year's ending – 1936

In the autumn of 1936 Dylan Thomas's second book *Twenty-Five Poems* was finally published. The reviews it received in literary journals – on the whole very praising, though with some reservations – established him as a poet. On 15th November, the *Sunday Times* featured a review of the book by Edith Sitwell, which was almost hyperbolic in its praise: "The work of this very young man is on a huge scale, both in theme and structurally ... I could not name one poet of this ... generation, who shows so great a promise, and even so great an achievement." The review, before such a wide audience, made Dylan Thomas famous.

Much as Dylan had blazed his own trail to this moment, he had also been greatly helped by the strong ground of support of his closest friends in Swansea. Thomas Taig commented: "very few seem to realize what an important part Fred Janes played in Dylan's whole life ... as a sort of mentor".[98] Every word of *Twenty-Five Poems* had also been shared with and tested on Vernon. It was entirely fitting, therefore, that these three should have met on this day to celebrate the hour. According to Dylan Thomas's biographer Paul Ferris: "The day the review appeared, Alfred Janes remembered going down to Pennard on the bus with Thomas to visit Vernon Watkins; the Swansea gang were still together."[99]

As for Vernon, in another poem he wrote in 1936, called 'Art Poétique'[100], he reflects again on the polarity between his own kind of *musical* poetry and Dylan Thomas's *sculptured* poetry – between, that is, *breath* and *clay*. Dylan Thomas, who so strongly favoured his own side of the polarity, had been harshly critical, when they first met, of the failings in Vernon's earlier poetry. As 1936 ended, with his new poetry being born, Vernon could say, as if responding directly to Dylan:

> I foster the unformed, lover of breath not clay.
> Slay in me what I have made; in what I am making you cannot slay.

His new-found confidence also made him write angrily to Faber's about their failure to answer him regarding the publication of his Masque 'The Influences'. He had never heard back from T.S. Eliot, whose literary advice he had been seeking on the Masque, but Watkins was still very much hoping that Faber's would agree to publish it[101] and by December was furious that such an eminent firm as Faber's had not even had the courtesy to reply to him: "I am working in an office where letters have to be answered by return and it seems odd to me that replies should take weeks even months." Faber's wrote back in sincere apology that they were unable to find his manuscript. On December 28th Vernon Watkins was honest enough to admit: "You have found the courage to tell me that you cannot find my Masque, but how can I find enough to tell you that it is here all the time?" He did in fact know perfectly well where the Masque was, but had naively imagined them being so excited by it that they would have agreed to publish it without even needing to refer to the manuscript.[102] Wondering, presumably, what on earth they must have thought of him, he jokingly corrected them: "My address is 'Heatherslade', not 'Heathenslade'. I hope this was a typing blemish."

CHAPTER EIGHT

'Wales' and Ireland (1937–1938)

"my reticence was broken"

Vernon's wings had at last reached maturity and in 1937 he became more and more able to use them. Even at their first meeting Dylan Thomas had tried to persuade Watkins to publish his poetry and he had, as we have seen, been attempting to have his Masque published. In early 1937 a young writer, Keidrych Rhys, conceived the idea of a new magazine for new literature written in English whose authors came from Wales. Dylan Thomas was central to Rhys's idea from beginning. Thomas wrote to Rhys in February 1937: "You say … that you're looking to me for a lead" and was happy to give all the help he could, saying: "I know most of the Welsh artists, in & out of Wales"[1].

The magazine was to be called 'Wales', and Thomas took on to gather contributions for the opening issue. He immediately approached Vernon, who after some hesitation gave Dylan 'Griefs of the Sea' and 'Old Triton Time' for publication.

Watkins was happy to discover, he said later, that publication "did not affect composition at all." There would also, however, be a liberation for him in finally speaking to an audience: "the damage was done. A contact was made, and my reticence was broken."[2] His first appearance in print, therefore, as the new poet he had become, *was* an important moment for him and 1937 found him, for the most part, in buoyant and expectant mood.

Self-portrait as Wilfred Owen

At the beginning of June, the month the first issue of *Wales* would appear, Watkins gave a paper on Wilfred Owen, probably in Cardiff.[3] He described how it had come about: "*I was asked to write a paper for*

Princeton University on Auden, Spender and Day Lewis. I replied that I did not write about living poets, but asked whether anyone had written a paper on Wilfred Owen. The reply was that no one in Princeton had heard of Owen. This astonished me ... "[4]

Watkins, in other words, had made a clear and deliberate choice *not* to speak about the contemporary literary scene, which he saw little value in, and of which his non-friend Christopher Isherwood was a part, and to speak instead about the kind of poet that *did* matter to him. Furthermore, Watkins's paper about Wilfred Owen was in many ways a *self-portrait*, referring to aspects of Wilfred Owen which were equally true of himself. Owen, therefore: was partly Welsh; he started writing poetry very young – "when he was ten or eleven"; "by the time he was twenty he had written an immense amount of verse, mainly of a derivative kind"; "Yeats, more than any other, had taught him an exquisite sensitiveness to words"; and: *"Owen made a bonfire of nearly all his early work."*[5] And unlike the fashionable contemporaries Vernon had refused to write about, who along with Isherwood were currently enjoying the limelight, Owen had no interest whatsoever in literary 'reputation' or 'celebrity': "Because he was less concerned with finding himself a place in English literature than with speaking to the individual conscience, he escapes the limelight of criticism. He himself wanted none. '*And I want no limelight*', he remarks in a letter to his mother in May 1918, '*and celebrity is the last infirmity I desire.*'"[6]

Addressing his Welsh audience in 1937 Vernon was even prepared to answer back his belovéd Yeats. Watkins refers to how Yeats, as editor of the *Oxford Book of English Verse – 1892-1935*, had "ignored Owen's poetry completely", and how Yeats had justified this by stating:

'Passive suffering is not a theme for poetry.'

Watkins memorably put the record straight:

"Yeats, you see, has dismissed Owen's poetry in a single sentence. Owen, had he read that sentence, might have said under his breath:

'Passive poetry is not a theme for suffering',

but Owen always lacked Yeats's faith in epigrams. He would soon have discovered that poetry is a theme for everything, and that everything is a theme for poetry."

Vernon's friendship with his polar opposite, Dylan Thomas, then enabled him to speak delightedly of the need to reconcile all contraries:

"Indeed every dogmatic statement about poetry is true and false at the same time ... Poetry is the finest essence of all knowledge, poetry is a celebration of ignorance, poetry is memorable speech, poetry is the desire to drive out memory, poetry is a rarification of emotions, poetry is a sexual perversion ... poetry is exploration. And, as a friend of mine (whom you saw not long ago) told me the other day: 'Poetry is a kind of plumbing.'"[7]

"Master, master ... "

In the second week of June, with his poetry on the brink of being published and having just given something of his own poetic manifesto via Wilfred Owen, he continued the seeming *announcement* of his own arrival by heading off to Ireland on his holidays. It soon became clear what had drawn him there – the wish to bow down in homage at the feet of his poetic master, Yeats, in whose footsteps he was following:

"what shall I do when I see him? I have been practising salaams on my bedroom carpet, kissing the foot of the bed with the words 'Master, master ... ' I can't run in with my flageolet for I forgot to bring it with me. Perhaps, at Coolaney, I can find a reed."[8]

Despite his self-mockery the image is startling, revealing Vernon almost back in the rapt state of his seventeen year-old self, who had immersed himself in the Middle Eastern world of Flecker's *Hassan*. His arrival in Ireland and the prospect of seeing Yeats did in fact bring on a momentary relapse into his former impassioned state, for which he immediately suffered: "I was desolate and sick with an old passion – I was really sick, almost at once; so went to bed and slept the clock round." The next day, "the sickness has departed, Dieu merci" and his usual holiday vigour had returned: "I'm going to bike to Killarney today, though it's very far – about 80 miles. I may take the bus part of the way."

He managed to find the Yeats's telephone number and spoke to

George Yeats, who informed him William Butler was not there. A year later, when Watkins *did* finally meet Yeats, George told him how irritated she had been by his self-deprecating manner: "You said very firmly 'The name is Watkins. I know you don't know it.' And I did know it. I felt like kicking you in the pants."

Watkins also found his way to Yeats's Tower at Thoor Ballylee and wrote a poem about it: 'Yeats' Tower'. It was a fitting end to his pilgrimage, "The Tower" having been the first book of Yeats' poetry Watkins had bought.

'Wales'

Almost as soon as he was back from Ireland, '*Wales*' appeared, boldly announcing the "renaissance"[9] of English literature currently being launched by Welsh writers:

> "British culture is a fact, but the English contribution to it is very small.
>
> There is actually no such thing as 'English' culture; a few individuals may be highly cultured, but the people as a whole are crass.
>
> The Kelt's heritage is as clear as sunlight, yet the burden of English literature has also fallen upon him. The greatest of present-day poets are Kelts.
>
> We publish this journal in English so that it may spread far beyond the frontiers of Wales, and because we realise the beauty of the English language better than the English themselves, who have so shamefully misused it.
>
> We are beyond the bigotry of unintelligent fascist nationalism.
> Though we write in English, we are rooted in Wales."[10]

Dylan Thomas, the young champion of all this, wrote to congratulate Rhys: "I've had the first number of 'Wales' … what a good number it is … Didn't Watkins's longer poem look well?"[11] He was referring, of course, to 'Griefs of the Sea'. When Watkins received his copy, however, he was horrified. Dylan had *changed* the poem, altering two lines and missing out two lines altogether. For all his love of the anarchic Dylan:

Griefs of the Sea

It is fitting to mourn dead sailors,
To crown the sea with a blind wreath of foam
Though the deaf wave hear nothing.

It is fitting to fling off clothing
To enter the sea with plunge of white seawreaths
Broken by the limbs that love the waters, fear the stars,
Though the blind wave grope under eyes that see, limbs that wonder,
Though the blind wave grope forward to the sand
With a greedy, silvered hand.

It is a horrible sound, the low wind's whistle
Across the seaweeds on the beach at night.
From stone to stone through hissing caves it passes
Up the curved cliff, and shakes the prickly thistle
And spreads its hatred through the grasses.

In spite of that wicked sound
It is fitting on the curved cliff to remember the drowned,
To imagine them clearly for whom the sea no longer cares,
To deny the language of the thistle, to meet their foot-firm tread
Across the dark-sown tares,
Who were skilful and erect, magnificent types of godhead,
To resist the dogging wind, to accuse the sea-god;
Yet in that gesture of anger we must admit
We were quarrelling with a phantom unawares.

For the sea turns whose every drop is counted
And the sand turns whose every grain a holy hourglass holds
And the weeds turn beneath the sea, the sifted life slips free,
And the wave turns surrendering from its folds
All things that are not sea, and thrown off is the spirit
By the sea, the riderless horse which they once mounted.
                                             VERNON WATKINS.

Vernon Watkins's poem 'Griefs of the Sea', in 'Wales 1', altered by Dylan Thomas and changed back again by hand by Watkins.

"to alter a poem without the other's consent was unthinkable." The usually affable Vernon exploded in anger: "This is just to wish you an extra sweat in your worst nightmare for altering 'Griefs of the Sea'." He then went back to Morgan and Higgs, where he had first found *18 Poems*, and secretly corrected Dylan's changes to the poem in every copy of 'Wales': "The task of altering the pile of copies of *Wales* in the bookshop was laborious and illicit, but I did it in the next few days."[12] Some time later a repentant Dylan replied:

"Dear Vernon,
If, in some weeks' time, you see a dog-like shape with a torn tail and a spaniel eye, its tail between its legs, come cringing and snuffling up Heatherslade gravel, it will be me ... It will deserve your anger. But, really, the Grief of the Sea was this: I was fooling about with a copy of the poem, playing the pleasant, time-wasting game of altering, unasked-for, somebody else's work; and then, when I met Keidrych with the manuscripts I had collected, blindly and carelessly I must have included among them the for-my-own-benefit, not-to-be-shown copy instead of the original. I hope you forgive me: that's the truth."[13]

Dylan immediately went on to tell Vernon the "big and simple" news of his marriage to Caitlin Macnamara, the daughter of the Irish painter Augustus John: "I think you'll like her very much, she looks like the princess on the top of the Christmas tree, or like a stage Wendy; but for God's sake don't tell her that. Write as soon as you can, and bless me ... "Which Vernon did. "I wrote a letter which began with a curse, and in a few days I had the gentlest of replies with the news that he had just been married; so my blessing instantly followed."

Dylan looked forward to taking over, with Vernon, the editorship of 'Wales': "when Keidrych goes up to Cambridge next year I shall probably – *and with you as colleague, or whatever it is, if you'd be* – take it all over. And no more Nigel Heseltine when we do: he can crawl back into the woodwork, or lift up his stone again."

The inclusion of the work of Nigel Heseltine (who turned out not even to be Welsh but English) in 'Wales' had been Dylan's particular bête noire from the beginning. After lambasting Heseltine, Dylan had told Keidrych Rhys: "if, by Christ, things like Heseltine's (& there must be a lot of that sort of thing being excreted) are going to go in, it's about time Something Was Done."[14]

T.S. Eliot meanwhile had finally written back about Vernon's Masque, though not at all as Vernon might have hoped, but rather giving detailed reasons for "the failure of the Masque."[15] Eliot spoke of its "tendency to monotony" and of its too close similarity to Yeats, in both rhythm and vocabulary. The Masque, said Eliot, was: "an interesting experiment which should be useful to you, but … is not in itself satisfactory for publication." Watkins was not remotely to be put off. He replied to Eliot on July 3rd telling him: "although I have borrowed the dresses from Mr Yeats and even had my dancers trained in his measures, I cannot find in any one of his plays the particular allegory which is the subject of the Masque." Vernon went on: "And because this allegory seems to me as profound as anything in the whole of art (- it is, indeed, touched upon in your late single poems for which I have a very great admiration) I feel I cannot discard the Masque in the way you mention." Far from giving up on the Masque Vernon therefore intended to: "attempt a new version with your criticism to guide me."

"dazzling days"
Vernon remained in heightened spirits throughout the summer. In July he finished his poem 'The Sunbather', which might well be the most unusual poem about sunbathing ever written. Strange to extremity, almost to the point of humour, it beautifully reveals the profundity of Vernon's kind of "indolence". Lying "inert … on the saltgold sand", the dead appear and speak out loud to him. In response to "their frightened song" he gives them: "The beat that consoles them most, his blood."[16]

In August Vernon told his friend Francis Dufau-Labeyrie of his summer joys: "In a few days more I shall return to the sea. I have been bathing every day, in the morning naked and in the evening suitably clothed; and we have had dazzling days. Monday was a day of supernatural brilliance. But the sea was always running back. I shall catch it as soon as I can and bring it home in my hand, and send it in an envelope to you."[17]

Vernon Watkins at Hunt's Bay, July 1937.

The bank seems to have been merely a hindrance that he took, unbothered, in his stride: "I race at full speed after lunch knocking over men and women indiscriminately until I arrive late at the office; murmuring Yeats under the terrible accusing clocks."[18]

At the end of August, Vernon was still in unstoppable mood: "I swam out a great way yesterday & brought in a huge plank nearly 20 foot long, from a ship." Though the giddying heights of the summer also led to a fall on his bicycle at full-speed, dressed only in swimming trunks: "I am now clothed in an almost entirely new skin." As for the old one: "The flaying is slow."

He was also seeing much of Dylan and Caitlin. Echoing Dylan's "big and simple" words about his marriage, Vernon told Francis:

"Not a great deal of news. Yes, of course, there's a lot of news: one big item. Dylan came home with his wife Caitlin ('Caitlin ni Houlihan') last week and the first day he was home he came over here to supper. She is a very beautiful and very nice girl, with wonderful gold hair like the incarnation of light, and still blue eyes like flowers. When she smokes a cigarette she looks very like Dylan ... "

According to Gwen Watkins: "Caitlin simply became part of the romantic aura in which Dylan lived in Vernon's mind ... She had entered the charmed circle in which Dylan lived, and was thereafter to be immune from criticism, as he was."[19] "*Caitlin ni Houlihan*" certainly suggests this, making Caitlin part of the mythology of this exuberant Irish-Welsh Summer. The genius that had held sway in Ireland was moving to Wales! The photographs Vernon took of Dylan and Caitlin playing croquet that summer at Heatherslade have become so famous that their current copyright costs make it impossible to include theme here.[20] They all walked together through Bishopston Valley wood[21] and Vernon's words to Francis make tangible the mood of those days: "What a miraculous world it is, and how everything is transfigured by a touch! Touch a pine and the effect is quite extraordinary – the whole nature of the tree is changed. It leaps out of a photographic world into a breathing one. Then the scent of sweet-briar – how utterly undefinable. We should touch, smell things always … "[22]

Critical help to Dylan
"What should he say?"

Poetically, both individually and in the help they gave each other, Dylan's and Vernon's work grew ever stronger. Their "affinity" and their trust in each other as poets and as friends were unquestionably of great support to Dylan in the particular assault he was launching on the poetic bastions of the day.

At the end of 1936, Dylan had refused to review W.H. Auden, not feeling capable of doing so: "I'm not close enough to him, he's not sufficiently my cup of tea, for me to enjoy his new poems very much or to talk about them constructively (with a few exceptions)"[23]. In 1937 W.H. Auden celebrated his 30th birthday and the poetry magazine 'New Verse' ran a double number celebrating him as the pre-eminent poet of the time – ("We salute in Auden … the first English poet for many years who is a poet all the way round"[24]) and asked Dylan Thomas to join the chorus of praise. Dylan walked into the Kardomah one morning, where Vernon was sitting with Fred Janes and John Prichard, and "said that the Editor of 'New Verse' had asked him for a tribute to Auden … *What should he say?*"[25] Vernon not only through his sure sense as a reader of poetry but also through his experience of the great gulf between himself and Auden's close friend and colleague, Christopher Isherwood, was happy and able to help. Vernon wrote some notes about Auden for Dylan, who was then able to adopt a confident stance regarding all of Auden's work to date. The 23 year-old Dylan, seven years younger than Auden, ended his contribution with the triumphant quip: "P.S. Congratulations on Auden's seventieth birthday."

Vernon offered such help to Dylan on other occasions too. In February 1938 Keidrych Rhys asked Dylan Thomas to review for 'Wales' David Jones's *In Parenthesis*. Dylan replied: "I'm afraid I can't ... my knowledge of the book isn't too sure." The following month Dylan's bête noire Nigel Heseltine wrote instead on Jones's book, stating: "*In Parenthesis* is more likely to make our national peculiarities international than the mouthings of D.T." Dylan angrily asked Rhys: "Do you agree not to publish Nigel Heseltine in future?"[26] and then asked Vernon to write a second, completely different review of *In Parenthesis*, which appeared in the following issue.[27]

Later in 1938 *The Harvard Advocate* prepared a special issue devoted to T.S. Eliot and also asked Dylan Thomas for a contribution. Dylan wrote "a heap of notes, none of which seems really satisfactory" and again turned to Vernon for help: "Do please tell me a few things, just as you helped me with that little Auden appreciation. Just a few comments or notes."[28] It is not known what came of this, as the issue when it appeared[29] contained no contribution by Dylan, but it is easy to see why Dylan had hoped to co-run *Wales* with Vernon. Dylan also knew that for all the critical help of this kind Vernon could offer, Vernon would only ever write as a poet. As Vernon had written: "I am not a critic, and I am not a biographer ... A poet will never learn anything from critics except the negative art of how *not* to write."[30]

Criticism of Vernon's poetry

As for their help with each other's poetry, Vernon described that after the publication of his second book: "Dylan sent me his poems more or less as he finished them. I typed them for him, and we discussed them in letters if we could not see each other. I typed all the poems for his next book, *The Map of Love* (1939) ... The excitement I felt when I opened these poems was always great, and they usually came one at a time."[31]

Vernon also sent Dylan many of the poems he had been writing, with Dylan writing on October 25th, 1937: "Thank you for the poems. I like them all. My respect for them is always increased when I read them again, and in typescript. 'Mana' is magnificent."

Vernon had told Francis Dufau-Labeyrie two weeks earlier that he had just finished 'Mana', proudly proclaiming: "You must like every word of it now. It is really superb. It excites me as much as Owen's greatest poems and that is a great excitement. I oughtn't to say this, but of course I can – I can say anything to you … . in every language of boasting, in every sort of ecstatic term, until the immoderate gust has passed through me."[32] Three days later, "the immoderate gust" having passed, he told Francis: "I have found out that 'Mana' is not quite right. It ought to be one of the greatest poems in the world, but it just isn't."[33] It was Dylan, inevitably, who had shaken any complacency Vernon may have had regarding the poem. Dylan disliked the opening line, but subjected one line particularly to his mercilessly humorous critique – *'Laid in the long grey shadow of our weeping thought'*: "This, to me, has far too many weak words. They … elongate a thin nothing: a long, grey, weeping sausage."[34]

Altogether, Vernon's exposure of his poetry to the eyes of others was not without its challenges, as he had already seen with 'Griefs of the Sea'. When the third issue of 'Wales' misprinted the title of his poem 'Yeats' Tower' he fulminated: "What bloody fools they are to print my poem as *Yeat's Tower*! Did they really? I think 20 years penal servitude would be a lenient punishment for such a mistake."[35] Worse, however, the poem itself received considerable criticism, making Vernon envisage an opposing support movement for the poem called the "Anti-Yeats's-Tower-Firing-Squad."[36] Even Francis found the poem's refrain weak ("O under grass, O under grass, the secret"), to which Vernon replied: "I cannot unfortunately defend it … But I love it & can't alter it both of which things are inexplicable."[37] One comment the poem led to had a significant influence on Vernon. Keidrych Rhys urged him: "*Try and write a poem that could only be written in 1937 and only by you.*"[38]

'WALES' AND IRELAND (1937-1938) 157

Vernon accepted the challenge and wrote in response a highly autobiographical poem, which certainly no one else could have written. Identifying himself as a young Welsh coal-miner, and as the Biblical Joseph, Watkins depicted in miniature his whole life-story. The poem was called 'The Collier'. It begins with the earthquake at his birth and then moves to his equivalent of being "cast ... down a pit", his taking up work in the bank: "You will get your chain of gold, my lad,/ But not for a likely time." The pit collapses on the collier, just as the bank became an entombment for Watkins. For the collier, though, as for Watkins, this death-experience transforms into an experience of resurrection:

> And white on my limbs is the linen sheet
> And gold on my neck the sun.

It became the poem which would open Watkins's first book.

Dylan greatly liked 'The Collier', he often spoke it at readings, and immediately offered to have it published for Vernon in 'Life and Letters'. He was far harsher about two other poems Vernon sent him at the same time, writing of one of them, 'The Windows': "The poem ... is a serious failure ... I mean it is a serious poem which fails. But don't mind my rudeness, I'll tell you my real and detailed objections to the poem later. They might amuse you anyway."[39] When Dylan told Vernon that he "inevitably" preferred such ballads as "The Collier" to "the long and complicated poems" Vernon must have answered that he had to follow his inspiration wherever it took him. Dylan replied: "You are right to write poems of all kinds; I only write poems of allsorts, and like the Liquorice sweets, they all taste the same."[40]

Poetic Workshop

During 1938 and 1939 the co-working between Vernon Watkins and Dylan Thomas was at its busiest. Dylan was writing the poems he would include in his next book *The Map of Love* (1939) and not only sent each one to Vernon, asking for his comments and suggestions, but Vernon typed them all for Dylan as well.

Reading Dylan Thomas's letters to Vernon Watkins during these years we gain the sense of being in the midst of Dylan's hectic, often chaotic poetic workshop, with poems needing to be worked through and corrected, others needing to be typed and sent off to magazines, poetry readings needing to be prepared, clothes sometimes needing to be borrowed and with the whole venture, of course, needing to survive financially.

The demands on Vernon were frequent and intense:

"I wonder if you would type a couple of copies of the poem for me – and let me have them as quickly as you can." (13th November, 1937.)

"I have another favour to ask … The time … is alarmingly short … It's blackmail to say I'm relying on you, but I crookedly am. I respect your judgement, & your typing. Love & admiration, as always. DYLAN." (20th Nov. 37)

"Here are 4 poems … Could you type these out for me? … Don't be too harsh about these poems until they're typed; I always think typescript lends some sort of certainty: at least, if the things are bad then, they appear to be bad with conviction." (21st March, 1938)

With regard to staying afloat financially, Vernon was again the most obvious person for Dylan to turn to:

"God, I almost forgot. Are you rich, temporarily? Would you like to lend me some money, a pound, or at the very most, two pounds … I can get a few pounds elsewhere – though not, Mr. Watkins, with such lack of embarrassment as I can ask you for it." (July 1937)

Four years later he would be saying: "See if you can squeeze another drop from your borrowed-to-death body. I'm not going to tell you how grateful I am and have always been; … I hope I am spoiling nothing. It is just that I am useless, & have nowhere to turn." (May 1941)

Vernon, as far as is known, never failed to help Dylan, when asked. He said of his small gifts of money that they "matter(ed) so much to him and not at all to me."[41] Vernon *was*, however, making an exception for Dylan. When his close friend Francis asked for similar help, Vernon was prepared to lend but not *give* him money, explaining: "the money I earn from the bank always appears to me to be a sort of trust, possibly for my sisters or my mother, & although I pay my mother and father some money every month (for my keep) *I don't feel really free to give away the rest except casually and occasionally.*"[42] And when Francis asked Vernon to type some poems out for him, he replied that he was: "momentarily tired of Secretary-work – If I were a quick typist it would be easy."[43]

It is as though Dylan and he were involved in a joint poetic project, consisting of *both* of their lives and works. The wilder, Dionysian path that Dylan was on, if not ultimately more difficult, was the more dangerous of the two, and Vernon would always do all he could to help Dylan negotiate it.

Portrait of a Friend

Vernon's inner reliability led Dylan sometimes jokingly to exaggerate the Dionysian side of his nature – and sometimes to be wholly honest about the toll life was having on him. Sometimes he would do both at the same time.

On 7th February 1938 Dylan wrote to Vernon: "the self-drama continues: bluff after bluff until I see myself as one … Send me poems, & I'll send you some. Mine, not through humility or knowledge of less competence – will be more unsatisfactory. At the moment I am, in action, a person of words, & not as I should be: a person of words in action."

The writing of poetry was seemingly being replaced in Dylan by the life he was living, causing him to send Vernon a photograph of himself, an image of the "tough" pose he was currently presenting to the world: "Why I want you to think of me, – photographically, when I'm not about – as a tough, I don't know. Anyway, it's very big; you can write a poem on the back, draw whiskers on it, or advertise Kensitas in the front window."

Through Vernon, who remained solely devoted to poetry in a way he could no longer be, Dylan was able to "touch base" with another part of himself and he signed off particularly warmly: "My love to you & write soon. I hope to see you before the summer … I miss you. DYLAN."[44]

The letter and above all the photograph touched Vernon very deeply. The photograph, which arrived "cracked" in the envelope through being folded, made Vernon muse deeply on all that Dylan meant to him. It led to Vernon's poem 'Portrait of a Friend'. Soon after meeting Dylan,

Vernon had written of how the lofty may learn from the basest and most "down to earth": "*Great men on thrones envy the bastard's hut/ Where cradled may swing the true, may grow the strong.*"[45] Exactly this is needed to understand the whole riddle of Dylan's existence. 'Portrait of a Friend' ends:

> *The superhuman, crowned*
> *Saints must enter this drowned*
> *Tide-race of the mind*
> *To guess or understand*
> *The face of this cracked prophet*
> *Which from its patient pall*
> *I slowly take,*
> *Drop the envelope,*
> *Compel his disturbing shape,*
> *And write these words on a wall*
> *Maybe for a third man's sake.*

The "third man" is the one who can unite the two worlds of Dylan and Vernon. If Vernon had, however, been thinking of anyone in particular, it might well have been Keidrych Rhys, for the poem was an even better answer than 'The Collier' to the demand: "Try and write a poem that could only be written in 1937 and only by you."[46] Dylan, the "cracked prophet", replied when he received it: "Thank you a lot … for the poem and the money. I liked both immensely. The poem, I think, is altogether successful."[47]

"Yeats – Ireland"
"I'd like you to take over the baton"

If Dylan Thomas may be seen as the heir of Gerard Manley Hopkins, Vernon Watkins may be seen as that of William Butler Yeats. This has, to date, been seldom recognized, except by Kathleen Raine, who after saying that she had never "hoped or attempted to emulate (Yeats's) poetic skills" stated: "*the only English poet for whom that could be claimed is Vernon Watkins.*"[48] The editor of the Everyman edition of Yeats's

Poems even stated that Yeats *had* no immediate successors: "in many ways Yeats's poetry has seemed to be an end. Few poets followed his example, either in theme or style. The great poets of the next generation regarded him suspiciously ... Eliot and Auden were equally perplexed in their relation to Yeats's work ... Auden ... even asserts that noone could remember a line of Yeats's poems."[49] None of this is at all true of Vernon Watkins, who told Yeats, when he finally met him, that: "after six or seven years I could remember every single word of a poem of his without reading it again."[50]

Vernon Watkins knocked at Yeats's door three times before the latter answered. His first trip to Ireland had been in June 1937, giving rise to his poem 'Yeats' Tower'. He had sent this poem to Yeats, with the issue of 'Wales' in which it was published, together with a photograph he had taken of Thoor Ballylee. He told Francis of this in February 1938, adding: "But I only addressed it to Yeats – Dublin – or else Yeats – Ireland. Could it have got there? I've had no reply."[51] A month later Vernon finally heard back from Yeats from the South of France, thanking him for everything he had sent. Yeats's words on his poem more than made up for all the previous criticism it had received:

> "I find your poem 'Yeats' Tower' rich, strange and moving, and the repetition of that line at the end of every stanza is not only right but essential to the whole. It is a strange, beautiful line. I am not quite certain that I always get your meaning, but I always find beauty."[52]

Watkins had also asked if he could visit Yeats, to which Yeats replied that he would be back in Dublin at the end of April: "If you should happen to be in Ireland at any date after that I shall be delighted to see you."

Vernon told Francis of "my Yeats' letter which I wear next to my heart"[53] and more than ever looked forward to returning to Ireland in May, during his next week's holiday. He wanted Francis to accompany him,[54] but this was impossible and so Vernon went back to Ireland on his own. As soon as he was there he telephoned Yeats for the second time and again spoke to Mrs. Yeats, who again told him that Yeats wasn't available:

"George (it must have been George) said he 'would be sure to be in Dublin in June'. I had a nice talk with her on the phone – a short one."[55]

On Vernon's last night in Dublin he went to a play – *The New Gossoon* – at the Abbey Theatre. Though he described this as "the climax" of his trip, it was scant compensation for what his imagination had been hoping for:

"But (O my sorrow) this week they are doing the 'Playboy of the Western World' and to-night (I think) Yeats returns to Dublin … If I had been in Dublin this week I would have asked him to go with me to it, which would have been cheek, but I think we should have gone – We would have keened together."[56]

Watkins's attention shifted, as it did so often throughout his life, between W.B. Yeats and Dylan Thomas and on his way back from Ireland he cycled across Wales to stay with Dylan, telling Francis: "I've just come back from my holiday which was wonderful … I biked about 400 miles altogether – about 150 in Ireland and about 250 in Wales … balancing on castle turrets, being attacked by swarms of flies (I had a hornet in my shirt for four miles) … the last of Wales was Laugharne … I stayed there with Dylan and Caitlin."[57]

Watkins's main two-week holiday was in June, as he had already mentioned to George Yeats, asking her whether Yeats would then be in Dublin. Hearing that he would be, Vernon on his return immediately started preparing for his third visit to Yeats. He would spend his first week with his sister Dorothy in France and the second in Ireland. He again asked Francis to accompany him: "Can you come to Ireland for the second week of my fortnight, meeting me in Dublin or somewhere, preferably with a bike or strong shoes? I'd like you to take over the baton from Dot".[58] A few days later he was insisting: "Ireland on the 20th? … I'll write to Yeats again & ask if we can see him. What do you think? … I think we must go and see Yeats together."[59]

"Ami de Dax"

Before addressing the meeting which finally took place between Vernon Watkins and W.B. Yeats, we shall take a brief look at Watkins's close friend and travelling companion, Francis Dufau-Labeyrie.

While a student of English literature at the Sorbonne, aged 20, he had

Francis Dufau-Labeyrie in Ireland
- (June 1938)
(photograph by Vernon Watkins)

got a job giving French conversation classes at the Swansea Grammar School. Dylan Thomas's father, D.J. Thomas, asked Dufau-Labeyrie to write an article for the school magazine and on reading it D.J. Thomas said: "I like what you write ... you ought to meet my son some day. He wants to become the poet-laureate, or something like that." Soon afterwards, in early 1937, Francis was invited to the Kardomah Café, where he met Dylan, Vernon, Fred Janes, Tom Warner and Charles Fisher. After this, though he went out on a few drunken evenings with Dylan, "a closer relationship developed between Vernon and me, perhaps because of his interest in the literature of the continent, particularly in German and French poetry."[60]

Their friendship continued to grow and Francis became a wonderful companion for Vernon. "Why is it that I enjoy my week-ends with you such a lot? There's something incalculable about them", wrote Vernon and they enjoyed a wide-ranging, humorous correspondence together. Francis both wrote and translated poetry, but his errors in English inspired in Vernon a child-like joy in punning and word-play. For example, when Francis wrote 'oisters' Vernon corrected him: "oysters are spelt with a wye/wigh/wie", then penned a limerick to underline the lesson:

> "An old man who lived upon oysters
> Ran up and down stairs in the cloysters
> He scattered their shells
> Like a thousand farewells
> On the Gentiles the Jews and the Joysters."[61]

Vernon being far the more confident of the two, communicatively,[62] there was a strange reversal of the roles he and Dylan usually played in their friendship. Thus, in his friendship with Francis, it was Vernon who played Dylan's part while Francis took on Vernon's.

The clearest example of this was when Vernon made corrections to the translation of a poem that Francis submitted to 'Wales'. Remembering what Dylan had done to 'Griefs of the Sea', Vernon wrote: "In case you wish me a double extra-sweat when you see the translation in print, I'd better tell you what alterations I've made." Soon afterwards, though, Vernon wrote to tell Francis of "a most unlucky thing". He had sent Keidrych the wrong copy of the poem by mistake, and "unfortunately it has already gone to press, Dylan says. I'm really awfully sorry about it". He finally admitted: "It's all untrue. As far as I know … I did send Keidrych the right copy. [Or didn't I?]"[63]

Much more seriously, in March 1938, Francis really was sorely wounded by Vernon's words and deeds, just as Vernon occasionally was by Dylan's. Shortly after Francis's translation was rejected by *Wales*,[64] Vernon wrote Francis a letter which, for Francis, shattered their friendship.[65] When Vernon understood what had happened he immediately wrote: "I'm sorry for the letter I sent you – please tear it up. I had to 'get it off my chest', as people say – I was like Etna pinned down by the weight of all kinds of unrealities. But you have terribly misinterpreted it." Vernon also wrote a poem about the dangers of letters and: "your dark, cheated eyes/ Reading my last which wounds you bitterly".[66] He goes on: "Forgive me, first. My temper is curious,/ Rash in love, gentle in afterthought,/ And strongest when the ribs of hate are burst./ *None came on certain love but by its loss.*"[67] Once they had emerged from this crisis in their friendship Vernon then wrote: "Nothing could alter my affection for you – Last weekend I thought its duration was threatened; now I know it is not."[68]

It was therefore with this re-won friend at his side, the Frenchman Dufau-Labeyrie, with whom Vernon could happily converse not only on English poetry but on European poetry as well, that Vernon set off for the third time to visit Yeats.

CHAPTER NINE

A Death and a Birth (1938–1939)

*Yeats In Dublin – Impending War –
A Horse's Head – A Death And A Birth*

Watkins did not leave his third attempt to visit Yeats to chance. The arrangement was made to meet Yeats at his Dublin home, Riversdale, at 4 p.m. on June 23rd.[1]

Watkins spent the first week of his Summer holiday with Dorothy in the fishing villages of Finistere in the west of Brittany, cycling and swimming, as well as sardine-fishing seven miles from shore at 4 o'clock in the morning, leading to his poem 'Sardine Fishers at Daybreak'.[2] Then, as planned, Vernon returned to London, from where he travelled straight to Dublin via Swansea and Fishguard. Francis Dufau-Labeyrie boarded the train in Swansea, where they failed to notice each other and so each presumed the other had missed the train. They finally bumped into each other in the train corridor and Vernon's description gives a clear picture of this bumbling pair on their journey to see Yeats.

"We got to Fishguard, *where we boarded the wrong boat*; ... finally we reached Dublin in a deluge. Neither of us had a coat of any kind. *After taking a tram in the wrong direction,* we found the Ivanhoe Hotel ... Then we waited for the rain to stop. It didn't, and after lunch we went to a Sports shop and bought a huge golf-umbrella to cover us both, and under this we walked all over Dublin."

They went to the Cuala Press where Elizabeth Yeats, the poet's sister, showed them around. Vernon would remain in contact with Elizabeth Yeats, buying from her many editions of Yeats's work, which when Vernon lost them 4 or 5 years later would be returned to him by Philip Larkin, initiating their friendship. After leaving the Cuala Press Vernon and Francis visited the Municipal Art Gallery in Dublin, which they found "extraordinarily interesting, full of portraits of people we knew largely through Yeats's or their own work" then "walked along the Liffey eating cherries."[3] The following day, Thursday 23rd, they took the bus to Rathfarnham, Dublin, then walked to "Riversdale".

June 23rd, 1938
Meeting with W.B. Yeats

George Yeats met them at the door, Vernon gave her some flowers – blue scabious and pink carnations[4] – and she brought them in to meet her husband, the poet. When Vernon finally stood in front of him, he didn't quite call out "Master, master … ", but performed some kind of polite equivalent: "Francis says that when I shook hands with him I raised one leg high like a ballet-dancer, and he and Mrs Yeats winked at each other."

George Yeats asked the two young men to "park ourselves on the chairs" opposite Yeats, and Vernon describes his first impression of the "great man" in front of him, the goal of his long poetic pilgrimage:

"He was still and very noble. Very like a portrait, his grey hair thrown back, his very sensitive mouth just parted, his large hands resting on the arms of the chair, and his eyes looking kindly at us, quietly, through strong glasses, one of which was shaded."

Yeats then "began talking at once, wonderfully, and about the things we wanted to talk about … we talked about 'Wales'.[5] He was interested to know who the group of writers were. I mentioned Dylan Thomas first … "

Watkins would describe this visit twice, first in the prose notes he wrote immediately after leaving Yeats and secondly in his long poem *Yeats in Dublin*, which gave an exact poetic record of their meeting and conversation. We shall use both in describing this event. Thus Yeats' questions about the magazine 'Wales' and Vernon's mention of Dylan Thomas reappear in the poem:

> 'Tell me about that young group
> Of Welsh writers,' he said,
> 'Whose poems in that paper you sent me
> The other day I read.'
> An image stands on Carmarthen sands
> With the black birds overhead.

Yeats was already aware of Dylan Thomas, telling Watkins he had "received a book of his poems from Edith Sitwell and had corresponded with her about them."

Yeats then launched into his own critique not only of Dylan Thomas but also of other young poets, stating that they "toiled too much, forgetting that the greatest poetry is always natural and always simple." They "dissected" too much, till nothing was left but "grains of intellect." They failed to understand, said Yeats, that the source of true poetry can never be reached by mere intellect. As Watkins noted Yeats's words: "Poetry is always luck – magical. Is made not by the intellect but *through the intellect to something much deeper*."[6]

This was the first of the things Yeats said in this interview which always remained central to Watkins's own creativity. He would write: "In art the real statements of power are those in which the whole intellect is involved, first in a suspension of power, and then in the renewal of power through grace."[7] A late poem states more simply: "No intellect complete/ Lacking the hand of grace".[8]

Vernon had waited ten years to meet Yeats, since first discovering *The Tower* in 1928. As the poem describes their moment of meeting:

> *After the ten years' journey ...*
> *I look him in the eyes.*

For Vernon it was a meeting with his poetic "Master" and thus he drank in the lessons he could learn from him. There is no doubt that Yeats also addressed Watkins sometimes as though he was passing on a teaching: "You must always try to get near the greatest intensity which we call Eternal Man."

By this time, however, Vernon was far from being merely a pupil and as Francis Dufau-Labeyrie described: "There was something intense in the rapport between Vernon and Yeats, some mysterious communication of the soul"[9]. As a result, the poem *Yeats in Dublin* that Vernon Watkins eventually wrote did not simply document everything Yeats had said, but was also a beautifully wrought poetic statement of what that "rapport" had consisted in. With regard to the teachings given by Yeats about poetry, as expressed in the poem, there is in fact little that the mature Vernon Watkins could not equally well have stated. The poem *Yeats in Dublin* can therefore be viewed, after Watkins's paper on Wilfred Owen, as his *second* poetic manifesto, albeit disguised as an exact record of their meeting.

This became clear as they moved from talking about Wales and Dylan Thomas[10] to criticizing the more politically-minded poetry emerging from England, such as that of W.H. Auden. It was Vernon Watkins who introduced the topic, attacking the whole emphasis of Auden's poetry: "I quote Auden and attack him for saying 'A poem must contain news' and 'a poet must be something of a reporter.'" Yeats agreed with Watkins, stating: "The reverse is true" and that: "that attitude to poetry is just materialism."

In *Yeats in Dublin* Watkins omits any mention of his own criticism of Auden and even tactfully omits Auden's name altogether, but instead has Yeats alone represent their viewpoint:

> 'My quarrel with those Londoners
> Is that they try
> To substitute psychology
> For the naked sky
> Of metaphysical movement,
> And drain the blood dry.
>
> All is materialism, all
> The catchwords they strew,
> Alien to the blood of man. – '
> One ranting slogan drew
> That "Poetry must have news in it":
> 'The reverse is true.'

Yeats clearly also took Watkins into his confidence as one "Kelt" to another – and spoke with him of how the intellectual character of English cultural life drained it of true strength and vigour. Yeats spoke of the barrenness of English culture compared with that of Ireland: "He compared the life of art in Ireland with the intelligentsia of London. The latter was barren intellect producing nothing."

> We have the folk in Ireland;
> The English make it up.
> How can a country's language thrive
> If an abstract shape
> Battening on the vigorous man
> Sucks the blood-drop?

Vernon Watkins, who remained in vigorous physical health throughout his life, strongly resonated with these words as well. They remind one of the comparison Yeats made between two portraits in Dublin's National Gallery. The first, Strozzi's portrait of a 'Venetian gentleman', shows what Yeats meant when he told Watkins: "*Learn what reason could not teach/From the marrow in the bone.*" The second, Sargent's painting of the American President Woodrow Wilson, exemplifies what Yeats meant by an "*abstract shape/Battening on the vigorous man*". Yeats writes: "Whatever thought broods in the dark eyes of that Venetian gentleman has drawn its life from his whole body … *his whole body thinks.* President Wilson lives only in the eyes …; the flesh about the mouth is dead, and the hands are dead, and *the clothes suggest no movement of his body*".[11]

They had some tea, after which Yeats withdrew saying: "he had been out of sorts lately – his heart was rather bad." Vernon suggested that he and Francis should leave but George Yeats urged them not to, telling them her husband "just needs to rest for a quarter of an hour, he likes to go upstairs, and then he comes back and is quite all right again." So after a short pause, during which Vernon and Francis talked with George, Yeats returned and they continued their conversation.

The only area of potential disagreement between Watkins and Yeats was when: "We talked of national movements." Yeats told Watkins: "Poetry must not be nationalist, but must be national."[12] Vernon struggled to understand the seeming limitation this puts on poetry:

> I questioned him: 'How can there be
> A national poetry?
> What can we make or what resist
> When all is like the sea?'

However much Vernon may have enjoyed the thought that a poetic torch was now being passed from Ireland to Wales,[13] he could not accept poetic genius being constrained within the bounds of nationhood and certainly not that it be linked with any kind of political activity. Watkins's thoughts turned again to the Celtic Christian bard Taliesin, whose poems are not "national myths" in the same way as are those of pre-Christian Ireland:

> 'Though leaders sway the crowd', I said,
> 'Power is underneath.
> The sword of Taliesin
> Would never fit a sheath.'

Yeats appeared to agree with Watkins, telling him that: "*The leaders and the poets/Are not in unison*" and giving the example of the differences between Hitler and the poet Stefan George. It was a bad example, as Stefan George's nationalist writings are in no way comparable to the Christ-centred universality of Taliesin that Watkins was seeking, but Watkins was unaware of this and happily took Yeats at his word. Watkins's approach to "national poetry" was different from Yeats's, as he would later make clear, but such was his devotion to Yeats that he appears hardly to have noticed this when they met.

Only when it came to poetry was Vernon confident enough to speak about the slight weaknesses in Yeats' early work compared with the later:

"I said how much I loved his late work. I said 'I can see nothing artificial in any of the late work – from 'The Tower' on; but in the early work I can see occasionally a little that's artificial, a little that's decoration.' Yes, he agreed. He said he was glad that I preferred the late work."

One of the very few topics of conversation that Watkins did *not* later include in *Yeats in Dublin* was the question of poetry and earning a living. Vernon Watkins directly asked what Yeats thought about the 'career choice' he had made: "*I asked Yeats whether he thought a man could write poetry all his life and yet work in an office.*" Yeats replied: "*I don't see why he shouldn't. Poetry cannot earn a living. That is a problem of the future. But volume means nothing; intensity is everything, and only life brings that.*" Watkins said *"that poetry required a contrast in living to its own intensity. I told Yeats I worked in a bank.*" Yeats hid whatever surprise he felt and only remarked that poets "*usually found the contrast in work that was somewhat connected with poetry …*"[14]

When it was time for Vernon and Francis to leave, Yeats said he was "sorry we had come so far for such a short time," and after shaking hands with them headed upstairs. George Yeats, as she had at tea-time, prevented the meeting ending prematurely and called Yeats back for a photograph:

"Just as he was going upstairs Mrs Yeats said 'I saw you had a camera and I'm sure you'ld like to photograph him.' I said that as he was tired it was better not to bother, but she took him by his arm and said 'It will be very easy' and walked with him outside." Yeats sat on the garden seat and Vernon took his photograph.

William Butler Yeats
(photograph by Vernon Watkins[15])

As Vernon looked at Yeats for the last time, he was suddenly almost overwhelmed by the moment. What would happen? What would pass between them? Did Yeats have any idea how deeply Vernon was connected to him and his work? Now was the moment when some kind of parting gesture, acknowledging their connection, should occur. Vernon leant towards Yeats, muttering some words about what Yeats meant to him and waited for Yeats to reach out and touch him, or do something to honour the mystery of their meeting and this moment. And Yeats made no response at all.

As Watkins later depicted this:

> *I lean down, crying: 'Touch me, lay hold on my Spring,*
> *Reach up, for I have loosened, tearing your skies,*
> *Fountains of light, ages of listening!'*
> *But the bound hands are folded, the fold its word denies.*

As he expressed it far more matter-of-factly in his notes: "I then thanked him for everything and said 'For ten years I have been greatly influenced by your work, more than by anyone else.' He made no comment."

"Yeats was behind us"

When Vernon and Francis left, after their two hour meeting, they made the "sudden decision" to hire bicycles and take the evening train to Galway. They raced to the station and saw their train from afar just about to leave: "Vernon frantically waved our rolled red umbrella to the amused conductor, who, from the rear van, waved back at us with a rolled red flag. He held the train for us. We threw our bicycles into that van, jumped aboard and off went the train to Galway."[16]

They arrived late at night "and most of the way I scribbled down recollections of what Yeats talked about, and handed the sheets to Francis to read as I finished them." The next morning they cycled north to Connemara, "against a gale in the wrong direction … on saddles that bruised us unmercifully".[17] The day after, in Francis's words: "We started back to Galway practically at dawn, amazed at our speed now that we were assisted by a wind blowing from the rear … I remember the vast openings of blue sky among slowly tumbling clouds, the sun over the marshlands, the flooded pools of waterlilies. A black hare crossed the road. "Yeats is behind us!" cried Vernon."

From Ireland Vernon and Francis cycled across Wales to Laugharne and stayed with Dylan and Caitlin. Fresh from the "oracle" of Yeats, Vernon perhaps expected Dylan to be as reverential as he was about everything the "Master" had uttered. If so, Vernon was quickly disillusioned, encountering Dylan's utter refusal to heed any given statements on how poetry should or shouldn't be.

"When I stayed with Dylan Thomas in Laugharne on my way back from seeing Yeats in Dublin in the Summer of 1938 I was struck by the difference between them. Both were men of undoubted genius, but whereas Yeats spoke like a musically controlled oracle, Dylan Thomas, with his abundant imagination and quick intelligence was prepared to challenge everything he said. Not that Dylan Thomas did not admire Yeats' poetry immensely, because he did. But he distrusted, at the age of twenty-three, pontifical statements, or statements that sounded pontifical. Yeats had told me: 'There must always be a quality of nonchalance in a poet's work.'[18] Dylan would not accept this. And Yeats had added: 'The young poets toil too much.' – 'He should come *here*', Dylan said."[19]

Dylan had every reason at that moment to challenge any statement that he was "toiling too much". Two months later he sent Vernon the poem beginning: "On no work of words now for three lean months in the bloody/Belly of the year".[20]

First three readers of 'Yeats in Dublin'

Vernon wrote to thank Yeats for their visit, but received no reply. Vernon told Francis on August 3rd: "I've not had a letter from (Yeats) – I must go and visit him again next year." In September, once Vernon had finished the first draft of *Yeats in Dublin*, he wrote to Yeats again, sending him a copy of the poem and asking permission to quote from their conversation.[21] A few weeks later, when Yeats still had not replied, Vernon began worrying that he disapproved of the poem: "with my usual romantic susceptibility I've made up my mind that he dislikes it. That is my usual reaction to a friend's silence. Yet I can never reconcile it to my conviction that a thing is good & the two strive together until an answer comes."[22] Finally on October 23rd, 4 months after their meeting, Yeats wrote to thank Watkins for the poem, saying: "I like to be thought of in that charming way, and certainly have no objection to your publishing the little scraps of conversation they contain."[23] Soon after, Vernon made a new version of the poem and immediately sent a copy to T.S. Eliot.[24] Eliot responded appreciatively[25], but added that he looked forward to seeing Watkins's poetry once it had "escaped from the influence of Yeats, as well as that of everyone else."[26]

Vernon replied with absolute certainty regarding the development of his own poetry, from early childhood until the present:

"If you mean to wait until I have 'escaped' from all influence you will have to wait a long time, because I work and develop very slowly, relying always on my original conception of verbal music which was in me when I was a very small child; it was latent and impotent then, but if I write a lucky line I always know instinctively and at once."[27]

Eliot assured him: "I enjoyed your Yeats poem so much that I shall be much interested to see your future work."[28]

Vernon Watkins, completely unknown as a poet except to readers of 'Wales', had chosen W.B. Yeats and T.S. Eliot as the first two readers of 'Yeats in Dublin' and would soon choose Dylan Thomas as the third.

After meeting in Laugharne on his return from Ireland he and Dylan had enjoyed a couple of carefree pre-war days together that Summer. Vernon had walked round the cliffs to see Dylan at Bishopston, "taking with me Lorca & a book of Welsh translations from Taliesin ... We read a lot of Lorca which is grand".[29] At the beginning of September Wyn Lewis's brother David had driven Vernon, Dorothy and Eric Falk to see Dylan in Laugharne. As Dorothy described: "Dylan was so impressed by the car that he insisted on driving it onto the vast stretch of Pendine Sands – where, to my horror, both Dylan and Vernon insisted on taking it in turns to drive ... they tore over the beach, until Eric and I implored them at least to stop and let us out." In Vernon's words: "I had no understanding of the controls, and Dylan's maximum speed was 10 miles an hour before the car came to rest in soft sand. Both potential drivers, we blamed the conditions; but, as far as I know, neither of us ever drove again."[30]

As for 'Yeats in Dublin' Dylan was tremendously praising of what Vernon had achieved: "Congratulations on the magnificent Yeats poem: so few faults in such noble danger; ... I think it's one of your most truly felt poems; that's not to say that other poems of yours are not true or felt, but only to say that the purity in it is never less than the poetry. What a poem for the old man after that historic interview."[31] Vernon must have been delighted to hear this from Dylan, but had no doubts in his own mind about the poem's worth. When the *London Mercury* turned it down it he told Francis: "It's immensely long – that may have been a reason. And perhaps too intimate a poem for a magazine. However, it is the best poem of its kind in the world."[32]

Dylan Thomas had also said he had a few "grumbles" about the poem, but Vernon, in this mood, was clearly not at all willing to hear them. Dylan was not to be put off and humorously persisted in throwing a little cold water over Vernon and showing him the comparative faults of the poem:

"Since you've apparently been taking lessons from John Pritchard in refusing to accept adverse criticism, I shall make my grumbles about your good Yeats poem illegible to invisibility. Here come the grumbles, hot, strong, and logical, but you can't see them." After an invisible gap, Dylan continued by telling Vernon that where *Yeats in Dublin* failed to be *effective* it was because it was *too true* to the exact words Yeats had used. "You can say to me that effectiveness is less than truth; I can only say that the truth must be made effectively true, and though every word of the truth be put down the result may well be a clot of *truths*."

Yeats in Dublin was eventually published in April 1939[33] – by which time Yeats had died and Europe was under threat of war – and Vernon's summer visit to Yeats and racing over Pendine sands with Dylan might have seemed like some idyll from a former time.

September/October 1938
The threat of European War

In March 1938 Hitler had taken over Austria, unopposed. In September, when Hitler demanded that Czechoslovakia yield Sudetenland to Germany, leading to the so-called Munich crisis, the threat of European war grew terrifyingly near, even in Britain. On September 15th the British Prime Minister Neville Chamberlain met with Hitler for three hours at his home, near Berchtesgaden. On September 17th Chamberlain told his cabinet that Hitler appeared to be "a man who could be relied upon when he had given his word".

Two days later, on September 19th, Vernon commented to Francis: "Czechoslovakia is on everyone's lips – Don't you think that all racial purists ought to be pissed on hard and long – or isn't that too good for them? Nothing can cleanse those who think they are consciously clean."

The Czechoslovakia crisis intensified through the rest of September then reached its false conclusion on September 29th and 30th in Munich. The leaders of Britain, France and Italy[34] met with Hitler – and capitulated with him, agreeing that Sudetenland be given to Germany. Prime Minister Chamberlain returned to England waving the paper they had signed, declaring they had secured "peace in our time". On October 1st Hitler marched into Sudetenland.

On the 14th October Dylan sent Vernon a "big poem" he had been working on, "provisionally called 'In September' ... only because it was a terrible war month." Caitlin and Dylan were to become parents in January and Dylan had written the poem for his unborn child, in the light – or the darkness – of the world situation. He told Vernon: "Remember this is a poem written to a child about to be born ... & telling it what a world it will see, what horrors and hells ... It's an optimistic, taking-everything poem. The two most important words are "Cry Joy"." Vernon suggested Dylan title the poem 'Poem in the Ninth Month' which Dylan immediately accepted.[35] He first published it with this title, though later changed it to: 'A Saint About to Fall'.

On the 18th October Dylan took part in a radio broadcast "sweetly called 'The Modern Muse'" and told Vernon: "Don't forget to listen to it ... I may as well go up to meet Auden, Spender, MacNeice, Day-Lewis & some others who'll be there."[36]

Dylan, perhaps in response to the more politically-aware poets he was reading with, gave an unforgettable reading of his poem beginning 'The hand that signed the paper felled a city'. Written in 1933, it could not have spoken more pertinently to Neville Chamberlain's paper-signing in Munich two weeks before. Dylan Thomas would later become famous for the extraordinary power of his reading voice, but this, rightly, is the first recording of his that has survived.[37]

The broadcast was at 10.30 at night, but Vernon, for all his efforts, missed hearing Dylan. He went to a concert that night in Swansea and afterwards: *"took a bus to Mrs. James's, broke in on her & without overture or explanation switched on the wireless. Why? – For Dylan's broadcast ... I didn't hear Dylan ... we just missed him."* He did hear almost everyone else and was unimpressed, continuing to Francis: *"we heard Macneice & Spender & Day Lewis and a few others. What a lot reputation does for people. My poems are better than theirs & nobody knows. Even you don't know. I say this from instinct not pride."*[38]

The attitudes of Dylan Thomas and Vernon Watkins to the world situation in late 1938 were, in fact, remarkably similar. Dylan had written in July to Henry Treece: "You are right when you suggest that I think a squirrel stumbling at least of equal importance as Hitler's invasions, murder in Spain ... the fascist anger ... but I am aware of these things as well."[39] Vernon, likewise, seemed wholly to overlook the real dangers and to be strangely convinced of his own greater perspective. Before hearing a lecture in Swansea (by Stephen King-Hall) "on the European situation!" he overconfidently – and surprisingly vulgarly – told Francis: *"Who knows it better than I?* Hitler is at this moment shitting, Pound is drunk, Mussolini's skipping to get his weight down, the Pope is eating a sandwich, the Czech Jewish refugees are sleeping in old newspapers, Nazis ranting everywhere – 'the arse-belching of preachers' – Pound's phrase."[40]

And just as Dylan in 1939, when Vernon asked him what he wanted for Christmas, replied "a war-escaper", so Vernon in 1938 was having absurd thoughts about how the horrors of war might be avoided altogether. The government, he joked to Francis, had been uninterested in his inventions:

"I had a plan in case of air-raids to mirage all industrial towns on to the water ... so that they would look like lakes; and another plan for everyone to talk in a foreign language ... so that the pilots would think they were over another country ... An alternative plan was that everyone should be supplied with a gas-inflatable balloon-parachute and rise from the ground to a sufficient height as the bombs fell."[41]

Like Dylan as well, the truth may have been that Vernon, finely sensitive as he was, found the reality of what was happening, initially at least, too much to bear. He also confessed to Francis that when the Munich crisis had been at its height he had reverted to how he had behaved as a small child:

"When the crisis was at its highest, when it was almost war, I did a thing I used to do as a small boy – opened my bible with my eyes closed & put a finger on a passage. My finger fell on this, in Zepheniah: – 'Woe unto her that is rebellious and polluted, to the oppressing city.' That very line. Don't you think that's extraordinary?"

Exactly at the time of the Munich crisis Vernon suddenly also saw the newspaper poster one day – 'Pearl White is dead' – and this too plunged him back into memories of his childhood.[42] Pearl White had been the American film star whose films he had watched as a boy during the First World War. So strongly had she affected the children, like Watkins, who watched her repeatedly escaping, on screen, from almost certain death, that they always gave her a central role in "our mock street-wars". Now, in 1938, her death and the nearness of war had become real. This led to Watkins's poem 'Elegy on the Heroine of Childhood' that he wrote "between the Munich Crisis of 1938 and Jan 1939".[43]

Watkins described himself, aged 60, as one who was "totally unskilled in politics, yet deeply concerned with human behaviour."[44] This was in fact already true of him in 1938, aged 32. Far as he was from detailed political insight into the world situation, he was deeply concerned with the need for *human beings* to change. This involved, though, for him, more than mere political change: *"I would like a complete revolution but not the way people are asking for it"*, he wrote. *"The incontinent disgust at the times is itself a right disgust but it would be better to see human beings in spite of it, for their own sake, independent of political creeds."* [45]

From this perspective, despite the horrors of the Nazi government, which he was well aware of, as his Jewish friend from Nuremberg, Frau Hechinger, had asked him help her gain asylum in Britain,[46] he could never view the people of Germany nationalistically, nor lose sight of the spiritual and artistic gifts of true German culture. As if appealing to this, in October, he translated Novalis's hymn 'When All Become Untrue' ('Wenn Alle Untreu Werden') and sent it to Dylan.

From this perspective too, no-one was exempt from Vernon's criticisms for their failings as human beings, whoever they might be. After the propagandist lecture he had heard by Stephen King-Hall, the "spokesman for Government and Press agreement", he told Francis: "It was absurd ... We stumbled into the room where the lecturer wasn't, but a hat and coat talked."[47]

Even in the Kardomah Café, in the intensity of those days, Vernon not only had no wish to engage in what he saw as superficial political discussion but also, with Dylan and Fred Janes away, was unusually impatient with the human inadequacies of everyone else:

"I'm afraid I antagonized Tom & a few others by rushing into the Kardomah & out again immediately ... to juggle European balls at that hour was too much. Tom is too courteous, Fisher too theatrically vile, Prichard too maliciously self-interested. Fred alone is a complete man & he wasn't there."[48]

New Year's Eve, 1938/9
"Midnight. Midnight. Midnight. Midnight." (VW)
"On the tip of the tongue of the year" (DT)
On New Year's Eve at the end of 1938, the year that had seen so much in common between Dylan and Vernon, they experienced at the same time, though in different places, something like a shared dream or vision, of momentous importance for both of them, particularly for Vernon.

The situation in Europe had been rapidly worsening. On 'Kristallnacht', on November 9th, Jews were attacked and Jewish premises were destroyed across Germany. On December 31st, during the day, a clear statement was made that the year ahead, in all likelihood, would bring a Second World War. Neville Chamberlain, who had granted Hitler's demands regarding Czechoslovakia, was to visit Italy's fascist Prime Minister Benito Mussolini in January. *If* Chamberlain also granted Mussolini's territorial demands, then, it was officially predicted,[49] Hitler would claim parts of France (Alsace-Lorraine) and would move into Soviet Ukraine, leading to war with both France and Russia.

That New Year's night Dylan Thomas had a dream of a *blind singing horse* in a cage, whose bars, on which the horse was standing, grew steadily hotter until they were red-hot, at which point a man called out: 'He sings better now.'[50] The horse became an image for Dylan of himself, blind and singing, as he suffered the times he was living in. It led to a poem, whose first title was 'January 1939', which Dylan, according to his biographer, "intended as a poem or prayer for the New Year."[51] The poem – later called: 'Because the Pleasure-Bird Whistles' – in Dylan's own words: "has a figure in it *standing suffering on the tip of the new year* and refusing, blindly, to look back at, if you like, the lessons of the past year to help him."[52] Dylan likewise refuses to look back at the fears of the previous year and offers his blessing, such as it is, on the present moment and the year ahead. The poem ends: "Over the past table I repeat this present grace."

As for Vernon, on New Year's Eve 1938 he had been working very late at the bank, as it was the day the year's accounts had to be completed. He returned home to Heatherslade at about quarter to midnight and immediately turned on the radio. There was a broadcast on, from his father's village of Taff's Well, of the ancient Welsh ritual of the Mari Lwyd, where a white horse's skull covered in ribbons was carried from house to house by singers and revellers, who challenged, in a rhyming contest, the people indoors. As midnight approached, "I had a distinct vision, such as one sometimes has when one is tired".[53] "As I listened, it seemed to me that the old custom assumed terrifying proportions, for not only drunken and holy people, *but the dead themselves* seemed to have come to the house."[54] This experience of 'the dead themselves', in large numbers, encountering in terrifying manner the living inside their houses, in this moment out of time between the years: "was a kind of reconciliation of contraries, an eternal moment of contradictions, and my *Ballad of the Mari Lwyd* began to take shape."[55]

The 24 year-old Dylan, like the blind horse in his poem, really was now singing better and better. In 1938, according to Vernon, Dylan "suddenly reached maturity, both in verse and prose, beyond anything he had achieved before."[56] In prose, as Vernon put it: "He would now write about real people; his verse would move in the direction of the living voice. He had broken the shell of symbolic time and come out into real time."[57] In verse, Vernon described the poem Dylan sent him on December 29th – 'Once it was the colour of saying' – as "the turning-point in Dylan Thomas's work"[58] Dylan's new stories and poems would eventually make up his third book, *The Map of Love*[59], which would open with the New Year prayer: 'Because the Pleasure-Bird Whistles'.

Vernon's New Year's Eve vision, on the cusp of the year when he would turn 33, led to the poem ('The Ballad of the Mari Lwyd') which quite definitely marked his own "turning-point". It would form the central title-poem to his first book and would have, according to the poet David Wright, an "electric" impact on the poetry-reading public.

January, 1939
W.B. Yeats's death & Llewellyn Thomas's birth

Vernon Watkins described that for the previous ten years: *"each new poem of (Yeats's) was confirmed by my own metaphysical experience"*.[60] It was always a significant occasion for him, therefore, when Yeats's most recent poems were published in the 'London Mercury'.

In March 1938, when 'Lapis Lazuli' appeared, he described how he "got the figures wrong all day at the bank". In December 1938, when the first of Yeats's 'Last Poems' appeared,[61] Watkins was amazed to discover that Yeats, speaking of himself towards the end of his life, had written: "I, through the terrible *novelty of light*, stalk on, stalk on." ('High Talk') For Watkins had written in *The Influences*, as if about Yeats himself: "Who but the unafraid of time can sing/ Out of sheer joy, the *novelty of day*?" Vernon excitedly wrote to Francis: "Extraordinary that Yeats should use 'novelty of light' when I use 'novelty of day' in the 4th line from the end of the Masque, & my line was written at least 3 years ago."[62]

In January 1939, 'The Mercury' had three more poems by Yeats.[63] The last of them, 'The Circus Animal's Desertion', ends: "*Now that my ladder's gone/ I must lie down where all the ladders start/ In the foul rag and bone shop of the heart.*" Vernon, on reading these words, had a brief visionary experience: "At once, when I read those words, I saw a coffin".[64] On Sunday January 23rd, Vernon read out the whole of

'The Circus Animal's Desertion' to his friend Rene Wauquier.[65] Five days afterwards, on January 28th, W.B. Yeats died in the South of France. When Vernon heard the news of his death, from his mother who had heard it on the radio, he felt he was hearing about something he knew already: "I had no actual premonition of immediate death, yet the news of his death came as no surprise. I was in this room (the windows) and Mother shouted through the partition. I said 'I know' quite evenly."[66]

Francis rang Vernon soon afterwards, having also heard the news. As Vernon told him: "When you rang up, I was still in a pretty incoherent state. It is the splendour of the latest poems and of that wonderful visit which fuse and dazzle."

The following day, January 30th, Yeats was buried in the hillside village in Southern France that Vernon had visited nearly twelve years before: "Yeats was buried today at Roquebrune, which I know, and where, in 1927, I had tea … while two troubadours sang songs."[67]

Among the songs they had sung, as Vernon now recalled, had been: "Verlaine's beautiful 'Il pleure dans mon coeur' which brought tears to my eyes." Fitting as it was to remember this, Vernon was a very different person from the nostalgic, unhappy youth he had been in 1927. Yeats himself had been instrumental in helping Vernon overcome that earlier self. Rather than any traditionally grieving poem, therefore, Vernon wrote a poem for W.B. Yeats, called 'A Prayer Against Time',[68] in Yeats's own spirit. It begins:

> *God, let me not know grief*
> *Where time is uppermost (.)*

Its last stanza, resounding with Yeats's words: "Be secret and exult", concludes with Watkins's meeting with Yeats at Riversholme shortly before his death, yet with his poetic creativity as great as ever:

> *I have been luckier than*
> *All others in one thing,*
> *Devoted secret time*
> *To one love, one alone;*
> *Found then that dying man*
> *Exulting in new rhyme:*
> *The river standing,*
> *All but miracle gone.*

Vernon wrote a second poem about Yeats's death, called 'The Mummy'.[69] Recalling his apparent pre-knowledge of Yeats's death, so that on hearing of it: *"I said 'I know' quite evenly"*, the last lines of 'The Mummy' speak of how Vernon: "heard a great friend's death without a change of voice."

'What shudder of birth and death? What shakes me most?'[70]
The news of the death of W.B. Yeats's was immediately joined, for Vernon, by Dylan Thomas's latest news: "This is just to tell you that Caitlin & I have a son aged 48 hours. Its name is Llewellyn Thomas. It is red-faced, very angry, & blue-eyed. Bit blue, bit green. It does not like the world. Caitlin is well, & beautiful. I'm sorry Yeats is dead. What a loss of the great poems he would write. Aged 73, he died in his prime."[71] Caitlin also wrote to Vernon: "Llewellyn … is a very intriguing person … his head is long and fibrous, & his face squashed red & angry like Dylan – … It's marvellous to have shed my burden at last!"[72]

Llewellyn Thomas had been born two days after Yeats had died and the two events would always remain linked for Vernon. Vernon became Llewellyn's godfather and wrote a series of poems for him. In one of them Vernon depicted Yeats as the 'Dalai Lama', (whose successor, traditionally, is born almost immediately after his death), and told his godson:

> *You were gathered in the seam*
> *That sewed the great man's burial shroud (.)*[73]

Dylan told Vernon that of all the poems: "I liked ... the Dalai Lama poem particularly." Vernon gave everything he earned from them to Dylan and Caitlin for Llewellyn, and to help secure a bed they could no longer afford paying for. Dylan gratefully wrote: "Thank you for the bedsaver; it has. Lovely of you, and one day I will buy you a bank all for yourself."[74]

CHAPTER TEN

'Sailors on the Moving Land' (1939–1941)

The Outbreak Of War – 'Sailors On The Moving Land'

In early 1939, a movement was begun in Cardiff to found a "New Wales Society"[1] with the stated aim that the "Welshman who writes in English" should not have to work "in the midst of a cosmopolitan confusion of poetasters and literary racketeers" but should "try and realise himself within his own society, Wales."

Dylan Thomas on being asked to become a member remarked that he did not like the idea of "societies, groups or manifestos", adding: "I'm selfish enough not to feel worried very much about the writer in his miserable artistic loneliness, whether it's in Wales or Paris or London; I don't see why it should be lonely anyway."[2]

Vernon Watkins replied in different words but in a remarkably similar spirit:

"I hate conferences, manifestos, groups, movements, etc … I feel that people write best when they write independently of groups."

In June 1938, Vernon Watkins had directly asked W.B. Yeats about what value, if any, there might be in a "national poetry". Watkins recorded his question and Yeats's answer in 'Yeats in Dublin':

> I questioned him: 'How can there be
> A national poetry?
> What can we make or what resist
> When all is like the sea?'
> He said: 'You must resist the stream
> Of mechanical apathy.'[3]

Watkins used Yeats's words now in answering the request to join this national – or even nationalist – movement for Welsh poetry. What Yeats was asking for, thought Watkins, was better served by creating great literature than by sitting and talking about it:

"Resistance to a mechanical way of living can be sustained better by excellent writing than by excellent conversation".

As Watkins ruthlessly went on: *"those nationalists who are most bitter at this moment should try to distinguish between the imperfections of their country and the imperfection of their style."*[4]

This was in fact perhaps the one issue on which Watkins profoundly disagreed with Yeats. Keidrych Rhys, one of the three founders of the "New Wales Society", had tried in March 1938 to persuade Watkins to link himself to their cause by asking: "Did you know Yeats believes in National Poetry?" Vernon, for all his love of Yeats, was wholly able to criticize him where necessary. Referring, during the war years, to "Yeats, the great nationalist", he commented: "the worst of Yeats's last work is found in his praise of war; it presents an arrogant blindness, and the technique also stumbles."[5]

What was important for Watkins about Yeats had nothing to do with nationalism or political causes, but with the universal character of his individual imagination. Watkins continued in his letter to W.T. Davies:

"Manifesto is to me one of the ugly words that I don't like, yet I would like to 'take London'. The age is vile, the worst things at the top, but I don't know of a single man who has gone out of his imagination and by that reason achieved a tenth of what Yeats achieved by going back into his."

Watkins therefore gave a clear though courteous "no" to the offer to circumscribe his free imagination within the bounds of Welsh writing. He ended his letter: "*You can count on my friendship, if not on my support.*"[6]

A few years later, in a questionnaire, Watkins made clear that like other non-English poets of the English language, such as W.B. Yeats or Gerard Manley Hopkins or Dylan Thomas, he wished his poetry to be able to speak to everyone:

"*Do you consider yourself an Anglo-Welsh writer?*"

VW: "No. I am a Welshman, and an English poet. Wales is my native country, and English the native language of my imagination."

"*For whom do you write?*"

VW: "*Everybody*; and, more particularly, for a succession of natures stretching as far back and as far into the Future as possible for whom the values of the imagination are at once first and unchanging."[7]

Not surprisingly, therefore, Watkins now sought for a wider and more appropriate audience for his poetry than could be reached through the journal 'Wales'.[8] T.S. Eliot having said no to publishing his Masque in 1937, Watkins, after revising it, had asked Elizabeth Yeats, the poet's sister, if the Cuala Press (set up to publish Yeats's poetry) would publish it. Miss Yeats had replied that Cuala could perhaps *print* the book, at Watkins's expense, but not 'publish' it.[9] On May 17th, 1939, however, she informed Watkins of the Directors' statement "there would be not time to do a book for you … so there it is for the present." Watkins, having had no success with the publishing companies of W.B. Yeats or T.S. Eliot, next sent his Masque to Dent's, the publishers of Dylan Thomas.

With his lyric poetry too, Watkins now began sending the new poems he wished to have published to the 'London Mercury'[10] or 'Life and Letters', rather than to 'Wales'[11]. *Not* that Watkins had suddenly changed his tune and become ambitious in relation to publishing. After T.S. Eliot wrote to him, after 'Yeats in Dublin' had appeared in print,[12] Watkins replied: "*I am very glad that you will be interested to see my future work.*" This in no way, however, made him hasten to send Eliot new poems. Instead he told Eliot:

"It is very difficult to be a true poet … I distrust a reputation of any kind, and I admire your ability to resist it completely … I have to go warily, & *I shall publish as little as possible*, writing as much as possible at the same time.[13]

Life, Love and Llewellyn

The first half of 1939 was altogether a busy, happy time for Vernon.

By March, when his annual banking exams came around, which he had repeatedly failed, he had too much on to give them any thought.

Describing the banking exams as "my annual conundrum" he added: "I am serene about it as only those can be who have made no preparation. The fact is, I've been too much occupied to open a book. I shall enjoy, though, framing my ingenious and imaginative answers."[14]

The time he did have, at night, he spent writing and rewriting the Ballad inspired by his vision on New Year's Eve 1938. During the first four months of the year he worked at it "almost every night." In March he told his friend Francis: "It's been written at least half-a-dozen times since I wrote to you about it, each time a quite new vision appearing."[15]

Watkins was a remarkably prolific poet and told Eliot:

"My danger is always facility, but I insist on abundance and refuse to be cramped. That is why I often write a poem a great many times, always making a new poem."[16] Thus the Ballad in no way interfered with him writing at the same time quite different poems, such as 'A Lover's Words'. ("*Come down, dear love, be quick./ Now must our limbs great follies/ Fly through the zodiac.*") As Watkins since his transformational experience of 1928 had had no ordinary 'romantic interests' at all, it might well appear strange to suddenly hear him writing of "naked limbs flying ... under the sheet awake". He told Francis: "Perhaps this theme is not one you would expect from me but I felt compelled to write it. It *is* my theme too."[17]

As romantic love was an almost constant presence in Francis's life, who in early 1939 was contemplating marriage, Vernon in his letters to Francis at this time discussed the theme of love, and his own peculiar relation to it, far more openly than elsewhere.

After a long bicycle trip he innocently told Francis: "At the last sweetshop you would have kissed the maid ... but I only made her laugh while our lives flew for a moment into a mutual bit of butterscotch. It's no good. I cannot be romantic." He then disclosed the real complexity of this, that he in fact saw no need for love to have any 'sensual counterpart': "I'm in a hell of a mess about women, as you know, my imaginative love having no sensual counterpart; this doesn't trouble me, because I've never believed much in natural things."[18]

This didn't hinder Vernon from offering Francis surprisingly confident advice concerning his relationships and his thoughts of marriage: "I've always deplored your indiscriminate affection for women which seems to me the opposite to any form of true love, but if you like the girl a hell of a lot, if she's a constant presence, not heatedly near, but very near in great distance ... & if her voice would not change if you were to leave her forever, I think she must be the one ... People aren't changed by marriage: only the world is changed. They exist before and after it."

Francis did decide to get married and asked Vernon to be best man. Vernon, strangely prefiguring what would one day happen at his own marriage, answered: "a very happy marriage to you, I wish I could be there. You must consider me your best absent-man, and my ghost-hand will pass you the ghost-ring."[19]

While this banter was going on Vernon was asked to be Llewellyn Thomas's godfather and told Francis: "You must congratulate me as well, because I'm now a father. Don't be alarmed. Dylan made me godfather to his child & he was proxy for me. He rushed into the house last Saturday & asked me to come to the christening but I had to perform the blessing by proxy."[20]

Vernon, bachelor as he was, loved the role of godfather and took it very seriously – with regard to the presents he gave perhaps too seriously. He wrote Llewellyn poem after poem, publishing three of them in the March 1940 issue of 'Life and Letters'.[21] Dylan was happy with such godfatherly offerings: "As for Llewellyn, a poem in his stocking is more than he deserves – unless you think, as I think, that everybody deserves everything or nothing. I can't pretend that he will admire the poem ... but we will."[22] Caitlin asked, though, whether they might receive something more practical, like "undervests and/or nappies. Is that too dull?"[23]

In March the last of Yeats's *Late Poems* were published in 'The London Mercury'.[24] 'The London Mercury' was then subsumed into 'Life and Letters', whose April edition included Watkins's 'Yeats in Dublin' – which both Yeats and Dylan Thomas had already appreciated, soon to be joined by T.S. Eliot. They were full and lively months and Vernon told Francis: "I'm incredibly happy ... for a lot of reasons – all unreasonable."[25] Going beyond what was "reasonable" was indeed the key to happiness for Vernon, enabling him to go beyond what Eliot had declared possible, as he inspiringly told Francis, who had written to him feeling "fed up":

"I hope that you are now your impossible, insubordinate, irrational, irrepressible self again, not that possible, subordinate, rational, repressed self which is moody, therefore not established. I was for many years more miserable than I like to remember, and I only became truly happy when I realized that things I had thought fixed were moving and that happiness was bound to be paradoxical. All the things that I love seem to exist miraculously in spite of the leaden and denying things which did their best to pin me down when I was a very young boy growing up. I have little use for a happiness which doesn't touch all the points of sorrow at the same time. Eliot says that human beings can only bear a very little of reality but I think man is designed to bear a great deal intuitively and very little rationally. Insofar as we believe in everything as a vision and a miracle we are capable of bearing reality and also of being intensely happy; it is because Yeats has discovered this that he has written so much poetry that I love, – lyric poetry which I find equal to any of the last 500 years – but of course time is of no account."[26]

Above all, though, the months of March to May 1939 saw the culmination of Vernon's practical, poetic help to Dylan. Dylan was completing his third book of poetry, *The Map of Love*. Vernon had been sent all of the book's poems by Dylan "more or less as he finished them" and had typed them out for Dylan as well.[27] On five occasions[28] Dylan asked Vernon to help him with last-minute revisions or to go through the proofs: "Can you come down Saturday – for, if possible, the weekend? Please try, I need your help a lot. It really is important to me." When he didn't hear back Dylan wrote to Vernon twice, once to the bank, in case he left home before the post arrived, and once to Heatherslade in case Vernon had a moment to prepare: "if, and I hope terribly that you can, you do come, you might want to … get a few things, pyjamas perhaps … I need you urgently to rewrite a poem with me that belongs to the final proofs … which have to be sent off almost at once."[29]

Vernon's devotion to Dylan meant there could be no question of his *not* going, even if it meant cycling the 40 miles between Gower and

Laugharne with no lights, which was no problem going there on Saturday afternoon, but more of one coming back on Sunday night: "I spent last week-end with Dylan at Laugharne. He's much bigger all round – 12 stone 8 – but otherwise very much the same. And I cycled home in the dark without a lamp of any kind."[30]

Vernon was the only person with whom Dylan could work on his poetry in this way. Soon after the weekend, like an immediate expression of thanks, Dylan told Vernon that his "way of criticizing" was "the most helpful there is for me, and I want it to go on." Even if Vernon occasionally made suggestions that "seem completely to misunderstand my meaning", he always made them: "*as nobody else has done – though this is a late and wrong place for a recommendation of your complete intellectual honesty, a thing we needn't talk about – without rancour, affectation, or the felt need to surprise.*"[31]

In the same letter Dylan sent Vernon a poem beginning 'Friend by enemy I call you out" about the deceitfulness of many so-called friends. Above it he wrote: 'TO OTHERS THAN YOU'. Vernon often modestly said that the only concrete help he had given Dylan was in persuading him to use titles for his poems. 'To Others Than You' was in fact the very first title Dylan used that was different from the poem's opening words.

'The Influences'

Ten days after Vernon's 33rd birthday, on July 6th and 7th 1939, his Masque '*The Influences*' – which he saw as his most significant creation to date, "my *Faust*", as he named it to T.S. Eliot – was at last to have two performances at the Little Theatre in Swansea.

Vernon had now wholly rewritten it, telling Francis: "at the moment the Masque dominates all. I've put all I know into the new vision & my heart is set on it."[32] It failed to move the directors at Dent's, however, and like Faber and Cuala before them they refused to publish it: "Dent's have cast it off as a publishing project. I can't & shan't afford their price; but for refusing it may all the Directors have boils on their bottoms for life, and so belie the name of Dent's."[33]

Vernon *had*, though, been successful in interesting Thomas Taig in the Masque, who not only produced these two Swansea performances but also generated huge interest in the event in the literary community of Wales. The performances took place at the height of the activity surrounding the creation of a "Cymdeithas Cymru Newydd" ("New Wales Society") for the promotion of a new Welsh National Literature. As so many Welsh writers had been invited to the Vernon Watkins's Masque Keidrych Rhys felt the event would provide an excellent opportunity for a meeting of "Cymdeithas Cymru Newydd" and wrote to Pennar Davies, his colleague: "There will be a lot of the boys there. We could hold a conference in Fred Janes's studio."

A more unlikely or inappropriate setting for a meeting of writers aiming to bring about 'social change'[34] would be hard to imagine. Watkins's poetic *Masque*, far from being activist, did not even include what would normally be seen as *action*. He told T.S. Eliot: "All the dramatic action, in a sense, takes place inside the skull."[35] Thus Watkins saw no need for any kind of outer staging: "It could be beautifully done, as I see it in my forehead, with no dramatization at all, but simply a succession of patterns, like a vision".[36]

Watkins's ideal audience, therefore, consisted of those able to experience poetry most intensely – Yeats being first on the list. For Watkins the *Masque* was: "as dramatic as anything in the world, if produced as I imagine it and for the people I imagine. They may not exist, but that would be an accident of history & not my fault. *Yeats is one of them*."[37]

Yeats being dead, Watkins invited Eliot. Ignoring Eliot's thorough rejection of the first version of the *Masque*, Watkins told Eliot of his latest 'brainwave': "You say in your letter that you would be much interested to see my future work. It has suddenly occurred to me that you might like to see the performance of my Masque 'The Influences' ... at Swansea Little Theatre on July 6th and July 7th ... I hope you will not judge the idea too hastily ... I could arrange rooms for you in Swansea or out here."[38] Eliot declined.

Four days before the premiere Watkins wrote to Peter Hellings, a 17 year-old aspiring poet from Swansea: *"Everyone with any interest in poetry should be there. It's taken a hell of a time but it's done now & it will one day open people's eyes & ears."*[39]

There is no doubt, though, that the person Vernon most hoped would be there was Dylan Thomas. The Masque had largely been inspired by his first meeting with Dylan Thomas. The two "Influences" depicted in the Masque, that of the old sage who seeks to overcome death and time and that of the child-like youth who celebrates life and the present moment, bore a relationship, as the two great influences on Vernon Watkins, to W.B. Yeats and Dylan Thomas, respectively. Much more immediately, though, they relate to Vernon Watkins himself and Dylan Thomas – and the touch with which the Masque ends, from which "art is born", relates not only to their meeting as friends but also to the mysterious bond between their opposite yet complementary poetic gifts. The riddle of these *two poets* of genius, brought up a few stone-throws from each other in Swansea, lay right at the very heart of the whole "literary renaissance" in Wales – and the *Masque* was to put this on stage, in the form of an allegory, in front of the literary community of Wales.

But Dylan never came to see it.

On first hearing about the performances of the Masque Dylan had been delighted, telling Vernon: "You want a big audience, of word-boys as well as theatre boys".[40] He would, he said, review it for 'Life and Letters' and planned to be there for the premiere. Shortly before the performances, however, Dylan wrote and told Vernon "with great regret, that we *may* not be able to come to your play." If Richard Hughes could bring him and Caitlin by car: "we'll be able to; if not, not. I'd hate to have to miss the play, more than I can tell you ... we *will* try."[41]

Vernon's hopes were suddenly raised on the day of the first performance – "I've just had a wire from Dylan to say he's coming"[42] – but in the end, though Richard Hughes *did* travel by car from Laugharne, Dylan and Caitlin *didn't* come with him. They were, Vernon reported to Francis, "kept away by horrible colds (so Hughes said)".[43] Whatever Vernon's immediate feelings were about Dylan's excuse, he kept them to himself, and was soon, as always, understanding and forgiving. Eighteen years later, however, when an interviewer asked if Dylan had not treated him "rather carelessly" at the Masque, Vernon said nothing about any "horrible colds" but replied, with equal understanding and forgiveness: "well, that was a question of money ... unfortunately he ran out of funds, he certainly would have come."[44]

With the performance itself Vernon was delighted. He told T.S. Eliot:

"The Masque was a great and wonderful success ... What a pity you were unable to see it! It held the audience completely." [45] Dylan Thomas's old friend Charlie Fisher reviewed the Masque for the Swansea Evening Post and commented on its complete lack of action: "*Movement, when it occurs, seems a definite intrusion, which is an odd thing to say about any piece written for the theatre.*" He did agree, though, that the audience had been "held": "Contrary to some fears the argument between the two great influences ... was not at all difficult to understand."[46]

The Masque, in fact, was so successful that the producer Thomas Taig immediately planned a further production at the Mercury Theatre in London, in a programme of pieces by new Welsh writers, to be hosted by Dylan Thomas. It was this prospect of a London performance in September that led Vernon, on the same day that he wrote to Eliot about the Masque, to state boldly to W.T. Davies:

"*I would like to 'take London'* ... but I don't know of a single man who has gone out of his imagination and by that reason achieved a tenth of what Yeats achieved by going back into his – the noblest and most powerful attack and one that will eventually destroy it."[47]

"Everything ... depends on Hitler, Poland, & insanity."

As August went by the European situation grew ever darker and world war ever nearer. This was the moment Dylan Thomas's *The Map of Love* was published and he rightly told Vernon: "my book couldn't have come out in a viler month".[48] However much Vernon and Thomas Taig may have been looking forward to the Mercury Theatre event, by the end of August it seemed increasingly unreal to Dylan Thomas:

"This war ... fills me with such horror and lassitude that I can't easily think about the London programme .... Everything – including all our happiness – depends on Hitler, Poland, & insanity."[49]

As Dylan was to have been the host of the whole event, Vernon and Thomas Taig drove to Laugharne to discuss it with him on Sunday September 3rd. While driving they heard on the car radio Prime Minister Chamberlain's declaration of war with Germany. Dylan Thomas heard it too.

Thomas Taig gives a vivid description of how Dylan was when they arrived: "my recollection is of someone so deeply affected by the horror,

> Now running
>
> Repeat Performance of the Stupendous Success—
>
> ## "The War to End War"
>
> or
>
> "MAKING the WORLD SAFE for DEMOCRACY"
>
> Previously ran for over four years, 1914—1918
>
> Adolf Hitler as "The Villain"
> (formerly played by KAISER BILL)
>
> STARTLING   BIGGER & BETTER
> IMPROVEMENTS!   BOMBS!
>
> WHOLE TOWNS BLOWN SKY-HIGH!
> (complete with inhabitants)
>
> The Craziest Show the World has ever seen
>
> Millions of FREE Gifts of wooden legs, etc.
>
> BOOK NOW at nearest Recruiting Office
>
> Entire proceeds for benefit of Profiteers
>
> To be followed shortly by
> "The War to End War to end War"

Back cover of 'Wales' – October 1939

the enormity of the thing, that he always recurs to me as a kind of animal caught in a trap ... It lasted ... the rest of that day. Dylan was not quite there – and that was unusual for Dylan. *There are some artists who are ... always sort of floating off, but Dylan was immediate and his contact was always live, but not on that occasion* – he seemed to be overwhelmed."[50]

Vernon, too, couldn't fail to notice the scale of impact the news had on Dylan. Referring to this particular day Vernon wrote: "The advent of war filled Dylan with horror, and the war itself was a nightmare from which he never completely recovered."[51]

Immediately after the outbreak of war, the October issue of 'Wales'[52] printed a biting satire on its back cover against the whole international conspiracy that had brought about the present war.

This may well have been partly inspired by Osbert Sitwell's savagely satirical poem 'The Next War', written in November 1918. Although it is impossible to imagine Dylan Thomas authoring the back cover of 'Wales', its bitter humour and pacifist sentiments were nonetheless not far from his own stance. He wrote to Vernon in September 1939: "I intend registering as a conscientious objector as soon as necessary" and described himself as "a never-fighter".[53]

Vernon Watkins, for all his affinity with Dylan Thomas, did not share Dylan's relationship to the war. Vernon was not permitted to sign up immediately, the banks being deemed an essential service, but joined the local Home Guard – patrolling the Gower with, among others, "Mr. Nunga, a magnificent Zulu, who, though born in Ladysmith, South Africa, had worked for eighteen years in the Steel works at Llanelli."[54] Working in the bank by day, "fighting" for the Home Guard at weekends, and never ceasing to be "a poet first", Vernon seems like one of the prototypes for *Dad's Army* and no more likely than Dylan ever to have been actually sent to the front. Nonetheless, their attitudes to the war were different, and in October 1939 when Dylan Thomas invited several

Vernon Watkins and Dylan Thomas
(probably 1936)

contemporary writers to create a public 'Objection to War', which he intended to publish in 'Life and Letters', there is no evidence that he asked Vernon to contribute.[55]

In early October, Keidrych Rhys was to be married, with Dylan as best man, and Dylan asked Vernon if he had "a respectable suit you can lend me, or, rather, trust me with". Vernon obliged and gave the suit as a gift.[56] There is a photograph of Vernon standing next to Dylan, who may well be wearing another one of Vernon's suits. The photograph is probably from a few years earlier, as Dylan is far thinner than in other photographs at that time, but it is the only image there is of the two poets standing side-by-side:

The Last Poems of Yeats

In July or August 1939, Vernon had, as he often did, kept a few days free at the end of his holidays to stay with Dylan in Laugharne.[57] Among all else they did, Vernon recited to Dylan some of Yeats's extraordinary last poems, which had recently been published. ('Lapis Lazuli', 'The Statues', 'Long-Legged Fly' and 'Notes for the Delphic Oracle'.) In November Dylan was to give a reading to the English Club at Cambridge and turned to Vernon for help: "I want to read one of yours – what do you suggest?" and asked Vernon to copy out: "some of the very last Yeats, some of those lovely poems you said down here a few months ago when we were walking down a hill."

These four poems by Yeats belonged, for Vernon, among the greatest poetry ever written. Soon after reading them he wrote to T.S. Eliot: "Have you … seen the four poems by Yeats in … the London Mercury? That poetry seems to me as great as Shakespeare, and even purer. It is just bafflingly pure."[58] They inevitably made him think as well of his own meeting with Yeats at the time these poems were being written. And now Vernon copied them for that other recipient of his unconditional admiration as a poet, Dylan Thomas, who Vernon had stayed with straight after visiting Yeats and who had immediately set about challenging Yeats's words.

The presence of these two opposite geniuses within him, as he copied out Yeats for Dylan, didn't so much lead him to write a poem as to a poem simply presenting itself to him fully-formed, as he described to

Francis: *"I have never heard a poem – not even 'Griefs of the Sea' which I heard coming out of the grass of the cliffs of Pennard and Hunt's Bay – in quite that way. What Yeats called an "articulation in the air". It was momentary and extraordinary. The whole poem took place in less than a second."*[59] Vernon called the poem 'The Last Poems of Yeats', which is written in couplets, such as:

> *A young man challenges an old.*
> *A fierce man praises a moon that's cold.*
>
> *An old man and a young man fight*
> *And each puts out the other's light.*

He immediately sent it to 'Life and Letters', where it appeared in December 1939. Oddly, though, Watkins never republished it. That Autumn he had also written a long essay on Yeats's late poems ('Yeats and the Oracles'),[60] and envisaged a book consisting of this essay, 'The Last Poems of Yeats' and 'Yeats in Dublin', as his own tribute to the miraculous fruition of Yeats's genius at the end of his life. The book, however, perhaps because of copyright issues over the many poems by Yeats in the essay, never came about.[61]

"a serious failure" & "a grand redemption"

Dylan was delighted with "the great Yeats poems" and promised Vernon he would "read them all" at Cambridge. Vernon had also sent his own poem 'The Windows' to Dylan, which Dylan called: "a serious failure, I think – I mean it is a serious poem which fails." It was Dylan's last written criticism of one of Vernon's poems. At the end of the same letter Dylan spoke, by contrast, of the poem Vernon had written for Dylan, 'Portrait of a Friend', just published in 'Life and Letters': "which I thought had only your poem to redeem it this month; but what a grand redemption. Very much love from DYLAN."

The Ballad of the Mari Lwyd

Dylan and Vernon spent much of Christmas together that year. In early December Dylan told Henry Treece he'd be in Swansea for Christmas "with Vernon Watkins and other queer men for company."[62] With war no longer a threat, as it had been a year before, but an ever more horrific reality, Dylan replied when Vernon asked what he wanted for Christmas: "Oh, that's nice. I want a war-escaper – a sort of ladder, I think, attached to a balloon, – or a portable ivory tower or a new plush womb to escape back into. Or a lotion for invisibility."[63] In mid-December, Dylan looked forward to their Christmas Eve, amidst smoke, alcohol and ink for poetry: "we'll smoke your ridiculous cigarettes and buy bathfuls of cointreau, bitter, biddy, or ink."[64] As Christmas approached, having finished his book *Portrait of the Artist as a Young Dog*, Dylan now had: "*nothing to do but wait for Swansea, marble-town, city of laughter, little Dublin, home of at least 2 great men.*"

A year before, on New Year's Eve 1938/9, Dylan and Vernon had had their simultaneous dream-visions – Dylan's of a blind horse singing and Vernon's of the skull of a white horse, the Mari Lwyd.

Dylan's dream had led him to write 'Because the Pleasure-Bird Whistles', which had a strange line about the 'hunger' of the dead, and the challenging effect of this upon the living:

> "*If the dead starve*, their stomachs turn to tumble
> An upright man in the antipodes".

Vernon's vision now led, exactly one year later, to a startling and haunting 600-line ballad, which brought the challenge to the living of the *hunger* of the dead dramatically and viscerally to life for a whole generation of readers and listeners. The poet David Wright was one of those confronted by the poem's almost mesmerizing, darkly illuminating genius when it appeared. He referred to it as: "Watkins's great piece of luck, for which when it came he was well prepared" and wrote: "For my generation the impact of 'The Ballad of the Mari Lwyd' was almost as electric as that of Auden's 'Paid on Both Sides' had been a decade earlier."[65] The Welsh poet Glyn Jones described how until then he had seen Watkins as: "a rather remote and Shelleyan poet ... whose excellence I could see rather than feel. 'The Ballad of the Mari Lwyd', by contrast, he found "haunting and magical" with "a sort of vigour, a coarse life and vitality, which (I) could experience to the full. I could never after this experience read Vernon's poetry with the eyes of my former mood of mere liking and respect."[66]

Vernon had certainly been "well-prepared". To call the poem only a "piece of luck", however, was only true in the way that Watkins himself used the phrase – where, after great labour, a poem may suddenly fall into place "like the "click of a box".[67]

First there had been his vision, the year before, where the ritual of the Mari Lwyd "assumed terrifying proportions, for not only drunken and holy people, *but the dead themselves* seemed to have come to the house."[68] For three or four months Vernon had then worked at the poem every night – with neither the form, title or content of the poem yet being clear for him. In early March he told Francis he had just "*finished* a new ballad" and "thought (after the Ballad of the Rough Sea) of calling this the Ballad of Rough Stuff." The poem was in fact still only in its first beginnings and he was soon telling Francis: "Last night I went on with my Ballad of Rough Stuff – the Mari Lwyd – *all about food* … It's been written at least half-a-dozen times since I wrote to you about it, each time a quite new vision appearing."[69] From all this work over four months he "kept nothing … except the stanza form." Only after a further two months' work "did the first verse of the final ballad come to me." And now, after the intense year of 1939 was over, as New Year's Eve returned: "the whole poem came, with the refrains".[70]

The narrator's opening words made the ballad's premise startlingly clear:

The dead return …
The Living … have cast them out, from their own fear, from their own fear of themselves …
The Living cringe and warm themselves at the fire, shrinking from that loneliness, that singleness of heart …
Terrified, they hear the dead tapping at the panes …
It is New Year's Night …
It is the moment of conscience …
Listen.

Gwen Watkins has written that the terror of the living, sitting by their warm firesides, unwilling to open themselves to the dead, reflects Vernon Watkins's struggle to open himself to the Dionysian, anarchic presence of Dylan Thomas in his life. Though this may partly be said to have been the theme of the Masque, *The Ballad of the Mari Lwyd* goes further than this. At least since the death of his grandfather Vernon had often written of his awareness of the presence of the dead. Sometimes this related to individuals he had known – his grandfather, David Cochrane, W.B. Yeats – but sometimes to vast numbers of the dead, on the other side of the thin veil of our ordinary consciousness: "The sky was filled with voices, voices of death."[71] This awareness had been part of his psychotic consciousness, prior to his breakdown and "rebirth" in 1928. But it was an even stronger part of his mature consciousness that developed from that experience. In poem after poem he would speak not only of his awareness of the dead but also of his *relationship* to them: "For the dead live, and I am of their kind." ('Gravestones') In this sense it was *Vernon* who was closer to the "rejected" dead who were "*tapping at the panes*", and Dylan who was more likely to be at home among those eating and drinking inside.

For the 'union of contraries' enacted in 'The Ballad of the Mari Lwyd' – like that in Blake's *Marriage of Heaven and Hell* – defies customary definitions. The hosts of souls outside the doors, bearing the ribboned skull of a White Horse, the Mari Lwyd, are *both* anarchically opposed to the conventional order *and* sacred – "drunken and holy people". They were, moreover, "the dead themselves", seeking to connect with the living, just as the living must reconcile with the dead. The moment of midnight between one year and another was, for Vernon Watkins, the moment 'out of time' where this became possible. He wrote, and he meant it:

"I have attempted to bring together those who are separated. The last breath of the year is their threshold, the moment of supreme forgiveness, confusion and understanding, the profane and sacred moment impossible to realize while the clock-hands divide the Living from the Dead."[72]

Quietness stretches the pendulum's chain
To the limit where terrors start,
Where the dead and the living find again
They beat with the selfsame heart ...

(Voice)
Dread and quiet, evil and good:
Frost in the night has mixed their blood.
Thieving and giving, good and evil:
The beggar's a saint, and the saint a devil.

Mari Lwyd, Lwyd Mari:
A sacred thing through the night they carry.

Betrayed are the living, betrayed the dead:
All are confused by a horse's head.

Midnight. Midnight. Midnight. Midnight.
Hark at the hands of the clock.
Lazarus comes in a shroud so white
Out of the hands of the clock.
While baskets are gathered of loaves of light,
Rape is picking the lock.
Hungering fingers, bones of the night,
Knock, knock, knock ...

(Loud and near)
'None can look out and bear that sight,
None can bear that shock.
The Mari's shadow is too bright,
Her brilliance is too black.
None can bear that terror
When the pendulum swings back
Of the stiff and stuffed and stifled thing
Gleaming in the sack.'

Midnight. Midnight. Midnight. Midnight.
Hark at the hands of the clock.

Watkins was immediately aware he had created a large and original work of genius, which spoke both with the voice of ancient ritual and with the urgent war-struck voice of the present. With a completely different urgency than before regarding publication he sent it (on March 7th) to Eliot: *"I have at last written a poem in my own idiom which I want to put straight into print. Will you be good enough to tell me whether Faber and Faber would undertake its publication, and how much that would cost. The poem is "The Ballad of the Mari Lwyd", and its length about 600 lines."*[73]

Vernon could only describe the after-effect on him of writing the Ballad by the word "happiness". (That he did not mean this superficially can be seen by his words: "I have little use for a happiness which doesn't touch all the points of sorrow at the same time.")[74] After his first book had appeared, he wrote to a friend about the Ballad: *"that poem has made me very happy, and it was that one which persuaded me to publish. I feel a great gratitude and an unsatisfied longing."*[75] He must have said something similar to Dylan Thomas, who wrote: *"I want very much to see the long-waited-for Ballad ... I'm glad you're happy from it. It must be very good."*[76] (March 6th) Despite Dylan's reminder at the end of his letter ("But let me have the ballad ... I have only the prologue with me here") Vernon would *not* let him see it, because the ballad "at that moment, after the long period of composition, seemed to me too recently finished to send away."[77] Yet *on the same day* that Vernon received Dylan's letter he sent the ballad to T.S. Eliot, asking that it be "put straight into print"! The truth was that Vernon really had found his "own idiom", and no longer had any need or wish to hear Dylan's comments before publication.

To Vernon's refusal Dylan replied: "Sorry you can't send the Ballad. I must see it soon." Dylan did suggest one alteration to the prologue – that rather than repeat its opening words at the end it should finish with the word: "Listen." Vernon took the advice, and Dylan later borrowed the advice back again in *Under Milk Wood*, whose prologue calls out to the audience three times: "Listen."

Meanwhile, Vernon arranged to meet T.S. Eliot in London as soon as possible: "I want very much to discuss the prospect of publishing the Ballad which I sent you. I have set my heart on publishing it."[78]

The fall of France – June 1940
'Elegy for the Soldiers'

Vernon's first godchild, Llewellyn Thomas, born when Yeats died, had helped bring Vernon back to the realities of newborn life. His second godchild, Francis's daughter, Danielle Dufau-Labeyrie, would bring him into the immediate realities of World War Two.

In January 1940, three months into the war, Vernon was still far from any realistic relationship to what was happening in mainland Europe. He told Francis: "I'm bored with the bloody war" and genuinely felt that France, on the brink of occupation by Nazi Germany, might be a good place for his springtime holiday:

There was a similar degree of unreality about his relationship to being a godparent, let alone a parent himself: *"I may really take a part of my holiday there in the Spring, or is that absurd? I don't want to come as a soldier – I'm not one yet – but as a visitor. Are there any in France now, and are they allowed? Or are they all suspect? Alternatively I may take a holiday in Germany as a spy."*[79]

"Am I allowed to be a godfather? You know I haven't the necessary experience – of fatherhood, I mean; my children have so far been invisible and my wife a four-dimensional heavenly body, not even an anti-self, but a magnetic, molten, and erotic nebula, suddenly changing into a vast distant statue, then a statue very near. Does this disqualify me? *Let the Pope decide."*[80]

Vernon innocently arranged to fly to Paris on May 11th, hoping to be there for the birth and even perhaps the christening of his godchild. On May 10th the Nazi invasion of France began. Winston Churchill became British Prime Minister on the same day. Vernon's prescience – or lack of it – regarding world events was identical to that of his parents, who had taken their family to Brittany on holiday as World War One broke out. That day, May 10th, Vernon met T.S. Eliot for the first time in London, for a "valuable and memorable" interview. Vernon later told Eliot how his holiday plans had collapsed: "I couldn't go to France as the 'planes were full." The 'planes, one imagines, were simply not open to civilian passengers, though they would indeed have been fully occupied bringing people out of France. Vernon's goddaughter, Danielle, was born in Paris on May 16th.

Dylan Thomas, Wyn Lewis and Vernon Watkins at Rhossili – May 1940

This meant, of course, that Vernon could spend more time with Dylan, who was in Bishopston for the middle two weeks of May. They went to the *Marriage of Figaro* in Swansea, which Vernon must also have played on his record player out into the garden at Heatherslade, for, in Dylan's words: "Beethoven accompanied our croquet". Wyn Lewis drove Vernon, Dylan and Caitlin to Rhossili, and the four of them walked out across the causeway to the Worm's Head. Dylan and Vernon were so engrossed in conversation that Wyn and Caitlin were already back on the mainland when Vernon realized he and Dylan had been almost cut off by the tide – "you nearly caught us napping on the Worm", wrote Dylan, "and what would a stranger, hearing suddenly, make of that?"[81]

Around the same time Vernon made another trip to Rhossili with Wyn Lewis's brother, David. It was a typical Vernon adventure, demanding considerable strength and even courage and at the same time naively clueless regarding certain realities in space and time. The two men set off from Heatherslade Bay below where they lived, in a heavy double canoe, planning to row the length of the southern coast of Gower and then camp on Rhossili beach. They misjudged the journey and it was completely dark when they finally dragged their canoe up onto the sands. They were immediately confronted by the Home Guard, who thought they might be German airmen or spies. Vernon, who was always quick to see the humour in a situation, shouted at them in German, before then trying to explain who they were.[82] As Vernon was also translating a lot of German poetry at this time, as he would do throughout the war, Dylan Thomas wrote: "Perhaps we're both marked. You translate Hoelderlin & swear in German to the Home Guard; I have no visible means of support, & have been known to call the war bloody and silly. I hope there's a special censor for our letters."[83]

None of this, though, could take away Vernon's profound worry about what was happening in France, above all with Francis and his family. Francis had recently joined the French Army and Vernon was well aware of the extreme danger he would be in, if indeed he was still alive. And no communication was now possible with him. For Vernon, who was a bachelor and looked likely to remain so, Francis had been an incredibly important friend over recent years, for whom he felt deep brotherly affection and love.

As the Nazi invasion of France continued, Vernon poured his grief and worry into a poem "for a French Friend before the Fall of France".[84] Yeats had told them both two years before: "You must resist the stream/ Of mechanical apathy." The danger was now far greater than this. Imagining Francis's death from an unseen bullet or bomb, Vernon ends the poem's first section: "But grief, grief is the sum,/ Grief at mechanical death."

The poem is dense and complex. But when France fell completely, with German troops marching unopposed into Paris on June 14th, Vernon wrote more directly than he ever would again about the war, imagining the possible circumstances of Francis's death. It was not a style that suited Vernon or that he did at all well, and he never attempted to publish the poem, called 'Elegy for the Soldiers'.

France, blown wide like a rose beneath the metallic invader,
Sinks ... black planes ... dived, machine-gunning refugees.
The roads were heaped with dead ... Legions of fire-belching tanks pressed
On, over pits, bodies, lives, limbs mangled, upturned eyes, crushed children.

Only the last two lines, speaking of Francis's 'dark-haired head', come near to the more usual voice of Vernon Watkins's poetry:

> O compassionate waters, bathe sweetly tonight the voice silenced by lust,
> And the neglected, unknown, dark-haired head that bleeds in the dust.

Swansea and the Battle of Britain
Intelligence and the Motorcycle

The German occupation of France was soon to have a much more immediate impact on Vernon's and on everyone else's life in Swansea and the British Isles. From France German bombers were now in easy range of Britain and Swansea, with its importance as a port for both troops and weapons, was directly targeted. Uncannily, the bombing of Swansea began on the morning of Vernon's birthday – "heralded by a golden flare which lit the sky ablaze at 3.30am on June 27 1940. Guided by this glow, the Luftwaffe easily found their target and dropped 10 High Explosives over the east side of Swansea."[85] There were no casualties from this first raid but it succeeded in "striking real fear, shock and trepidation into the hearts of Swansea's civilians."[86]

On July 10th the Battle of Britain began and lasted for three and a half months. Dylan asked Vernon: "Are you frightened these nights?" and told him how he would "wake up out of burning birdman dreams – they were frying aviators one night in a huge frying pan: it sounds whimsical now, it was appalling then".[87]

Dylan, who was living in Wiltshire, also told Vernon of what he had experienced on a trip to London: "Guns on the top of Selfridges. A 'plane brought down in Tottenham Court Road. White-faced taxis still trembling through the streets."[88] Vernon told Dylan of the situation in Swansea and Gower. None of Vernon's letters having survived, we can only learn of what he wrote through Dylan's replies: "you said ... that bombs were falling on the cliffs. I hope they missed you ... I can't imagine Gower bombed. High explosives at Pennard ... And Union Street ashen. This is all too near."[89]

Dylan, having first stated he was a conscientious objector, had finally been exempted from the army on health grounds. As nothing stood in the way of Vernon being called up he applied to the army and was immediately offered a job in the "Field Security Police."[90] The one big snag was that "this involved looking after a motor-cycle and understanding its engine which I could not do."[91] Dylan on hearing about this was flabbergasted: "you joining the army; dear God. Have you joined, or are you conscripted? Do tell me everything about it. And why a motorcycle driver? I know what your motor-driving's like from Pendine Sands. I'm not going to say you're barmy, but the chaps who engaged you to drive on public roads must be very strange little men."[92]

Only through Watkins's letters to T.S. Eliot has it been possible to solve this riddle. For Watkins revealed to Eliot that what he called the "Field Security Police" was, in fact, none other than the *Intelligence Corps* – who would swiftly have accepted him because of his excellent German. It was as a member of the Intelligence Corps that Vernon needed to ride a motorbike and he would also have been obliged *not* to reveal the nature of his work. It was this that made the whole idea of his being employed as a military motorcyclist so baffling and absurd to Dylan.

Dylan was, however, being utterly realistic about Vernon's practical incapabilities and gave him an excellent piece of advice, which Vernon did later attempt to follow: "Be an R.A.F. officer. You're too senile to be made to fly, and there's obviously more time to write poems when you're an officer than when you're creeping round corners slow as snails on your motorised scooter."[93]

In September 1940, as battle raged in the air, Dylan also advised his absent-minded poetic friend: "Don't forget: cover the croquet lawn, bury your poems in a stout box, & don't stare at the sky too much. The wrong wings are up there."[94]

"Have you any time for writing now?"

In the same month Dylan, who was now writing more prose than poetry, asked Vernon: "Have you any time for writing now? Will you let me see something new? ... I haven't settled down to a poem for a long time. I want to, & I will soon, but it mustn't be nightmarish."[95]

Vernon, who wrote no prose fiction, neither now nor at any other time in his life stopped writing poetry – on many different themes and in many different shapes and sizes.

In July 1940, he read a newspaper report that the Austrian-Bohemian writer Franz Werfel had been shot dead in Paris. With his imagination awake to the sufferings in France, Vernon immediately responded to the murder of a spiritually attuned artist like himself: "calculating bullets against the artist ... They have struck." The poem was called 'The Shooting of Werfel' and Watkins sent it to Eliot to be included in his first book. In November reports appeared that Werfel might still be alive and Watkins, not wanting this to invalidate his poem, told Eliot that a quotation from the original newspaper report about Werfel's death *"will make the question of fact insignificant. If he is alive, I shall read it to him one day. But I am sure he is dead."*[96] Within a few months the truth became clear, as Watkins dutifully informed Eliot: "Werfel is alive, in America. I do not want this to affect the inclusion of the poem."[97]

Watkins also now wrote a whole spate of ballads, whose deep blood-based rhythms seemed fitting for the darkness the world was going through. Some of them have apocalyptic themes, such as *Ballad of the Deluge*, where Noah addresses God amidst the destruction of the world. The ballad ends:

> Noah said 'God,
> After I am dead
> There shall be no crime
> Like the lack of love
> In the crucial hour
> When I stood in time.
> Let the rains fall.
> Hardly we dare live.
> By a slender thread
> You uphold us all.'

He wrote a cycle of fourteen *Equinoctial Ballads*, which, celebrating the time of the year when day and night are equal, have to do with the balancing of opposites or with *living* paradox. As he would write: "To believe in a paradox is a half-truth; the whole truth is to live it as well."[98]

In the *Equinoctial Ballads* this appears in the mysterious recurring storyline of a person who balances both sun and moon:

> When the sun and the moon are level
> And the sky has a fish's scales
> I stand by the foxy foam
> On that groaning shingle of Wales.[99]

> The sun and the moon know nothing,
> And between them I know less.[100]

> O why was I born of two?
> Why had I not one
> To feed me, to dress me,
> The moon or the sun? [101]

'Ballad of the Long-Legged Bait'
Christmas 1940 to April 1941

Between late December 1940 and the beginning of May 1941 Dylan and Caitlin Thomas lived mainly at Dylan's parents' house in Bishopston. During this time Dylan himself worked on a ballad, the only one he ever published: 'The Ballad of the Long-Legged Bait'. Dylan had always enjoyed Vernon's "excellent ballads" and 'The Ballad of the Long-Legged Bait' is undoubtedly partly influenced by them. The end of Dylan's ballad might almost be a picture of sun-and-moon-struck, long-legged Vernon himself:

> Goodbye, good luck, struck the sun and the moon,
> To the fisherman lost on the land.
> He stands alone at the door of his home,
> With his long-legged heart in his hand.

Dylan was in fact obliquely describing himself. But one of the most remarkable poems Vernon Watkins ever wrote about Dylan Thomas, written now, in January 1941, shows that their shared sense of being out of their native element – of being "*fisherm(e)n lost on the land*" –

was one they had talked about with one another. The poem – included in the appendix and never published in any of Watkins's books[102] – was called "*Sailors on the Moving Land*. For Dylan Thomas." The poem describes a drunken encounter between the two poets at the beginning of the war – an encounter whose intensity borders on clairvoyance. It probably took place on one of the very first evenings – if not *the* first evening – when the two poets remet during Dylan's four-month stay in Bishopston.

Sailors on the Moving Land
The final draft of this poem bears the dedication: 'For a friend *on the eve of war*'. This would suggest that the poem describes an evening near the outbreak of war in September 1939. The poem may indeed have echoes in it of the afternoon Dylan and Vernon spent in the pub in Laugharne on September 3rd, 1939, the day Britain had declared war on Germany. 'Sailors on the Moving Land', however, clearly describes an evening in Mumbles, Swansea, and Watkins wrote its first draft in January 1941. As it was in February 1941 that the war hit Swansea in earnest, when non-stop bombing-raids over three days and nights razed much of the town to the ground, there are good reasons why Vernon, who had not yet been called up for war-time service, should have later looked on January 1941 as 'the eve of war'.[103]

After Vernon finished work that evening he cycled to Mumbles to meet Dylan, his preferred means of getting in to work ever since 1939.[104] They were "sailors on the moving land" for numerous reasons. Already at their first meeting in Cwmndonkin Drive Dylan had asked out loud about Vernon: "Shall I welcome the sailor?" ('Ears in the Turrets Hear'). The land was "moving" not only through their becoming increasingly drunk, but also because, with the world at war, the ground underneath their and everyone else's feet was becoming ever more unstable: "the stones move towards them when they meet".

Dylan and Vernon had not seen each other for more than six months, since May the previous year. Not only this, but their meetings in May had had an extrovert character – walking to the Worm's Head, going to the opera – and had allowed for no really intimate sharing between them. And much had profoundly changed since the outbreak of war, particularly for Dylan. It was at this night-time meeting, with the ground shifting beneath them, that they would finally be able to gaze into each other's souls. In order to enter the inner deeps that Dylan was going through, Vernon would need to abandon all 'day-time' knowledge:

> *It is not knowledge makes the night more grand.*
> *What night reveals day cannot understand.*

They step into the Mermaid Pub in Mumbles, where, with the help of alcohol, they will be asked to lay themselves bare to one another:

> *Two sailors on the moving land,*
> *By the deceiving sea, we met;*
> *And the salt Mermaid cried:*
> **Give what you hide into each other's hand,**
> **Give what you hide.**

Like the Graeae in Greek myth, who shared one clairvoyant eye between them, Dylan and Vernon "passed an eye as talkers pass a saying", taking turns to answer this impossible question. It was Dylan who spoke first:

> *you, with terror in your head,*
> *Shook philosophy out of your ears,*
> *Snatched a great light, and said*
> *"I have a cage of darkness, hiding*
> *The great white innocent bird, the albatross".*

Sensing a dark abyss, in himself and in the world, beyond which no words could be said, Dylan hurls down a gauntlet to Vernon:

> *I know the horrible gulf from which we ran.*
> *Speak, if you know the place where speech began.*[105]

And Vernon *is* able to speak – beyond this abyss of nothingness or death. He had already shown in the *Ballad of the Mari Lwyd* that the

'Dead', as a living reality, ask that people become aware of them. He therefore answers Dylan's challenge in riddling, almost Sibylline words. His response is most comprehensible in an earlier draft of the poem where he describes himself as one who has been: "left/ With Palinurus in the creek/ To speak those words the living cannot speak."

To Dylan's words about the "horrible gulf" and the utter hopelessness of the times, Vernon drunkenly replies:

> **"Not within time, but out of time we dare**
> **Give hope a meaning and define despair.**
> Within time we must wait
> For recognition of a tomb-heard fate
> In the eyes' word the dying would not spare."[106]

Dylan and Vernon stagger out afterwards onto the "stampeding earth" then struggle uphill towards Bishopston, where Dylan was staying with his parents, pushing and falling over Vernon's bicycle. Dylan at one point told Vernon that he seemed like the devil himself, with the silhouetted handlebars looking like horns. Drunk to the point of seeing double, they were therefore:

> *Two men with a bicycle, two men with horns,*
> *Two shadowed quarrellers pushing two moons.*

After leaving Dylan, Vernon somehow managed to walk or cycle the two or three miles between Bishopston and Pennard.

The following morning, even before he was awake, Vernon felt his lips muttering words he was unable to understand: "'*Able to touch*'." As he wakes, he hears himself speaking the whole sentence of which this was part:

> "*I woke, saying:*
> '*I was able to touch his sorrow.*'"

The experience had a huge effect on Vernon. It has often been wondered how Vernon could be so accepting of even the worst aspects of

Dylan's behaviour over the years. An answer may be that Vernon *understood* them. He had touched, in this night, the abyss which Dylan experienced. He had always known of the "great white innocent bird" in Dylan, and he knew now as well of the "cage of darkness" from which it was often unable to break free.

As to what this meant in real terms, we have heard Vernon describing the war as: "a nightmare from which (Dylan) never completely recovered."[107] Vernon also wrote that after the war Dylan: "could still go back to peace, but from there he could no longer go forward."[108] Vernon's certainty about this may well have been rooted in his experience of Dylan in this night. As for Vernon, his strange ability to answer the challenge laid down by Dylan and to speak when no speech seemed possible, showed that he himself, most unusually, *was* still able to "go forward to peace". The poet David Wright recognizes exactly this about Vernon Watkins's poetic voice during World War Two: "he is one of the very few who have the moral ability to scan the lineaments of our present predicament without turning into a stone, or rattling like a pebble. For the predicament in which we are all involved has now turned its face towards us, and that countenance is Gorgon: none can move and few can speak."[109]

The night was crucially important to Vernon in another way as well. Before the outbreak of war he had put all his hopes in his Masque, celebrating the two opposite poles Dylan and he represented, and which culminated in the "*moment of touch*" between them, bringing about more than either could accomplish individually. Dylan's not turning up at the Masque's first performance[110] had been a blow to Vernon. Not so much subjectively, for he was able to overcome the personal hurt he felt, but for what it meant in reality. Through Dylan's not being present, the 'moment of touch' between them, had, in a certain way, *not been able to happen*. However much the Masque may have celebrated it as an ideal, it remained unrealized.

Vernon had then hoped that the Masque would be put on in London, hosted by Dylan. This too had come to nothing, with the outbreak of war not only making the London performances impossible,[111] but also altering so much for Dylan. The possibility of the "moment of touch" had become ever more remote.

And now, despite everything, Vernon had awoken saying 'able to touch'. Not in some joyful way, before a wide audience, but with the two of them alone, in this seemingly most desperate and drunken of nights, the mystery of that touch between them took place nevertheless, though by now it involved empathizing with Dylan to the point where he could "touch his sorrow". Vernon remained faithful to what he experienced in this night for the rest of Dylan's life and beyond.[112]

A few months later Vernon sent 'Sailors on the Moving Land' to T.S. Eliot[113] – hoping to publish it with another war-time poem he had written – but Eliot saw no place for it. It is a pity, for this deeply personal statement by Watkins might have worked against the false image that appeared of Watkins somehow being the weaker of the two poets – which is as foolish as were one to speak about Coleridge as a weaker poet than Wordsworth.

Vernon Watkins as a War Poet

Only a few weeks after that night-time meeting between himself and Dylan Thomas the Swansea they had known was blown to pieces in three long nights of sustained bombing raids, between 19th and 21st of February, 1941. The Kardomah Café was but one of thousands of

Central Swansea after the Blitz – February 1941.

buildings that were destroyed. 230 people were killed and more than 400 injured.

The story of one death in particular, which "was vividly described to me by a friend who saw it happen", powerfully affected Vernon. During one of the air-raids "a woman left her air-raid shelter to fetch a cushion for her child who was crying and could not sleep." She was then "instantly killed by a bomb."[114] Vernon wrote a poem about the event, called 'The Spoils of War'[115]:

> She sprang, luminous on a wish,
> ... reaching for a cushion for her child in the shelter to sleep on,
> Crossed her own tombstone, then all the stars ran in.

After the poem had been published in 'The Listener' Watkins sent it to Eliot, saying: "It is the only war poem I have done or shall do, as I have thrown all my feeling into it." Watkins in fact wrote many other war poems, but in perhaps the greatest of them, his long poem *The Broken Sea*, written three years later, he made this incident the focus, wandering "alone in the blown-up city", for much that he felt about the war:

> World-confusion sent shudders through my brain;
> So I fixed my eye on a single death.

'Sea Music For My Sister Travelling'

Between March and June 1941 Vernon finished another long and unusual war-poem: 'Sea-Music for my Sister Travelling'. His sister Dorothy had made several voyages escorting refugee children across dangerous seas and Vernon, who had an ever-fertile imagination with regard to the sea, in all its forms and dangers, set about creating a poetic vessel for his fears and imaginings of what she was going through.

In Spring 1940 Dot had travelled from Liverpool to Canada with a group of 11 to 14 year-old children. A week later another ship on the same route was "lost through enemy action. 87 children were drowned and the British government then stopped all overseas group sailings of children until after the war."[116]

In September 1940 she had sailed nonetheless to Cape Town, and in

February 1941, hearing the news about the bombing of Swansea, she had immediately looked for a ship to travel home on. There were two ships she could have chosen, and seeing the other one sailing past her she regretted her choice, only to hear it had been sunk soon afterwards. During the eight week voyage from Capetown to Liverpool, "when shipping losses at sea through enemy action were probably at their highest", her ship, the S.S. Ulysses,[117] was obliged to keep "weaving to avoid submarines – 8 alarms in one day – bombed by a plane – but makes it."[118]

Had Vernon been with Dorothy, he may well have shared her stalwart, even jovial approach to her adventures: "In spite of the obvious dangers no-one seemed in the least afraid. I have always loved the sea, which never seemed as much of a threat as being buried by bombs or falling buildings on land." It was different, however, to think of her from afar. "*I cannot find a pattern for my fear*", he wrote, and this was wholly reflected in the long and sea-swept, musical form of his poem. The poem, he told Eliot: "took nine months, and is over three hundred lines … it is full of sea-music."[119] Vernon had also just read the poem to Dylan Thomas, who commented: "It was very nice seeing you … I loved Rilke and the scrabbling in the shrubbery and your Sea Music."[120]

Three years later, when Dylan wrote 'Ceremony after a Fire Raid', its third most musical section[121] would have unmistakeable echoes of Vernon's 'Sea-Music' in its repeated prepositions and its hypnotic, insistent rhythm. Without even knowing it, Dylan must somehow have been indebted to Vernon's earlier poem:

> *Between the appointed lips,*
> *Between death's tide and rocks which guide the ships,*
> *Between the speechless worshipper and John, the unuttered name,*
> *The dark is stricken dumb.*
> *I cannot find a pattern for my fear.*
> *Under the trumpets of your desecration,*
> *Under the dolphins of your consecration,*
> *Under the trumpets blown*
> *By winds converged on the cold cock of flame,*
> *(Brass turn-tale, screeching chanticleer,)*

I sacrifice my nightmares on a stone,
Till their blood mingles with the sun.
          (From: 'Sea-Music for my Sister Travelling' by Vernon Watkins.)

Into the organpipes and steeples
Of the luminous cathedrals,
Into the weathercocks' molten mouths
Rippling in twelve-winded circles,
Into the dead clock burning the hour
Over the urn of Sabbaths
Over the whirling ditch of daybreak
Over the sun's hovel and the slum of fire ...
          (From: 'Ceremony After a Fire Raid' by Dylan Thomas.)

Intelligence Corps

As banking was a 'reserved' profession, meaning that that employees were not allowed to leave their jobs, Vernon had so far been held back from military service. By June 1941, however, he was due to be called up, for as he understatedly told Eliot about his position in the bank: "I am not really a 'Key' man."

He revealed to Eliot, though, as we have referred to earlier, his difficult situation regarding the Intelligence Corps:

> "My difficulty about joining up is that I have already been accepted for the Intelligence Corps and as soon as I cease to be reserved (June 1st, I think) I am supposed to let the authorities know. I like making poems better than anything in the world, so I shan't like the army, but I can't very well tell them that."[122]

The motorcycle problem hadn't gone away, and Dylan was still worrying and laughing about it in May 1941. When Vernon was struggling with alternative titles for his first book, Dylan wrote: "we must see you before your new 'Confession of a Dirt-Track Rider'." At the end of May Vernon at last plucked up the courage to tell the authorities the task was beyond him, telling Eliot: "I've turned down the Intelligence Corps offer as I don't want to ride a motor-bike".[123] Dylan was delighted: "I'm glad you wrote, telling the officials you can only just turn on a bathroom tap. Be a censor: pry and erase. Don't be a cyclist or a parachutist or a mine-tester … or the first man on the *very* edge of Dover cliffs."[124]

"Gratitude of a Leper"
Letters to T.S. Eliot

Throughout this time, Vernon was in continual correspondence with Eliot regarding the publication of his first book.

Vernon's hopes that Faber might publish his Ballad of the Mari Lwyd soon after his first meeting with Eliot, in May 1940, had not materialized. "It was a great disappointment not to have the poem printed then",[125] he told Eliot in July. Eliot was far from discouraging, however, about the ballad, leading Watkins to write in October: "*Your last remark was 'There is something queer about it', which I like better than any criticism, however favourable. I would like very much for it to be published this Christmas. Is it possible?*"[126] Eliot asked Watkins to make a varied selection of his poems to accompany the Ballad and told him this might be published by Spring.[127] Watkins replied with his usual combination of profundity and bumbling naïveté. He wrote: "*I have now made the selection. They are all poems of the soul. I find I cannot write about anything else*". He added that one difficulty in creating a selection had been his great number of drafts, in which his final version was often hidden: "*it was not easy for me to find the poems I wanted because I so often forget to throw away the drafts; in fact two of the poems I'm sending I have been looking for for six days and only just found.*"[128] Watkins was definite, however, that there was nothing haphazard about his selection. He wanted the poems: "*all included and preferably in that order. I chose what seemed to me the precise number of poems to form a unity of their own, and to balance the Ballad as it stands.*"[129] On December 9th, Eliot told Watkins: "I have now satisfied myself that I like your poems; it remains to try to persuade others to like them too"[130] and on March 28th 1941 Eliot confirmed that Faber would publish the book in this form.

Six months "to arrive where we started from"

If all this had proceeded swiftly enough, it took Eliot and Watkins *six months* to agree upon the book's title. This seemingly simple issue led to something like a metaphysical and critical sparring contest between the younger and the older poet.

Watkins's first choice – *Ballad of Mari Lwyd and Other Poems* – was rejected by Eliot in December. A series of other rejected titles followed: *Poems; The Music in the Eyes; Griefs of the Sea; These Leaves are Numbered; Half-Way Histories*. Eliot suggested *Words for the Dead*, which Watkins in turn rejected, saying: "*it suggests a séance – the very opposite to my meaning.*" He elaborated on what his own meaning was: "*That the dead give most to a man and produce the most generous love in him I am certain; and a true conception of the living can only be illuminated by that love.*"[131] He stated matter-of-factly: "Practical men serve the living, but poets serve the dead." Watkins then seemingly casually threw in: "Would you like an entirely different title like *Gratitude of a Leper*?"

Two days later he revealed that *Gratitude of a Leper* had not been such a casual suggestion after all: "*You are sure to see the tremendous implications of this title ... I hope you'll say Yes.*"[132] The title was that of a profoundly confessional poem Watkins had recently written, connecting his spiritually transformative experience thirteen years previously with the story of the ten lepers healed by Christ, of whom only one returned to express his gratitude:[133]

> *Since but for Christ, my body would be in earth*
> *Thirteen years, as men count on calendars,*
> *And a thousand eternities in each moment as I must count on the soul,*
> *I exult ...* [134]

When Eliot was unimpressed, Watkins put it down to Eliot's limitations, which he had spoken of to Francis: "*Eliot says that human beings can only bear a very little of reality but I think man is designed to bear a great deal intuitively and very little rationally.*"[135] He now told Eliot himself that perhaps his title described too intense a reality: "*I remember your saying that human beings can bear very little reality, and from that point of view perhaps a negative, impersonal and general title is better than the intensely positive and real title I have chosen."* "If you want a general title", proffered Watkins, "I can only think of The Turning of the Stars",[136] above which Eliot or someone else at Faber's scrawled 'NO'. Eliot somewhat exasperatedly wrote: "I am writing a final appeal for an inspiration from you. I am so sorry about this protracted agony."[137]

Dylan Thomas, who was privy to the potential absurdity of all this, chimed in: *"Any more about your leprous collection? Perhaps the volume should be surgically bound? I do hope it comes out this summer, just before the gas."*[138]

Despite Dylan jokingly and Eliot seriously telling Vernon that in the poetic culture reigned over by the likes of Auden and Spender the "leper" title would be disastrous, Vernon's certainty about it grew and grew:

> "sales or no sales, 'Gratitude of a Leper' is the best title for it. I am as sure of it as Baudelaire was of 'Les Fleurs du Mal'.
> I can see the objections of your sales committee. My own instinct is that, after an initial recoil from the title, the public would come round to it … In an age of unbelief it is important to have belief; I have belief, and it seems to me important to state it."

He added for good measure: *"I do not feel contemporary with Auden, Spender, Macneice or Day Lewis, all of whose poetry I dislike. Yeats has been my great tutor."*[139]

In June Watkins made a peace offering, saying that if the poem 'Prime Colours' might be included, the book could be called: *Friends and Enemies*. Eliot agreed and sent the proofs to Watkins, only to be told: "After reading the proofs I don't find *Friends and Enemies* a satisfactory title. I am sorry to disappoint you again."[140] Which brought them back to *Gratitude of a Leper* – although Vernon now saw its one failing: "*The fault in the leper's title is that it points too recurrently to the author."*

Eliot and Faber's seized on this tiny chink in the Leper's armour and returned to the very first title Watkins had suggested. On June 21st Eliot wrote to Watkins: *"my committee has now come back to the beginning of things* and voted decisively for THE BALLAD OF THE MARI LWYD and Other Poems as the title. I hope that it will not grieve you to return to your first love."[141] Watkins immediately replied: *"how terribly glad I am that you & the committee have, after all, chosen the original 'Mari Lwyd' title for the book. I am sure that it is the best title."*[142]

Whether coincidentally or not, it was at this exact time that Eliot wrote his first draft of 'Little Gidding', telling of the need: "to arrive where we started/ And know the place for the first time".[143]

The Dry Salvages
"The only criticism I can make"

All that remained was for Watkins to try and pass across to Eliot what he had learned through eventually rejecting *Gratitude of a Leper*.

Watkins had asked (on June 16th) if he might see Eliot's recently written poem *The Dry Salvages* (the third of the *Four Quartets*.) Eliot sent him a copy and Watkins wrote back on July 1st: "I thought I would just say, on very thin perishable paper, how much I love the new poem 'The Dry Salvages'." After expressing his praises he added that he had but one small criticism to make – that at one point Eliot *drew attention to himself* – through the words "I have said before".[144]

Watkins spoke as one religious or metaphysical poet to another:

"There's nothing wrong in this ... Yet I'm almost certain that in a poem like this it breaks the devotion. A poem is a supreme act of faith. The great discovery is that all tends to humility, and the great task is to revise all the processes of time which in the old days led up to fame and faith's antithesis – reputation. I think your parenthetical phrase tends to suspend the process of faith in the poem while there is a re-entry of the spectre of fame. You are, in that half-line, bringing an audience back. It is better to speak to nobody. The audience will always hear."[145]

Hard Times for Dylan

Though Vernon had not yet had his first book published, whereas Dylan Thomas was by now a well-known figure, their fortunes in many ways could hardly have been more contrasting. While Vernon was teaching T.S. Eliot about the self-renunciation demanded of the artist, Dylan was struggling with the compromises needed in order to sell his work: "My prosebook's going well, but I dislike it. It's the only really dashed-off piece of work I remember doing ... It's indecent and trivial."[146] Financially, Dylan was obliged to write beggingly to Vernon: "See if you can squeeze another drop from your borrowed-to-death body ... I hope I am spoiling nothing. It is just that I am useless, & have nowhere to turn."[147]

On August 22nd Vernon finally received his military call-up, demanding that he leave for the Air Force on September 4th. Whatever difficulties this might involve, he had an inner acceptance of the circumstances of his life that Dylan could no longer even dream of. Six days later, on August 28th, Dylan wrote to Vernon the most desperate of all the letters he sent him. His fortunes had reached their lowest point:

"We've been having an awful time, and I have felt like killing myself ... I would have written to you long before, but have been too miserable even to write Poem at the top of a clean page and then look out of the window at the millionaires catching buses. Are you, I don't hope, in the army? Soon perhaps ... I will be able to write to you about all the things we have always had, and will always have, to talk about together. We are prisoners now in a live melodrama and all the long villains with three halfpence are grinning in at us through the bars. Not the best bars either. Bless you, DYLAN."[148]

Publication of Ballad of the Mari Lwyd

Ballad of the Mari Lwyd and Other Poems was finally published in October 1941. On receiving his complimentary copies Vernon wrote to express his thanks to Eliot and everyone at Faber: *"the result seems altogether beautiful.* **Was lange wird, wird endlich schön.** *I never felt that proverb so strongly as now."*[149] So at home was Vernon with the depth and wealth of true German culture that he would have seen nothing remotely unusual in celebrating his book, while England was at war with Germany, with a German proverb.

The book reviews that appeared were, for the most part, extraordinarily positive. *The Spectator* announced: "How rare it is to discover a new poet."[150] Henry Reed, a couple of years later, but before

Watkins's second book had appeared, wrote: "*Vernon Watkins I have difficulty writing about. I find him at times very hard to understand, sometimes impossible; yet if a premature judgement may be allowed, I believe him to be the one poet of his generation who holds out unequivocal promise of greatness.*"[151]

Vernon Watkins himself, predictably perhaps, but genuinely, would not allow himself to be waylaid by any thoughts of fame or cultural achievement. He wrote a sonnet: 'On the Publication of my Book', stating that he could not respond to any such critical judgements:

> *For every moment is a judgement, not*
> *An envious court where witnesses may lie,*
> *But the last judgement, the last pitch of thought*
> *When all that is not love must surely die (.)*[152]

On November 17th he wrote in a similar spirit to Peter Hellings: "I hate the publicity I'm getting now because it's linked with all kinds of misconceptions. Soon I'll be disguised in an Air Policeman's helmet ... There's no public. There are only individual contacts ... my book was really a gift to me. I've nothing to be proud of."[153] He wrote on the same day to Elizabeth Iorwerth, who had played the dancer in his Masque: "I'm terribly glad the book has come out in spite of the war, but I would gladly do without publicity if only it would otherwise reach the individuals I want it to reach ... One has to be like a child always ... There's only the thread which binds us to the roots that are in death, and the generosity of the dead makes us infinitely humble."[154]

He was 35. It was at this age that Wordsworth had completed *Intimations of Immortality*, after which he had never been able to regain the poetic heights of his earlier years. Coleridge's lyrical genius had also left him by this age. Shelley had died aged 29 and Keats at 25. By the time Dylan Thomas was 35 he had written all but three of his *Collected Poems*. Yet Vernon Watkins, with the appearance of his first book, was only at the beginning of his work. Six further substantial volumes of his poetry would appear in his life-time, three would be brought out posthumously, and his complete work is still far from having been published. All the poetry quoted in this first part of his biography has therefore been taken either from his juvenilia or from his earliest published work.

"Almost immediately after the publication of this first book of poems I left Swansea for the R.A.F."
Dylan Thomas had told Vernon: "Be an R.A.F. officer" – telling him this would give him his best chance, within the limitations of military life, of continuing to write poetry. Vernon attempted to follow Dylan's advice but was turned down as an officer and was made to choose between being an R.A.F. policeman or a cook. Having hardly cooked anything in his life the choice was simple. As he told the probably bemused T.S. Eliot: "I shall be a policeman, which, as you said, will be 'disagreeable', but this is the only job open to me in the ranks as I have no mechanical ability."[155]

In December 1941 he therefore left Swansea, the bank and his parents' cliff-top home in Gower and was sent to Weston-super-Mare for an 8-week training course. His sister Dorothy describes both the change this meant for him and his unchanging character:

"He left the warmth of a comfortable home in the icy winter to share a freezing Nissen hut with forty other recruits ... For the first time in his life he was thrown into the close company of men drawn from every sort of background and occupation ... He continued, of course, to carry a book with him on all occasions. Once ... a well-meaning but patronising padre had asked him what he was reading. He retired discomforted when Vernon replied mildly that he was reading a book about the excavations at Ur."[156]

The cold and perhaps the shock led to him developing asthma and bronchitis, which he had never previously suffered from and hardly surprisingly he found the training "very dreary".[157] He was, however, extraordinarily resilient and would never lose either his humour or his poetry. As he had told T.S. Eliot on receiving his final call-up orders: *"Wherever I go I shall try to continue with what I am doing; I've always believed that everything is possible."*[158]

APPENDIX

Unpublished Poems by Vernon Watkins

Repton Poems

The Flower

Wouldst know the secret of our Life, my love?
– Life was a strange and lovely flower, which grew
Out of a magic seed, that God once threw
Upon the sleeping earth. And, from above,
He watched its petals tenderly unfold, –
Each faery leaflet timidly uncurled,
To greet the mystic glory of the world, –
And in their midst a passionate heart of gold.

The little flower looked up to God, and smiled …
But soon its head, – lovely, and petal-crowned -,
Drooped sadly down to its untimely end.
Wouldst know the tragedy of life, my friend?
Life was a seed which fell on stony ground, … –
And all we know of Heaven's a little child!

As

As I walked slowly past the little trees, –
As I trod softly o'er the faery grass, –
As I among the whispering flowers did pass,
And heard the murmurs of the tender breeze; –
As I looked up into the dreamy skies,
And as I heard the anger of the sea
Bursting against the rocks despairingly,
And surging back again with sullen cries; –
As I beheld the red sun disappear,
And as I saw, in their white purity,
The pale stars peeping slowly through the drear,
Darkening curtains of infinity, – ...
I forgot surplices and gowns uncouth,
And, for one blissful moment, saw the truth.   10/11/23

The above two poems were published anonymously in 'The Reptonian' at the end of 1923, when Vernon Watkins was 17. They are his first printed poems.

I stood in dark, sweet-scented solitude
Upon a little world ... The moon had kissed
The drooping flowers to sleep, in silken mist,
– Where they lay pale in soft dreams Heaven-imbued.
And, as I mused, the wild impassioned sound
– The swirling music of a bursting sea –
Fell on my ears ... and yet most tenderly

The moonlight smiled upon the sorrowful ground.
And through the mystery of the tremulous sky,
I heard the magic voice of Poesy,
– A might voice crying out into the Night,
– Yet a sad music stilled ... And in the light
Of the tearful moon I saw her lovely head
Uplifted for a song ... but silent, dead ...

V.P.W.

Published in 'The Reptonian' in March 1924.

Cambridge poems
Immortality

Since in the end we see
No fallacy, my friend,
In Time's enormous scheme
To outwit man and cheat him of his dream.

Though at the last in dust
We put our trust, the Past
Was wonderful and true:
Future we know not, but the Past we knew.

We understand: our fears
Count not the years God planned;
Yet could you call man blind,
Since he o'erlooks the hidden light behind?

We live one day, to learn
Beauty must turn to clay,
And Love, that lit our dark,
Flicker and tremble to a little spark.

And who shall prove that death
Steals not the breath of love
For ever? – or assume
That someone somewhere shall this light relume?

Yet who could be content
With argument so free
Of fancy? Who denies
Life's but a little paragraph of lies?

Ah, kind your rest if you,
Who only knew the best
From what had died in youth,
Yield to a stronger foe, the Unknown Truth.

Better unproved – the things
To which man clings, than loved
And lost again, for aye –
We die to live, e'en as we live to die.

V.P. Watkins

Written in January, 1925, when Watkins was 18. Published in: *Anthology of Contemporary Cambridgeshire and Hertfordshire Poetry.* London, Fowler Wright. 1928.

Stone Love

Since life goes over and the joy
The lover feels for blue-eyed boy,
Since vital beauty swiftly dies,
Beauty of cheek, of hair, of eyes,

Let me spend my fleeting hours
Entreating these unfaithful flowers
To vow their love before they part,
Restore faith to a faithless heart,

O bring me rather some rare cast,
Fair image of a fairer Past,
A passion carved in whitest stone
– Delight that lives when we are gone.

– A Grecian boy, a lover's head
Recovered from the dreamless dead,
Monuments of some buried lust,
Whose very beauty stirs their dust.

Show me but this, and I will swear
My model had more perfect hair;
And gaze in ravished, slow surprise,
Knowing his eyes were lovelier eyes.

February 1925.

Cardiff, 1929 – "three years ... war with time"
Document of a Live Poet

Examine me. I am the poet, sir,
Have known the change and then the counterchange;
Have seen the fresh front of desire cast down,
Have seen the swift light of the rose decay
To sepia, and lament that evil change;
Then genius, like the witless life of seeds,
Spring from the very shrouds where pomp was laid.
I set my heart on immortality,
Walked in a sacred darkness three long years,
Trusting no light but man's historic gleam
Secretly bent toward some more brilliant day
Where the reared walls of evil shall be cursed,
And these heroic pains unmastered reach
The death of joys and the true life of joy;
Where the slow motive seasons shall stand still
And a great trumpet summon from their tombs
Their joy, their childhood, and the loves of men.
How did I fare? I straight will tell you true.
First felt I like an exile from my kind,
Thereat grew proud and therewith reticent.
As on a map that men long hence will con
I saw the world, the legend of the towns;
Saw men by hate and their own scorn betrayed,
By all the vague deformities of fear,
Their lives misspent, seduced by lust of gold
Or lust of knowledge, scornful to be won;
Until at last, being tired of their false robes,
Their rustling lives were beckoned into graves.
All these I saw, then looked across the sea,
And felt a thrill more deep than lovers' songs.
It was the birds, my lovers who consoled
My single soul on their neglected shore.
Silent upon the craggy rocks I watched

Infinite azure cut by finite wings.
Then was my spirit spellbound like a shell,
Through which there flows the searhymes' hungry song,
So many sayings crowded to my lips
True exclamations of love's votaries
Heard from the oracles of antique verse.
Alas, my life was forfeit to regret
My deepest passion dedicate to pain.
For still life's counterfeit was in my eye
Though, in the stillness, in the wake of wings,
Purged for a moment by the lovely sea.
So three years long lasted my war with time.

Would you hear further? Pitched beyond reclaim
Of things that seemed to bear the brand of doom
The flowers, the birds, my brothers in farewell,
I drew my strength up like a proud deep wave
And cast myself upon the feet of life.
Frost-flowers upon the window, deep blue sky
Life surged through me, that ancient alphabet.
More clear, more true than it had ever been.
Life glowed to me, its falsehood all cast out.

(Handwriting similar to 1929 poems).

'Sailors on the Moving Land' –
Vernon Watkins and Dylan Thomas (1941)

FOOTPRINTS AT OYSTERMOUTH
(For a friend on the eve of war)

I sing the eternal tryst, the trivial date:
The morning's razor-blades, the shears of Fate.
The last words of a mummy wound
With casual daylight grow profound
And glitter like a letter on a plate.

Who can discern the distance crossed by these
Whose fingers cherish language night will freeze
To starry traffic overhead
Beyond the oysters' shifting bed
Where trains bring rumour to the tunnelled seas?

Footprints know imminent midnight out of reach.
The sun divides men, separating each
With aura, shade and centre
Which, if time's footsteps enter,
They frighten seagulls rising from the beach.

What may be found at dusk that hides so much?
Where there are jostling crowds no two can touch,
Yet after dusk there may be given,
Falling from sacramental heaven,
A word like driftwood drowning men may clutch.

And I have seen at night a street light bleach
Expectant features comfort could not reach.
Who knows what feet, hurrying through day's delaying,
Pausing at dusk, may stumble on a saying
That only night could teach?

A cry at dusk, the cry of children playing
Their game of hide-and-seek across the pavings
Running to hide, one staying
Counting, staying by the wall with anchorite's eyes,
Counting, weighing
Green Earth, calm green above the sea's ravings;
Walled from the edge of that estranging tide,
The young feet dancing kiss
Thought, and the tombstone's quarrelling silences;
They scatter, they dancing are still, where the watcher flies,
Pausing. Then is
The grinning skull at rest, and the tomb's engravings
Revised, in the tongue of birth. O the leaping foot
Is light upon miserhood,
And the night is sold for pennies.

Sitting in rows with manna crumbs to eat,
The people wait. Each doorstep is a seat.
War and its fires leave nothing vacant yet.
Through the lopped trees the dividing sun is bright.
Levelling the pavings in the way of tombs
Under the ragged ravens of Elijah Street.
It speaks the common language of the unwrinkled sheet,
Then drops. Deep darkness looms,
Rising. Then, then, through night
Men touch; they climb the eerie parapet.
Nothing is changed; the paving-stones are white;
But the stones move towards them when they meet.

It is not knowledge makes the night more grand.
Softly, as the waves reach forward to the land,
Compassion understands the sighs
Of people swimming to the eyes;
What night reveals day cannot understand.

The little deaths in the fishmonger's move,
Images of distracted love;
Then one man hurries on the theft
Of following feet, and one is left
In masking darkness with his robber's glove.

'I have a bicycle that is not mine.'

    'The round moon racing through the clouds is fine.'

'I have seen Lamprey's marble crossed by eels.'

    'Must we be mastered by the moving wheels?'

So to the inner smoke, the quarrelling air,
Angry jolting of a chair,
Edge of the darkness' knife; confessions of despair.

This water-skin has made all eyes oblique.
Another door, another door they seek,
Or tilted barrel turning round
To spill the questions of the drowned.
Yes, there are words the living cannot speak.

The bitter mermaid sang of her worst.
Neither throat could slake its thirst.

The crawling lobster moves about,
Then the eye of foam goes out.

Two sailors on the moving land,
By the deceiving sea, we met;
And the salt mermaid cried:
Give what you hide into each other's hand,
Give what you hide.

We passed an eye as talkers pass a saying,
And where our seats were set
In smoke of bitten cigarette
Circling extinguished words
Hauling the room of cords,
The hand was giving and the heart was praying,
The heart was giving and the hand was praying.
'We are caught in that encircling sea
And whirlpool of philosophy,
And I can feel that someone pulls the net.'

The bitter mermaid sang. We heard
The screaming woman-breasted bird.
Tritons of the sea shed tears,
But you, with terror in your head,
Shook philosophy out of your ears,
Snatched a great light, and said:

'I have a cage of darkness, hiding
The great white innocent bird, the albatross,
And where the waters toss,
This way and that way riding
White horses of the cradle or the fosse
To wordless islands and the One-Eyed Man.
I know the horrible gulf from which we ran.
Speak, if you know the place where speech began.'

'Flying with that hilarious foam for hair,
Their manes of mystery,
Hooves of the guilty sea
Cross and re-cross, words that deny a word,
Under the still, the steady-moving bird,
The cry of birth, the soul's cry answered late
In the eyes' word the dying would not spare.
To-night all words are deluged from the slate:
When will the shell close on the beak of air?'

AN EXACT MYSTERY

The gannet dropping on his bait
Hits the water, and is late.

Two eyes upon one side of a fish
Pronounce a dead fear and an unborn wish,
But speculation in the deep, dark sea is devilish.
O who would speculate or compare
Objects in the upper air?
In the abyssal deeps, all light is darkness there.
Moving, and at a loss for words,
Inside the sea-doors, near the moving hands,
We felt the labyrinth of the herds
Arrested, hesitant, like a clock run-down,
Moving to no fixed place, yet in that rout
Fine in their praise of lands,
Slow, docile giants with a bison's urge,
Met from cockcrow and mating-shout,
Their faces cut with diamonds,
Crosses of grief, betraying bonds,
Yet moving slowly like a town
Barnacled with ruin,
Moving enormous like a waterspout
Among the moving surge.

Against the raft of this rocked shore
Sea-dragons, monsters, tower and pounce;
They drain the blood of every door;
Shrinking from the scalloped shore
They drink the mountains, ounce by ounce.

A treadmill floor, London and Townhill falling
Mirrored in glasses lifted on a tray,
Joined with the drowning voices answering, calling,
Part of the evening flooding Swansea Bay,
Lives for the fisher-bird that feeds on loss,
Guarding the surface that no mind can cross.

Multitudinous darkness, the held flight
Of sailors' parrots that talk all tongues,
Loot and traffic of the night,
Golden rings and ladder-rungs
Of embarkation in the dark,
Dropped from the safety of the quay
To shipboard in an unknown sea,
A talking madhouse where night raves
Pulled by the force of wind and waves
Beating the door, the door and floor of dark,
Beating and meeting, meeting
The wave returning, beating
The windows of the ark,
The huge seas rising, huger seas retreating.

Time. Time. Time. Time.
Thunderbolts of death and birth.
Thunderbolts of rut and rout.
How many from the contemporary tomb
Who had found warmth and comfort here, stepped out
To the stampeding Earth.

So from Oystermouth's nets of Wales,
Followed by the fishes' tails
Past laverbread inside a sack
Hitched to a pole on bent man's back,
Past barrels, mussel-beds and creels,
Guiding ungovernable wheels,
Past alleys where a cat looked out,
Vanishing then, and made more black
That entrance when our eyes looked back,
Guiding our wheels we came to grief
Where the dull trees were lopped of every leaf;
Then climbed through darkness where you danced about,
Gay as a babbling thief.

Did I remark again the moon was round,
Or see the castle floating on its ground,
And that so excellent a sphere
Had somehow put us out of gear
So that we staggered towards the moon
Struggling with wheels? Soon, soon,
That circle in a spinning reel
Came back to meet us, overtook
All we had learned in life or book,
Zigzagged and flung us flat across the wheel.

Two with a bicycle, two men with horns.
Two shadowed quarrellers pushing two moons.

And morning, morning, morning followed fleet;
The playing pavings, gathering flying feet,
Hammered the dark of eyelids closed beneath their sunny sheet.

Sleep and retreat from oracles. Midnight,
An anchorite praying,
Refuses dawn, refuses to-morrow.
The lips stammer against the light.
Sleep holds them, forming the oracle, saying:
'Able to touch'. I woke, saying:
'I was able to touch his sorrow.'

First begun in 1941.
Published in 1949 under the title: 'Sailors on the Moving Land'
in: 'Life and Letters Today' (61).
The above is a revised, unpublished version from 1956.
Vernon Watkins did not attempt to publish it in this form.

Endnotes

ABBREVIATIONS:

'**DW**' **refers to:** *Vernon Phillips Watkins – The Early Years* – Dorothy Watkins. (Privately printed.)
'**GW/JT**' **refers to:** *Vernon Watkins on Dylan Thomas and Other Poets and Poetry*. Edited by Gwen Watkins and Jeff Towns. (Parthian 2013.)
'**NLW MS**' **refers to:** National Library of Wales Manuscripts.

CHAPTER ONE
BIRTH AND EARLY YEARS (1906-1920)

1. *South Wales Daily Post*, Wednesday 27th June and Thursday 28th June, 1906.
2. On June 27th, 2006, the BBC article 'An earthquake in Wales' described the epicentre as having been offshore from Swansea and said of the earthquake itself: "At 5.2 on the Richter scale it remains one of the UK's larger tremors, and was felt over much of south Wales." The day after the quake, on 28th June, 1906, the South Wales Daily Post spoke of it in more mysterious terms: "The extraordinary fact about Wednesday's 'quake' is that none of the seismographic apparati in the Principality appear to have recorded an earthquake at all. This is all the more surprising as the disturbance was so palpable – and no mere tremor – and so generally felt."
3. From 15,000 tons a year at the beginning of the 1870s, to a mere 11 tons in 1885.
4. Thomas (born 1860), Evan, Catherine, Mary, Sarah Ann, Jane, David, William (1st August, 1872), Daniel, Nan, Hannah (born 1877).
5. Evan Watkins "was widely known and greatly respected in the locality, and had taken an active part in public affairs, having been for several years chairman of the Pentrych School Board and a member of the Board of Guardians, in which capacities he did excellent service to the parish. Indeed it will be difficult to find a successor with such a thorough knowledge of parochial matters and so devoted to the public welfare. He was a staunch Noncorformist, and at the Bethlehem Congregational Church, Gwaelodygarth (of which church he was the secretary and a deacon) his loss will be keenly felt.") Obituary in *South Wales Echo*, 2nd December, 1895. 'Death of Mr. Evan Watkins, Tynewydd, Pentrych.'
6. From interviews by the author with Gwen Watkins, 2000.
Gwen Watkins added that Vernon Watkins's friend, Eric Falk, who was a lawyer, said William Watkins "had the best judgement he had known of any man in his life. He thought he should have been a judge." Gwen Watkins also described the influence on Vernon Watkins of his father's moral character and of his giving up his hopes of studying law in order to provide for his siblings: "His father's sacrifice, in so completely giving up everything he wanted, to look after not only his loved brothers

and sisters, but his hated stepmother as well – I think Vernon felt this very deeply – this tradition of integrity and sacrifice."

7 See Conway Thomas, 'Three Nesting Doves' in: 'A Carmarthenshire Antiquary', 2002.
8 The family had 3 womenservants and 2 menservants.
9 She was in all probability sent by Mary Williams, the widow of Dylan Thomas's great uncle Gwilym Marles, who ran the school during Sarah Phillips's time there. An undated prose note by Vernon Watkins states: "*Mrs Marles Thomas*, widow of the bard, was the Principal of the Girls' Collegiate School, Carmarthen, which my mother attended Kindergarten and Upper School. (Mother went on to London and Germany.) … Most progressive and scholarly woman, an ardent believer in Woman's Suffrage, and published, among other things, a Chronology of British History from the time of Egbert." (Jeff Towns Archive.)
10 Foreword to *The Golden Age and Dream Days* by Kenneth Grahame. Signet Classics. 1964.
11 From: *Twentieth Century Authors, A Biographical Dictionary*. Ed. Stanley J. Kunitz. (H.W. Wilson Company, 1955). "Vernon Phillips Watkins." Page 1052.
12 Letter to Meic Stephens, 29 Jan, 1967. NLW MS 2246E.
13 From: 'Introduction to a Reading at Carmarthen: 8th February, 1967. NLW Mss: 22480E.
14 'A Note on my own Poetry'. NLW: 22480E.
15 William Watkins was manager of Lloyds Bank in Bridgend between 1902 and 1908. He then became manager at Llanelli between 1908 and 1912. Soon after Vernon's younger sister Dorothy was born in Bridgend, in 1909, the family must have followed William Watkins to Llanelli.
16 From the poem 'Returning to Goleufryn' in *The Lady with the Unicorn*.
17 From 'Swansea Poems' (Gwen Watkins archive.) (Draft version of 'The Place and the Poem' – in *Vernon Watkins on Dylan Thomas and Other Poets and Poetry*. Edited by Gwen Watkins and Jeff Towns. (Parthian 2013.)
18 'Coal'. Unpublished poem by Vernon Watkins. NLW. Mss. 23756E.
19 Foreword to *The Golden Age and Dream Days* by Kenneth Grahame. Signet Classics. 1964.
20 *Vernon Phillips Watkins* – The Early Years – Dorothy Watkins. (Privately printed.)
21 John Prichard. 'Swansea and the Arts.' 1949 T Llên Publications. October 2000.
22 From: *Twentieth Century Authors, A Biographical Dictionary*. Ed. Stanley J. Kunitz. (H.W. Wilson Company, 1955). "Vernon Phillips Watkins." Page 1052.
23 'Poetry and Experience' – in *Vernon Watkins on Dylan Thomas and Other Poets and Poetry*. Edited by Gwen Watkins and Jeff Towns. (Parthian 2013.)
24 Unpublished MS – NLW – 22484E.
25 Marjorie Witts – 'Three Cheers for St. Anne's'.
26 'Swansea and the Arts' – Ty Llen Publications.
None of the family were clearly aware, either then or afterwards, of Sir Francis Younghusband's geopolitical activities, both in Tibet, where he is held to have been responsible for the deaths of hundreds of Tibetans in 1904, and in relation to the First World War. Unlike the Watkins family, Younghusband would have been completely aware of the outbreak of war, being a close friend of Lord Curzon, and

later founding the 'Fight for Right' campaign, set up in order to rally recruits for the war.

27 These Belgian refugees had been able to link with the sizeable community of Belgians already living in Swansea, which owed its origins to the metal-workers who had moved there to work in the copper industry in the 19th Century. (Swansea in the 18th and 19th centuries had been nicknamed 'Copperopolis'. At the peak of the Swansea copper industry [around 1820] an almost unbelievable "90% of the copper-smelting capacity of Britain was based within twenty miles of the city". See: http://www.channel4.com/programmes/time-team/articles/all/swansea-copperopolis.)

28 http://www.swanseasound.co.uk/news/local/wartime-refugees-remembered-at-swansea-library/

29 Accounts differ. Dorothy Watkins, Vernon's sister, who also appeared in the pageant, says Vernon represented Scotland. Gwen Watkins describes him dancing an 'Irish jig'.

30 Gwen Watkins, *Portrait of a Friend*, p.10.

31 DW.

32 Marjorie Witts – 'Three Cheers for St. Anne's'.

33 'From My Loitering' in *The Ballad of the Mari Lwyd*.

34 From the poem 'Returning to Goleufryn' in *The Lady with the Unicorn*.

35 "Cwondonkin Park is as it was when Dylan Thomas wrote his poem The Hunchback in the Park, except that the reservoir is dry; it has changed little since I, too, played in it as a child." In: 'Swansea' – published in The Texas Quarterly, 1961.

36 The quotations related to Watkins's experiences at the Uplands Cinema are taken from his poem: 'Elegy on the Heroine of Childhood – *in memory of Pearl White*' and his prose notes on the poem. He asks in the poem: 'Why was I left? What stairs had I to climb?', again referring to his being 'left' as a child, but also commenting on how near he was at the Uplands Cinema to the steep hill of Cwmdonkin Drive, which he might, hypothetically, even then have climbed and so encountered the infant Dylan Thomas.

37 There were two battles of Arras – the first in October 1914, the month that Dylan Thomas was born and the second in 1917, where the poet Edward Thomas was killed. The first is the correct one in time, but the second was probably the one that made Arras so significant for Vernon.

38 'Swansea' – essay by Vernon Watkins – Texas Quarterly, 1961.

39 'Notes for Cambridge Talk' – NLW MS 22480E.

40 *Twentieth Century Authors, A Biographical Dictionary*. Edited Stanley Kunitz. (H.W. Wilson Company, 1955) p.1052.

41 "Before he was ten ... he was a well established customer in Swansea's three bookshops, where he would spend hours at a time. Very soon all our presents to our parents ... were beautifully bound (volumes of poetry) in leather or suede, lovingly chosen by Vernon." Dorothy Watkins. (DW).

42 'Poetry and the Audience' – December 1963. NLW MS 22480E.

43 Ibid.

44 Tyttenhanger House was built in 1411 by the Abbot of St. Albans and remained in the possession of the Abbey until the dissolution. Cardinal Wolsey, as Abbot of St.

Albans, was at one point in charge of the house and Henry VIII and his Queen stayed in it for a fortnight in 1528 during the 'sweating sickness'. At the dissolution the house was acquired by Thomas Pope, whose neighbour, Nicholas Bacon, father of Sir Francis Bacon, he termed his "most true and assured friend." The house then passed to his descendant Thomas Pope Blount, who was knighted by James 1 at his accession in 1603.

45 *The Arms of the Infinite*, Christopher Barker, (Pomona, 2006). pp. 235-237.

46 'Introduction'. Feb 18th, 1953. (NLW. Mss. 22480E.)
He said in the same vein: "I thought Wordsworth's 'Prelude' very good; but I discovered, by counting the pages, that Longfellow's 'Tales of a Wayside Inn' was better. I had still to reckon up 'Don Juan', 'In Memoriam' and 'The Ring and the Book', when I was already engaged in writing long poems myself in a note-book of epic dimensions. Here I must record that a rival poem of Tennyson's 'Idylls of the King', which was intended to be one line longer, was left unfinished at my prep. School, to which I went when I was eleven, – a sad loss to English literature." (A Note on My Poetry – 22480E.)
There was, however, at least some variety in his writing: "But I didn't give all my time to my unfinished epic there. I remember coming home on holiday in the train and showing a man an alliterative poem I had made. He told me I should learn Greek." (Dec. '59?) NLW. MSS. 22480E.

47 'Poetry and Experience' – in GW/JT.

48 Elsewhere Watkins called this 'Arthurian epic' from his time at Tyttenhanger: "the most boring poem on record". Very little indeed, though, in Watkins's writing life would not later resurface in some new form. In 1955 he wrote the hauntingly beautiful poem 'Camelot' – of only 10 stanzas – which perhaps brings his childhood attempt to completion. 'Camelot' is the only poem Watkins ever wrote on an Arthurian theme, and begins: "She that was a queen stood here/ Where the kestrel hovers./ He was resting by the weir:/ He and she were lovers." (*In Cypress and Acacia*.)

CHAPTER TWO

REPTON (1920–1924)

1 Aldous Huxley, who also taught at Repton for a term, was of the same opinion, commenting: "Not until I taught at Repton did I realize the awful significance of the word bourgeoisie." *Victor Gollancz – A Biography* – Ruth Dudley Edwards; (Faber 2012); p. 102.

2 Geoffrey Fisher was "initiated" into the Old Reptonian Freemasonic Lodge on 11th January 1916 when he was 28 years old, at Freemasons' Hall, London. He was made a Master Mason on 9 January 1917. This was "the start to a long and continued successful Masonic career." Fisher also served as Grand Chaplain in the United Grand Lodge of England. (Masonic Quarterly Magazine. Issue 18, July 2006. 'Archbishop Fisher: A Godly Man and a Brother.' Available online.)

3 Somervell added: "and *what fun* it all was!" Quoted in: *Victor Gollancz* – Ruth Dudley Edwards. p. 124.

ENDNOTES 243

4   Ibid. p.123.
5   Ibid. p. 103. In this remarkable chapter on Gollancz's time at Repton (in the excellent biography of him by Ruth Dudley Edwards) there is much else on Gollancz's views and writings on education, based on his experience at Repton, such as: " There is only one way in which an older man can help a younger so to free himself; and that is by fostering his sense of joy … (B)y remodelling education so as to make it a means for releasing all those stores of spiritual and intellectual energy that lie hid in a child, we shall be doing more than we could ever do otherwise to render manifest that men and women are truly created in the image of God." p. 106.
6   Ibid. p.107.
7   According to Gollancz's biographer, Dudley Edwards. Ibid. p. 102.
8   Ibid p.110. Written by Ruth Dudley Edwards – quoting Victor Gollancz ('personal egotism and greed').
9   Ibid p. 98. Guy Snape had also proposed a motion in the school debating society, stating: "in the opinion of this house the dismemberment of Germany is absolutely essential for the future peace of Europe." Gollancz and David Somervell had opposed the motion. (Ibid. p. 109.)
10 Ibid. p. 99.
11 Ibid p. 119. This was described by a contemporary, who adds: "I can well remember boys who had been … called up … coming round the bedders on their last night at Repton and shaking hands with everyone, knowing, as we also knew, that in the following term, at the … services in Chapel on Friday evenings, we might hear their names read out … in the OR casualty list for that week. Moreover, the war showed no signs of ending."
12 Old Reptonian Lodge – No. 3725. 'Two Centenaries: Repton – The Lodge and the Great War'.
    By Bro. Ian McClary. (The 81st Festival of the Public School Lodge's Council. Held at Repton School.) 10th May, 2014. Page 3. (https://www.orl.org.uk/festival/Presentation_script.pdf)
13 The turnout was five times the usual number, and the wording of the motion was that: "in the opinion of this house it is disgraceful that Conscientious Objectors, whether genuine or not, should be disfranchised." *Victor Gollancz* – RDE. p.119.
14 Nicknamed 'The Pubber'.
15 It was co-published by the Repton School Book Shop and a Charing Cross Road bookshop "specializing in revolutionary literature." The bookshop was Henderson and Sons, which earned the nickname of 'The Bomb Shop' and was seen by some as 'a Bolshevik outpost'. *Victor Gollancz* – RDE. p.121.
16 Ibid, p.124.
17 Nothing shows more clearly the significance of Repton within the religious and cultural life of England at the time than that three successive Archbishops of Canterbury were closely connected with with Repton: William Temple (1942-1944), Geoffrey Fisher (1945-1961) and Michael Ramsey (1961-1974).
18 From *BOY – Tales of Childhood* by Roald Dahl. (Puffin, 2013). pp. 194, 190 & 173. Dahl says far more than this on his experiences at Repton. He adds: "All through my school life I was appalled by the fact that masters and senior boys were allowed literally to wound other boys, and sometimes quite severely. I couldn't get over it. I

never have got over it." p. 177. (Roald Dahl attended Repton between September 1929 and 1934.)
19 *Writers of Wales – Vernon Watkins* by Roland Mathias – University of Wales Press, 1974. p.14.
20 'Autobiographical note for: Poetry and the Audience'. December 1st, 1963. NLW. MS. 22480E.
21 "When I went to Public School I stopped writing for 18 months". *Poetry and Experience*.
22 In Watkins's second term he got the 'form reward' for being first in all subjects combined and for the next four terms got distinction cards for languages. Fisher's comments on Watkins's report are from December and August 1922 respectively.
23 *Poetry and Experience*. In his 'Autobiographical note for: Poetry and the Audience' (December 1st, 1963. NLW. MS. 22480E) he wrote: "Only when I went to Repton did I stop my writing of poetry for a year; but then, after hearing a lecture on Shelley, I immediately returned to it. It possessed me more than ever before."
24 *Vernon Watkins: Some Observations on Poetry*. Ed. Jenijoy LaBelle. The Anglo-Welsh Review. Number 65. 1979. Page 103.
25 *Shelley*. Undated sonnet in: NLW MSS 22463E. Probably written at the end of Watkins's time at Repton or during his year at Cambridge.
26 'Revisited Waters – for the Quartecentenary of Repton School, founded in 1557'. In *Affinities in Collected Poems of Vernon Watkins*. (Golgonooza Press. Ipswich. 1986).
27 'As' – dated 10/11/23. In 'The Reptonian', December 1923. pp. 212–213.
28 'The Second Pressure in Poetry'. GW/JT. Page 145.
29 Eric Falk was in the same house, Hall, as Isherwood and Vernon Watkins. Falk also kept up his friendship with Christopher Isherwood and thus maintains an interesting connection between the two radically different individuals, Watkins and Isherwood.
30 Letter to Eric Falk, May 19th, 1923. (NLW)
31 By the next letter a further 'craze' had developed for the Indian spiritual poetry of Rabindranath Tagore: "A craze for Tagore has been running through the best circles." Letter to Eric Falk, June 3rd, 1923. (NLW)
32 Watkins added: "I used to criticize people so much; and now, with a few loathsome exceptions, everybody's being glorious."
33 *Isherwood: A Life Revealed*. Peter Parker. (Random House, New York, 2004). p. 56.
34 Letter to Eric Falk, July 8th, 1923. (NLW) R.T.V. was Richard Vaughan, a young boy in Watkins's house.
35 Letter to Eric Falk from Richard Sykes. (NLW) Sykes adds: "For heaven's sake tear this letter up or burn it or something. It's positively immoral." Falk kept it all his life, perhaps to ensure this little part of Watkins's story did not remain untold.
36 Letter to Eric Falk, July 8th, 1923. (NLW)
37 *Victor Gollancz* – RDE. p. 121.
38 From *Repton. An Epic*. Begun September 1928. (NLW MSS. 22445C)
39 From Winston Churchill's obituary of Rupert Brooke. Available online at: (http://exhibits.lib.byu.edu/wwi/poets/rbobituary.html)
40 From *Repton. An Epic*. Begun September 1928. (NLW MSS. 22445C) (Emphasis added.)

41 Addressing his beloved, therefore, as a "Child of Eden", he once again praises the boy's body in terms that are both physical and spiritual: "Those eyes that are the Cherubim's/ O Child of Eden, thine!/ Those limbs that are God's very limbs/ Are thoughts more great than mine." (XXI)
42 Letter to Eric Falk, 21/8/24. (NLW)
43 Dorothy Watkins writes that Watkins had "several holidays in Germany while he was at Repton", concluding: "His final stay was with a very kindly Jewish family in Nuremberg. He soon spoke German fluently and learnt to love the poetry and music of that country." Gwen Watkins only recalls Vernon Watkins describing one German holiday from Repton, to Nuremberg in 1922. Both agree about his usual absent-minded antics while travelling. Dorothy writes: "Aged sixteen and travelling abroad on his own for the first time, Vernon was so afraid of losing the £50 his father had given him that he put a wad of notes into one of his shoes. He immediately forgot all about it and hours later could not understand why one of his feet was so uncomfortable." Gwen Watkins says that the money: "was so saturated with sweat that the bank would not at first accept it."
44 Letter to Eric Falk, July 8th, 1923. (NLW)
45 Watkins's translation of Jules Laforgue's 'Song of the little hypertrophic child' dates from 1923. It is published in *Selected Verse Translations* (Enitharmon, 1977).
46 Watkins wrote, in Reptonian schoolboy language: "(E)veryone ought to regard his fag as a coming man, and not as a coming bozer (the terms are not synonymous)". Letter to Falk, 14/11/23.
47 *Hassan. The Story of Hassan of Bagdad and how he came to make the Golden Journey to Samarkand.* First published in 1922, nearly 8 years after Flecker's death in 1915, it was put on to huge success in London in September 1923. The Repton production would almost certainly have been directed by Alec Macdonald.
48 The two lovers declare: "We have heard the Trumpets of Reality that drown the vain din of the Thing that Seems. We have walked with the Friend of Friends in the Garden of the Stars, and He is pitiable to poor lovers." When they are told: "This is Sufic doctrine, and most dangerous to the State" they reply: "Then a plague on the state!"
49 Letter to Eric Falk, 5/12/23 (NLW). Watkins played the comparatively minor role of the fickle female lover, Yasmin.
50 The Reptonian. December 1923.
51 Speaking about his poems to Eric Falk, Watkins told him: "2 are going into the Reptonian this term". (Letter of 14/11/23.) Taking Watkins at his word, it was easy to find these two anonymously printed poems. I am very grateful to the current librarian of Repton School, Paul Stevens, for his help with this.
52 See Appendix for both of these poems – 'The Flower' and 'As'.
53 This poem has never been published except within the pages of "The Reptonian" in March 1924. It is included in the appendix.
'(…)' indicates words have been left out by RR; ' … ' indicates the dots are part of the original poem.
54 Despite Watkins's loving idealism about Macdonald, nothing suggests that the latter in any way wrongly crossed any boundaries. He appears to have played the genuinely helpful role of a mentor, to whom Watkins was able, as best he could, to gain some

reflection on his own feelings and what he was going through: "I talked to him, also, about Public Schools, Idealism, a touchy part verging on keenness, the Fagging System & c. – upon which subjects, I think, he was fairly 'spot'."

55 After Macdonald's early death in 1949, a later headmaster of his credited him for exactly this: "He was not the conscientious and efficient schoolmaster; but he was something much rarer and more valuable. He was able to kindle sparks. That is the real gift of the teacher, for the sparks may flare up into great fires ... His interests were the things that endure: creations of the mind and spirit of man, poetry, painting, architecture, literature, music and ... history. Where there is no vision people perish. Efficiency without vision is of no use to a school. Alec Macdonald's great contribution ... was that he had the vision to see what really counts in education." [From: 'King's Connect (Old Vigornian)', Issue 23, July 2008. At: http://www.ksw.org.uk/files/connect%2023.pdf]

56 Letter to Eric Falk. 12/7/24. (NLW)

57 "O Fig, I had a wonderful time just round Speech Day ... Marjorie came down on the Tuesday, & Mother on Thursday." Marjorie was an important spiritual presence in Vernon's life. At this time, although pleased that some of his friends had been able to meet her, he doubted their ability to do so: "she is such a strange person, & you can't get to know her for years." (12/7/24)

58 "HOWE PRIZE POEM – The Japanese Disaster – by V.P. Watkins" in 'The Reptonian', June 1924.

59 "the san is a good place; – peaceful, blue, and free from the unwholesome taint of conventional barriers." After failed attempts to return to the life of the school, Watkins once again measured the passing of time: "I made frantic efforts at persuasion with sister to go down, & got an awful shock when I was told I couldn't. I went out into the garden and wept bitterly, but a streak of philosophy trickled into my tears, and by a skilful process of subtraction, I came to the conclusion that I had over a fortnight, and not just under a fortnight left of my last term." Letter to Falk, 12/7/24.

60 Watkins was referring to a very close friend of his at Repton and Cambridge, John Mervyn Upward, the younger brother of Edward Upward.

61 All quotations in this paragraph are from a letter to Falk of 12/7/24, addressed: The San, Repton.

62 *Lions and Shadows – An Education in the Twenties* by Christopher Isherwood. (Foursquare Books, London). pp. 46-47

63 From: *A Short History of Repton* by Alec Macdonald, (London 1929), pp. 235-236.

64 That Watkins was young for his age is shown not only by his 1923 Repton photograph, when he had just turned 17, but also by a school report when he was 16: "His mind is still very unformed and this comes out in his essays." School report of April 4th '23. Gwen Watkins Archive.

65 'As'. Written, as Watkins noted, on 10th November, 1923 – in other words on the eve of the first anniversary of the Armistice Day celebration of 1922.

66 From a photograph by Mr. G.B. Smith – included in *A Short History of Repton* by Alec Macdonald.

67 Denis Browne had in fact taught at Repton for less than a year in 1912. This would not have mattered, though, for the way his memory was honoured at Repton. The

teacher and friend of Vernon Watkins, Alec Macdonald, in his *Short History of Repton*, which is otherwise recognized to be an extremely accurate account, *mistakenly* wrote that Browne had been teaching at Repton when the First World War broke out: "Three masters were killed, namely, Denis Browne, the composer and friend of Rupert Brooke, who had just joined the staff as second music master … " (p.231) This must therefore have been the story that was told throughout the school.

68 Browne's description of Brooke's end has become very well-known: "… I sat with Rupert. At 4 o'clock he became weaker, and at 4:46 he died, with the sun shining all round his cabin, and the cool sea-breeze blowing through the door and the shaded windows. No one could have wished for a quieter or a calmer end than in that lovely bay, shielded by the mountains and fragrant with sage and thyme."

69 *Victor Gollancz* – RDE. Page 119.

70 The similarity of Watkins's feelings to the experiences of boys during the war even extends to the dread that could be attached to one's eighteenth birthday. During the war: "with a singular unimaginativeness … the War Office called up a boy precisely on his 18th Birthday." (Victor Gollancz – A Biography – Ruth Dudley Edwards; (Faber 2012); p.119.) Watkins would say when this moment arrived: "O, as Rupert would say, 'I'm as old as death'. I didn't know it would be quite as terrible as this to be eighteen years old." Letter to Falk. 24/6/23

71 The writer Harold Monro commented after Brooke's death : "One fears his memory being brought to the poster-grade. 'He did his duty. Will you do yours?'" Quoted in: *A Literary History of Cambridge* by Graham Chainey, (C.U.P.1995), p. 288.

72 The "Bloomsbury Group", to several of whom Brooke had been connected, and who, for the most part, shared none of his spiritual qualms concerning their sexuality.

73 From: *My Dear Boy: Gay Love Letters through the Centuries* (1998), edited by Rictor Norton. Norton's view that Brooke, in his 1914 sonnets, saw "desire for death as the only resolution to his inner conflict" is completely borne out in "I Peace", where "we who have known shame.. have found release" in the peace of death, "(w)here there's no ill, no grief … Naught broken save this body, lost but breath; /And the worst friend and enemy is but Death."

74 "A severe series of diseases in adolescence left the adult Marsh with fragile health, a wispy falsetto voice and, more cruelly, complete impotence. In a perverse way this disability may have protected him in an age when homosexual behaviour was still a criminal offence in Britain. For Marsh, himself strikingly handsome, was attracted to other young men but in a necessarily platonic way. As his biographer has written, Marsh 'cultivated a capacity for friendship which, untroubled by physical desire, could develop into a devotion characteristically feminine in its tenderness.'" From: 'Eddie Marsh: A Profile' by David Freeman in 'Finest Hour 131', Summer 2006, Page 30. (Online at The Churchill Centre website.)

75 For the view that Churchill's obituary of Brooke in The Times was written by Marsh, his Private Secretary, see: *Some Desperate Glory: The First World War the Poets Knew* by Max Egremont, (Picador 2014).

Edward Marsh wrote the 'Memoir' which was included in Rupert Brooke's *Collected Poems* in 1918, whose romantic character is seen in such lines as: "Here then, in the island where Theseus was buried, and whence the young Achilles and the young Pyrrhus were called to Troy, Rupert Brooke died and was buried on Friday, the 23rd of April, the day of Shakespeare and of St George."

There are many passages from Churchill's obituary of Brooke written in a similar spirit, as well as those with a more directly propagandist character:

"During the last few months of his life … the poet-soldier told with all the simple force of genius the sorrow of youth about to die, and the sure triumphant consolations of a sincere and valiant spirit. He expected to die; he was willing to die for the dear England whose beauty and majesty he knew; and he advanced towards the brink in perfect serenity, with absolute conviction of the rightness of his country's cause, and a heart devoid of hate for fellow-men.

"The thoughts to which he gave expression in the very few incomparable war sonnets which he has left behind will be shared by many thousands of young men moving resolutely and blithely forward into this, the hardest, the cruellest, and the least-rewarded of all the wars that men have fought."

From: Edward Marsh's 'Memoir', Section VIII, in Collected Poems of Rupert Brooke with a Memoir. (Available online at Wikisource.)

76   Edward Thomas wrote perceptively about Rupert Brooke, in a way which is relevant to Vernon Watkins's identification with Brooke. Firstly Edward Thomas acknowledged that Brooke could in some way be compared with Shelley. Secondly Edward Thomas pointed out the insufficiency in Brooke's poetry and in his thinking – that Brooke's work remained primarily an expression of his feelings: "*I think he succeeded in being youthful and … interesting … more than most poets since Shelley. But thought … gave him indigestion. He couldn't mix his thought or the result of it with his feeling. He could only think about his feeling … He was a rhetorician, dressing things up better than they needed.*" Quoted in: *Now All Roads Lead to France: The Last Years of Edward Thomas*. By Matthew Hollis. (Faber 2011)]

CHAPTER THREE

CAMBRIDGE (1924-1925)

1   Letter to Falk, 21/8/24
2   Watkins says he had made the decision on the advice of "several masters" but not only was Alec Macdonald the only teacher genuinely concerned that Watkins would not just leave Repton and go into banking, he had also been at Cambridge himself and knew the literary world there, having been editor of the 'Cambridge Review'.
3   On his entrance application, which he sent at the same time, Watkins completely unrealistically described his intention to study: "Modern Languages (Honours Course) & then Economics or Law." He also lists his credits in his Schools Certificate, in July 1922, which make clear what his natural gifts were: "French, Latin, Maths, English, Divinity."
4. Letter to Magdalene College, Cambridge, August 3rd, 1924. All the following documents regarding Watkins's application to Cambridge are in the Magdalene College Library.
5   Michael Ramsey, two years older than Vernon Watkins, had been a pupil at Repton

between 1918 and 1922. His elder brother, Frank Ramsey, was an extraordinarily gifted mathematician and philosopher, who died aged 26 in 1930.
6   Letter from A.S. Ramsey to VW – 9/8/24
7   Watkins's reply again revealed that he was by no means a free agent: "we have now been able to come to a decision regarding your kind letter of the 9th ... and my father has agreed to my going up to Cambridge in October." VW to Ramsey, 14/8/24
8   "Our 3 children having been born at intervals of about 2 years, we have, for several years had them all away at expensive schools and as this period has been one in which the cost of living and educational expenses have been high the expenditure has been heavy on us ... But as my salary is a fairly substantial one ... I would hate to trouble you." William Watkins to A.S. Ramsey.
9   Marjorie Watkins lived in a small flat in Bethnal Green and spent almost her entire working life working in connection with the St. Margaret's House Settlement in Victoria Park. This was started in 1889 and is still very active today. Marjorie also worked as an air-raid warden in Bethnal Green during World War Two.
10 Dorothy Watkins wrote a book about her lifetime in social work, called *Other People's Children – Adventures in Child Care*. Privately printed. 1993. (ISBN – 1872229158)
11 This is quoted by Dorothy Watkins, who also describes the constant presence of poetry. "We were at the Caswell bus stop ... when he (Alec Macdonald) opened a book of Hardy's and read in a resonant voice ... 'An Ancient to Ancients'. It made a profound impression on me."
12 Letter to Falk of 21/8/24. Watkins had written in his previous letter: "if you could come for a week at the beginning of September, we should all be intoxicated with joy." 12/7/24
13 Of Falk himself, for example: "it was astounding – He said that there was one thing lacking in your life, & that was love; ... He said that you'd have to be careful – (I think) mentioned homosexualism (?) (...) But he went on to say that it would be perfectly all right if you were careful, & met girls, treated them as friends, etc." Or of Vernon's older sister: "Marjorie he was tremendously struck with, & is frightfully anxious to meet her."
14 This refers to John Mervyn Upward, the younger brother of Christopher Isherwood's great friend, Edward Upward. (See also endnote 16.)
15 Letter to Eric Falk from 41, Garden Walk, Cambridge on 17/11/24. Cornelis van Stolk was born on June 11, 1905 and died in 1983. His father, mentioned in Watkins's letter, was Abraham van Stolk. (An article about him is available online: 'Altar to an Unknown God: The megalomanical thinking of the Rotterdam Nietzschean Abraham van Stolk (1874-1951)' by Dr. Ruben Buys.) Cornelis van Stolk was director of the 'Bloem- en Meelfabriek d'Blaauwe Molen N.V.' In 1942 he married Hermina Jacoba Hahn and they had two children – Abraham van Stolk (1945-1986) and Eveline van Stolk (1948-2013). It has sadly been impossible to discover any further information about his life.
16 The end of the letter also shows Watkins to have hardly in any way moved on yet from Repton in his consciousness: "Now I really must stop – Repton is calling for letters ... Are you going down for the Malvern match??? Try. I'd like to, but I fear it's impossible – Farewell, my love, & best of luck, V.P.W."

17 While at Repton Watkins had written of John Mervyn Upward: "I find that Upward's tasks are more sympathetic with mine than any other person's in the School – I *do* wish he were in the Hall." (5.12.24) Regarding his long conversation with Alec Macdonald, Watkins had written: "A large part of the conversation was about Upward, of course, whom I *love*".

18 Isherwood was two years older than Watkins and Upward three years. At Cambridge Isherwood was a year ahead of him and Upward two years.

19 If Cornelis van Stolk was indeed an "anthroposophist", it is of great interest, in that Watkins would have two further significant encounters with anthroposophy in his life. The founder of anthroposophy, Rudolf Steiner died in March, 1925 – in other words during the exact time when Vernon Watkins knew Cornelis van Stolk at Cambridge.

20 *Lions and Shadows* by Christopher Isherwood, (Four Square, 1963), page 64.

21 In this, Isherwood may be seen as the almost exact opposite of Watkins, whose striving may be seen as the search for how to reattain or rediscover a genuine naivety. That Isherwood named Watkins 'Percival' was possibly influenced by Watkins's initials "V.P.", which he always used at the time. The name 'Percival' though, as we have said, was a fitting one, being that of the naïve hero of the Grail stories.

22 Watkins had first met van Stolk some time previously and had talked with his sister Marjorie about him. In his letter Watkins expected that Falk would already have heard about van Stolk from Marjorie. By Nov. 17th, therefore, Isherwood and Upward would have been hearing Watkins's stories about van Stolk for some time.

23 Untitled poem, dated: Nov 20th, 1924. NLW MSS 22463e.
"The garden of enchantment" in the poem is unmistakably the Eden-like world Watkins had experienced at Repton. The poem addresses an unnamed "you", but is equally unmistakably addressed to Isherwood and Upward. Even before leaving Repton's "garden of enchantment" Watkins had said: "Isherwood cynically tells me that it's all only a beautiful dream, & I'm waking up to disillusionment now." (Letter to Falk – 12/7/24.)
'(…)' indicates words have been left out by RR; ' … ' indicates the 3 dots are part of the original poem.

24 Except for one small telling occasion, described in the following chapter.

25 'Immortality' – January 1925 (reworked in March 1925).

26 'Despair' – probably written, like 'Immortality', in 1925. These were two of the four poems by 'V.P. Watkins' published in: *Anthology of Contemporary Cambridgeshire and Hertfordshire Poetry*; (Fowler Wright, London, 1928.)

27 Written when Watkins was 18 and a half. NLW MS 22463E.

28 "Que la musique est la reine des arts" – January 23rd. "Soirée Poétique" – February 13th (1925). From a card listing the term's events at the 'Société Francaise de l'Université'. Gwen Watkins Archive.

29 Gwen Watkins – email to the author.

30 *Lions and Shadows* by Christopher Isherwood, (Four Square, 1963), pp.75-76.

31 'On reading some modern verse', March 1925. NLW MS 22463E.

32 *Lions and Shadows*, Christopher Isherwood, Foursquare Books, p. 26. Isherwood and Upward probably never knew that almost identical words would be written in all

seriousness about Vernon Watkins after his death, when Kathleen Raine called him: "the greatest lyric poet of my generation." ('The Poetry of Vernon Watkins' by Kathleen Raine, in: *Vernon Watkins 1906-1967*, ed. Leslie Norris; Faber 1970.)

33 *Lions and Shadows*, p.74.
34 "Vernon was over eighteen when he left school, but looked a great deal younger. Although intellectually advanced, he was in most ways very immature. His absorption in poetry and total lack of knowledge of all practical aspects of real life made him quite unfit to cope with the demands of self-sufficiency in university life." Dorothy Watkins, *Vernon Phillips Watkins – The Early Years*. p.15.
35 See endnote 72, chapter Two.
36 'A Note on my Poetry' – NLW MS 22480E.
37 'Poetry and the Audience' – NLW MS 22480E.
38 The pacifist 'Cambridge neutrality manifesto'. After WW1 was declared, however, on 4th August 1914 Benson stated: 'I'm not a Pacifist any more'. See: 'Magdalen College and the First World War'. Ged Martin. 2014. Available online.
39 In his voluminous diaries, extending to millions of words, in Pepys Library, Magdalene College, Cambridge.
40 His sister Marjorie, whose inner relationship to life was so close to his own, was living nearby at the time, having recently begun her life as a social worker in Bethnal Green, East London.
41 *Vernon Watkins* by Roland Mathias – 'Writers of Wales' series. (University of Wales Press, 1974) Page 22.
42 Diary entry of Tuesday 12th May, 1924. From A.C. Benson's diary – Feb. 22 to May 17, 1925 – property of: Pepys Library, Magdalene College, Cambridge.
43 A.C. Benson died on 16th June, 1925. Three weeks before the meeting with Watkins, Benson had dreams which might be seen as in some way heralding his own death: "My sixty-third birthday. I awoke after half-sad dreams. I looked out over a hedge and saw mamma in a grey dress making her way resolutely up the road; went to meet her and was greeted by an embrace. Then Maggie came, pale and silent, but smiling; then Beth, who declared herself with a great smile to be perfectly happy. All this moved me much, but I did not think of them as dead, till I awoke, and soon after slept again. It was a curious birthday." A.C. Benson, diary entry: April 24th, 1925.
44 'A Survey of the German Romantic Movement' in LMNTRE Poems (T Llen Publications, 1999)
45 His full marks were as follows:
Composition – 13/50 (French)   25/50 (German)
Translation – 26/50 (French)   22/50 (German)
Essay – 33/50 (French)   36/50 (German)
Literature and History   38/100 (French) 57/100 (German)
46 Letter from A.S. Ramsey to Vernon Watkins, 23rd June, 1925. (Magdalene College Archive, Cambridge.)
47 Regarding banking being the 'default' option, Geoffrey Fisher had written to A.S. Ramsey in his reference about Vernon: "Finance is a difficulty: it is the mother who wants him to go to the Varsity … If not the Varsity, the boy is to go into the Bank in which his father is." G.N. Burnham had written to Vernon soon after he had left

Repton, saying:
"Soon you will be
Banker
Poet
Bearer of the Glad News"
Letter from G.N. Burnham to VW, 4/9/24. (Jeff Towns Archive.)
Regarding Cambridge or some other profession being out of the question for Vernon, his sister Dorothy writes: "Our family had no private means, our expensive education had absorbed all my father's savings and it was essential that we should become self-supporting at the end of it. Nothing would persuade Vernon to go in for teaching, which would seem to have been the obvious choice, nor could he decide to work towards any other profession. After a year it seemed pointless for him to continue at Cambridge, and following endless discussions with his anxious parents he decided to leave the university and return to Wales, where he was immediately offered a job in Lloyds Bank. It was a difficult, painful decision but on Vernon's side a conscious choice. If he had to earn his living it would be in a way which made least demand on him, so that he would be free to concentrate his main energy in writing poetry. With his quick mind and facility for figures, banking presented no problem to Vernon, who was the only person I have ever met who could add up columns of pounds, shillings and pence at a glance." DW. Page 17.

48 The £5 grant offered to Watkins by the 'College Benefaction Fund' was described to him as the 'Mr. Peskett's Prize for Modern Languages'. It was not, however, given for his exam results, but out of understanding for the family's financial situation: "The Alfred Peskett Benefaction is in the Master's gift, and is annually bestowed by him upon poor and deserving students." ('The Cambridge University Calendar 1924/5' – section on Magdalene College.)

49 From: 'On the Passing of June', written 'June/July 1925'.

CHAPTER FOUR

CARDIFF (1925–1928)

1 'Address to the Poetry Society of Great Britain', 7th May, 1966. In: 'Poetry Wales', Vernon Watkins special issue, Spring 1977, Volume 12, No. 4.

2 He did sometimes see one friend from Swansea, Tommy Rice, but as Vernon's sister writes: "They could hardly have been more different". (See endnote 7.)

3 DW

4 'Document of A Live Poet'. Gwen Watkins Archive. (Included in the Appendix.)

5 'True Lovers' – published in 'New Selected Poems of Vernon Watkins', edited by Richard Ramsbotham. (Carcanet, 2006). In May 1929 Vernon Watkins would have the poem published in the prestigious London poetry journal "The London Mercury".

6 From 'Company', written in March, 1926. NLW: 22463E.

7 "One of Vernon's old Swansea friends, Tommy Rice, was also a reluctant clerk in Cardiff docks at this time, and they would often meet for supper ... They could

ENDNOTES

hardly have been more different ... though their love of tennis was a mutual bond." DW, p.18-19

8   From a page entitled 'NOTES' (towards one of his poetry readings) – Gwen Watkins archive. (Emphasis added.)
9   James Phillips had "a prodigious knowledge of the Bible", which he had read to his grandchildren in Welsh and according to Vernon Watkins not only "loved the prophets" but "went down singing". 'Inscription: for the Gravestone of my Grandfather', Nov.3rd, 1926, NLW Mss. 22463E.
10 My Grandfather Dying, Nov. 1926, NLW Mss. 22463E.
11 Watkins had written two further poems to his grandfather in the week after his death:
'Inscription; for the Gravestone of my Grandfather', on Nov. 3rd 1926 (NLW MS. 22463E):
"*Come round me, friends. Before I sink in the soil*
I'll tell a tale. Below this little mound,
Most free from trouble, one old man is lying ... "
and on the following day, the day of the funeral, a light song addressed to his mother: 'A Song', Nov. 4th 1926, (NLW MS. 22463E): "*Come away, Mother,/Laugh in the wind!/Soon shall another/Be gone out of mind.*"
12 "And in one moment's ecstasy I found/ Some certain footing to the rising star." The 'rising star' refers both to the spirit of his grandfather and to the young, aspiring and not wholly immodest poet.
'Return to a house where one had Died'. Nov 6th, 1924. NLW Mss. 22463E. (Emphasis added.)
13 These streets all still exist, but a further one has been added since then, which Watkins would have been happy about: 'Dylan Place'.
14 'Poetry and Experience' – GW/JT. (Emphasis added.)
15 VW to FDL, 'Thursday', 'probably early 1939'. Published in: 'Temenos 8'. pp. 151-152.
16 In NLW archive, with envelope dated: 24th December, 1926.
The complete letter reads: "Dear Fig,
Aren't the evenings closing in, Mrs. Fisher? We're approaching the last signpost of detachment, mon ami, & soon will be sending each other Christmas cards.
When shall we meet again on gallery? Buona notte – Vernon." 'Mrs. Fisher' was the wife of the Headmaster, Geoffrey Fisher. 'On gallery' refers to the upper gallery of one of Repton's oldest buildings where Watkins and Falk had often met.
17 He wrote a poem after leaving it, called 'The Vatican Closes'. NLW Mss. 22443C.
18 'In the Catacombs', NLW Mss. 22443C.
19 Interview with Vernon Watkins. 10th Oct. 1960. Published in: *The poet speaks: interviews with contemporary poets.* Ed. Peter Orr. (Routledge, 1966) pp. 267-271.
20 By the time of Keats's and Shelley's deaths in 1821 and 1822, respectively, the period of Wordsworth's and Coleridge's greatest inspiration had passed, Blake was towards the end of his life and was no longer writing poetry, and Byron's ironic genius, as in *Don Juan*, deliberately made no further attempt at a spiritually imaginative 'Romanticism'.
21 'In the Protestant Cemetery, Rome'. In: *Cypress and Acacia* in: CP.
22 Ibid.

23 'Keats's Grave', NLW Mss. 22443C. The poem ends: "This the world shall be, and Heaven/
Your eternal Pantheon."
24 'Children Playing', dated 'March 21st, 1929, Villa Borghese, Rome.'NLW Mss. 22443C.
25 This poem – in the notebook he named Rome 1927 – is untitled. The pages on which it is written are lightly smudged by rain, testifying to the fact that he was outside, in the Borghese Gardens, while writing it. NLW Mss. 22444B. (Emphasis added.)
26 His older sister, Marjorie, after graduating from Oxford, had taken up social work in the East End of London. Not long afterwards, she had contracted pleurisy, and during her convalescence had been advised to spend the winter in a warmer climate. She had gone to Menton in Southern France, and Dorothy, who had just left school, had accompanied her there.
27 DW.
28 VW to FDL, 30th January, 1939.
29 Dorothy falsely asserts that this 'Cambridge friend' was the left-wing writer and acquaintance of George Orwell, Frank Jellinek. Dorothy Watkins makes several large errors, however, in her brief memoir of her brother and Watkins never knew Jellinek and nor was he at Cambridge with him. It must therefore be assumed that she forgot the name of Vernon's "Cambridge friend", *Cornelis van Stolk*, and having heard of *Frank Jellinek*, confused the two. There is a similarity of both consonants and vowels in the two names.
30 DW, p. 16.
31 Letter to Falk from Cambridge, 17/11/1924.
32 From Wordsworth's 'Intimations of Immortality'.
The notebook containing 'The Prisoners' by Vernon Watkins is: NLW Mss 2244B.
33 'In the Protestant Cemetery, Rome'. The poem combines descriptions of how Vernon Watkins had been in 1927, when visiting Keats' and Shelley's graves, with actual descriptions of Keats and Shelley. Thus the words: "Confident that he would be/ Remembered by posterity" refer both to John Keats and also, unmistakably, to Vernon Watkins.
34 The story of Vernon Watkins asking his father if he could be supported to live in Italy for a year has been told before – for example by Roland Mathias – describing this as having happened immediately after Watkins left Cambridge. It was not realized, however, that Vernon had only gone to Italy a year and a half after leaving Cambridge. As Gwen Watkins writes: "Vernon asked his father if he could spend a year in Italy after the 1927 visit. It was certainly not until he had been romantically influenced by actually visiting the places of his imagination (he saw the Keats /Shelley house on that visit too, and the sofa where at that time you could see the stains of the death-sweat of Keats). He may also have felt the first signs of his approaching breakdown and realised that he must get away from Roath and the bank. Perhaps a year in Italy would really have prevented the crash, who knows?" (Email to RR – 17/7/2015)
35 "People had seen him dancing round his room naked … He did at least pull the curtains." Gwen Watkins – interview with the author, 2000.

36 At the end of the Blakes' garden in Hercules Buildings, Lambeth there was a summer-house: "Mr. Butts calling one day found Mr. and Mrs. Blake sitting in this summer-house, freed from 'those troublesome disguises' which have prevailed since the Fall. '*Come in!*' *cried Blake; 'it's only Adam and Eve, you know!*' Husband and wife had been reciting passages from Paradise Lost, in character, and the garden of Hercules Buildings had to represent the Garden of Eden: a little to the scandal of wondering neighbours, on more than one occasion." Alexander Gilchrist, *The Life of William Blake*, ed. Ruthven Todd (1942), pp. 96-97.

37 NLW Mss. 22480E, p.81.

38 'Poetry and Experience' – GW/JT

39 "One day in your 20s, reading Blake / You thought his prophetic books literally true."
'In Memory of Vernon Watkins' by Nelson Bentley, in *Vernon Watkins 1906–1967*, ed. Leslie Norris.
(Faber 1970)
In 1927, Watkins's second year in Cardiff, he changed from reading Milton exclusively to reading Blake. The powerful influence of Blake on his inner world and on his poetry becomes ever more clearly visible during 1927, from 'Byron Street' onwards. Many years later Watkins looked back on his time, and what Blake had done for him, in an unfinished poem:
I lived at first in self-deception,
Thinking the world, such fire was mine,
Must hang its fate on my next line.
The poems Milton did not write
Kept me awake through half the night.
Shelley enchained me, like Prometheus,
Nor could Plotinus, nor Boethius,
Deliver since they wrote in prose,
Chains that possessed me such as those.
Then Blake arrived, and by equating
Strength with sublimity, and rating
Beauty with pathos, set me free,
Dividing truth and falsity.
'Beginning of an autobiographical poem' in: 'Temenos 8', 1987, page 132. (Emphasis added.)

40 Emphases added by RR. Letter to Falk from 1927. NLW Mss. This letter has been falsely dated by Falk: 'Sept-Oct 1927'. It must in fact date from April 1927 at the latest, as it begins: "Thank you for your letter. I was most surprised and glad to get it when I was out in France ... Before that, I had had a week in Rome, which I'll tell you about later".

41 'Introduction'. 22480E p.1.

42 'Poetry and Experience' – GW/JT

43 "After leaving school I found that I liked most to read only one poet at a time. For a very long time I read Shelley only, then Keats only, then Milton only, then Shakespeare, then Blake. My own writing suffered from an inability to separate what I wanted to say from those great poets." 'Poetry and the Audience'. NLW 22480E p.34.

44   Vernon Watkins described this incident with the motorcyclist to Gwen Watkins – and made it clear that it was this event that triggered the 'spiritual emergency' he now entered upon. (Or that spun him into psychosis, in psychiatric terms.) This is undoubtedly the case. However, in absence of any records about it, it was assumed that the motorcycle accident then led Watkins to leave Cardiff and the bank the following day. It was also assumed that the motorcyclist crashed into the very lodgings where Watkins was living. This assumption has been made in all previous biographical descriptions of this incident. Finding the report of the accident in the South Wales News revealed that it happened on Newport Road, which Watkins walked down on his way home from the bank, and that Watkins's condition therefore continued to intensify for eight months after this, before he finally left Cardiff in December.

The text from the South Wales News, Friday April 13, 1928 (Plate 15) reads:
CONSTABLE KILLED – NEWPORT ROAD FATALITY. – SIDECAR CRASH WITH MOTOR-CAR.
A motor-cycle accident, with fatal consequences, occurred on the Cardiff-Newport road last night, when Police-constable Charles Davies, of the Cardiff City Police, received injuries, from which he died in the Cardiff Royal Infirmary.

   P.C. Davies was riding a motor-cycle combination in the direction of Cardiff, and was accompanied in the sidecar by Mr. George Davies.

   Proceeding in front of him was a motorcar, driven by Mr. B. Powell, a greengrocer, of Crichton-street, Cardiff, and by some means the wheel of the sidecar collided with the mudguard of the motor-car. The impact caused the combination to turn over, and P.C. Davies and the passenger were thrown out. They were attended to by passers-by, and later by Police-sergeant Taylor, St. Mellons, and were afterwards conveyed to the Cardiff Royal Infirmary, where P.C. Davies, who resided at Ordell-street, Splott, Cardiff, died.

     His companion, Mr. George Davies, of 7, Kerrycroy-street, received multiple injuries, but he is not in a serious condition.

The story on the same page - A MAESTEG EPIC – reads:
FIVE HOURS UNDER A "FALL" – HEROIC RESCUE EFFORTS.
For nearly five hours yesterday workmen and officials at the Maesteg Deep Colliery, Maesteg, were engaged in a heroic effort to rescue an entombed miner, Mr. David John Morgan, aged 36, single, residing with his parents at Llwydarth road, Maesteg, who was buried by a fall of roof.

   The rescuers were greatly handicapped in their work owing to falling debris, and it was with great difficulty that the victim was eventually recovered. Unfortunately, he was dead.

   Dr. Bell Thomas descended the mine immediately after the fall, and remained there until the recovery of the body.

45   'Document of a Live Poet'. Gwen Watkins Archive.
46   "*Surely I was blind*
Till that more heavenly darkness closed my eyes ...
Surely they saw not clear till sight was lost

And Night's refracting prism the image tossed."
This immediately enables Vernon Watkins to recognize why Goethe, unlike Newton, saw the colours to arise not from light alone but from light *and* darkness: *"not in vain/Great Goethe sought to prove/ Darkness an element with light combined/ To give the birth of colour".* His knowledge about Goethe's 'colour theory' and its difference from Newton's, would almost certainly have been gained from Cornelis van Stolk who was, according to Isherwood, an adherent of "anthroposophy", whose founder Rudolf Steiner spent 14 years editing and developing Goethe's scientific work.

47   This image of a slave chained to an oar at sea would recur several times in Vernon Watkins's poetry, for example in 'Art Poétique' (1937), which is referred to in Chapter Seven.
48   Four poems he had written while at Cambridge were published in *Anthology of Contemporary Cambridgeshire and Hertfordshire Poetry*; (Fowler Wright, London, 1928.)
49   "I remember the excitement this book gave me when I first opened it." *'Yeats and the Oracles.* Sources of Yeats' Later Poetry' by Vernon Watkins. In NLW Mss.
50   'Poetry and Experience' – GW/JT.
51   On one level it is not that important who this boy was, as Watkins makes quite clear that he is referring to an idealized experience of this boy *before* the onset of puberty, and that the man the boy would later on become was of no relevance for this 'Edenic' experience of him *before the Fall.* In that 'Edenic' world the boy is representative for Watkins of the divinity of childhood and, as such, has hardly any individualized features at all. The actual boy paeaned by Watkins throughout 'Repton: an Epic', was, however, almost certainly Richard Vaughan, who was two years younger than Watkins. In later life, Eric Falk would laugh with Watkins at how his one-time Adonis was now balding and overweight. Vaughan became a successful cricketer and died in 1966.
52   It might also be said that Watkins's ordinary sense of memory had become heightened, so that intensely remembered past experiences could suddenly appear completely present to him.
53   The preface to the epic began: "Sing the great birth of Love" and went on in Blakean style: – "*O that hand could write/What now my spirit feels; or finger spell/The language of my soul! ... / ... Who has ever writ/Between the eyelid and the sleeping eye?*"
54   Even after 90 sections it was still unfinished and it is oddly reminiscent, therefore, of the long unfinished epic he wrote at his preparatory school.
55   Thomas Shapley, b.1902. Watkins knew Shapley and his younger brother both from Swansea and Repton. Their father was a colleague of William Watkins in Lloyds Bank. According to Roland Mathias it was partly because of the Shapley family that Vernon had been sent to Repton.
56   "The everyday world hardly existed for me, except as a touchstone for protest and indignation." ('Poetry and Experience'. GW/JT)
57   Geoffrey to Rosamund Fisher, Repton, 5th December, 1928. (Repton School Archives.)
58   From the memoir of Rupert Norman Shepherd, who was in the same house as

Watkins at Repton between 1922 and 1926. (I am grateful to Paul Stevens, the current librarian at Repton College, for providing me with the previous two quotations and for further information relating to Watkins's time at Repton.)

59 "Kathleen Raine tells me that she considers you the best religious poet in England." Sister Mary Immaculate to Vernon Watkins. (December 1966 or January 1967.) NLW Mss 22486E.

60 See endnote 2. (Chapter 2)

61 Gwen Watkins – interview with the author – 2000. However one understands this, it leaves no doubt about the speed his mind was travelling at.

62 According to Roland Mathias Watkins shouted at Fisher that: "it was he, the uncomprehending Headmaster, who destroyed youth, that it had always been he." *Writers of Wales: Vernon Watkins* by Roland Mathias. (UWP 1974). Page 28.

63 "What is so interesting about this Headmaster is that he became a famous person later on. At the end of my third year he was suddenly appointed Bishop of Chester … I remember at the time trying to puzzle out how on earth a person could suddenly leap from being a schoolmaster to becoming a Bishop all in one jump, but there were bigger puzzles to come. From Chester, he was soon promoted again to become Bishop of London, and from there, after not all that many years, he bounced up the ladder once more to get the top job of them all, Archbishop of Canterbury! (…) Well, well, well! And this was the man who used to deliver the most vicious beatings to the boys under his care!" *Boy. Tales of Childhood* by Roald Dahl, Puffin Books, 1986. Chapter called: 'The Headmaster'. pp. 176-177. (Roald Dahl went to Repton in September 1929.)

64 Ibid. p.179. Victor Gollancz, Vernon Watkins and Roald Dahl all had similar views about Fisher. Little is known of Christopher Isherwood's views about Fisher, but Fisher clearly found Isherwood far more to his liking. At the end of Isherwood's time at Repton Fisher said of him: "His career here has been thoroughly to his credit and greatly to our benefit. He has been useful in many ways and I am very attached to him." *Isherwood. A Life Revealed* by Peter Parker. (Random House, 2004.) Page 65.

65 DW. Dorothy's words suggest that Watkins's parents were informed as soon as Watkins arrived at the school. It is certainly possible that Fisher alerted Watkins's parents soon after encountering Watkins on Wednesday, December 5th.

BEYOND TIME'S CHAIN

66 Untitled poem in: *New Selected Poems of Vernon Watkins* (Carcanet 2006)

67 The three poems are 'Document of a Live Poet' (included in the Appendix), 'Christ and Charon' (in *Cypress and Acacia* in CP) and 'Sonnet of Resurrection 7' (in 'New Selected Poems of Vernon Watkins', Carcanet 2006). The unattributed quotations in this chapter are all taken from one of these three poems.

68 The novel *Bliss* by Peter Carey (Faber 1981) opens with such a description. Perhaps the most well-known case is that of George C. Ritchie, who returned to life nine minutes after he had been pronounced dead and described his experience in: *Return from Tomorrow*. (Baker, USA. 1978). Most near-death experiences also involve an encounter with a "being of Light", who is often recognized as Christ. Experiences of

this kind have also been documented which, like Watkins's, do not involve the person nearly dying through an accident or illness, but occur in life, often but not always in the midst of intense crisis. See: *We experienced Christ. Spiritual Encounters with Jesus Christ* by Gunnar Hillerdal and Berndt Gustafsson (Temple Lodge, 2016). For a difficult but profound exploration of such experiences, see: *The New Experience of the Supersensible* by Jesaiah Ben-Aharon, (Temple Lodge, 1995).

69 In Gwen Watkins's words, he experienced himself being: "propelled inexorably towards this immensely deep pit and at the bottom was the actual weeping and wailing and gnashing of teeth. He said the gnashing of teeth was the worst – a terrible sound that he could hear – and he was aware that this was not hell but the hell of a spirit turned away from God." Gwen Watkins, interview with the author , 2000.

70 "and on the edge of that pit two arms came round him and drew him very gently back and he became aware that he was saved and that everybody could be saved – that this was possible – that there was salvation for everybody." Ibid.

71 ('Christ and Charon'.) Vernon Watkins would use variants of this phrase several times in his poetry. In his poem *Good Friday*, for example, the final stanza begins: "Come, Easter, come." An unpublished sonnet from 1933 ends: "For time is like a shadow that he spurns/ When from the East the sunshine clamours 'Come'." (See Chapter 6). The words strongly echo with the phrase "The time has come!" in mythology and fairy tales and even with Christ's words at the "raising" of Lazarus: 'Lazarus, come forth.' (*The Gospel of John*. 11:43)

72 'Document of a Live Poet'. Gwen Watkins Archive.

73 *Revelations*, Ch.1, verses 10-12 & 17.

74 "There is nearly always, in any serious poet, a moment of change, a pivotal crisis in time, that renews him." 'The Second Pressure in Poetry' in *Unicorn 10*, Spring 1963. In: GW/JT.

75 'Poetry and the Audience' – NLW MS 22480E.

76 The seventh of Watkins's sequence of eight 'Sonnets of Resurrection'. Six of these were published in *The Lady with the Unicorn*. This one exists in a single draft in the British Library. (BL MS 54159) It is included in: 'New Selected Poems of Vernon Watkins', (Carcanet, 2006).

77 'Document of a Live Poet'. Gwen Watkins Archive.

CHAPTER FIVE

'PIVOTAL CRISIS IN TIME' (1929)

1 'A Note on my Poetry'. NLW MS. 22480E.

2 'For Whom does a Poet Write?' (GW/JT. Page 138.) On another occasion he wrote: "In my twenty-third year I suddenly experienced a complete revolution of sensibility. I repudiated the verse I had written and knew that I could never again write a poem which would be dominated by time." ('Poetry and Experience' in: GW/JT. Page 156)

3 See passage with the Blake quotation in the previous chapter: 'Beyond Time's Chain'.

4 'Autobiographical Note to 'Poetry and the Audience', NLW. Mss. 22480E, p.34.

5   'Poems and the reading of Poetry. Introduction to poems read at Stratford-on-Avon.' August 1958. NLW. MS.
6   Notes for 'Cambridge Talk' – NLW MS 22480E
7   'Cellars' and 'The Auction'. March 1939. Jeff Towns Archive.
8   'The London Mercury' was a major monthly literary journal published between 1919 and 1939. It was edited by J.C. Squire until 1934.
9   'Poetry and Experience'. GW/JT.
10 A Gower neighbour, Ethel Ross, told Gwen Watkins she had seen Watkins roaming, mad-looking, through the Gower, after his breakdown.
11 'Remembering Vernon' by Ceri Richards in: *Vernon Watkins 1906-1967*. Ed. Leslie Norris. (Faber 1970)
12 Although Watkins had loved and lived in Gower since his childhood, he describes how his true relationship to its landscape only began in 1929. In his poem 'Document of a Live Poet' he refers to his incomplete relationship to the beauties of the natural world *before* his 1928/9 experience, for this was still at a time when: "Life's counterfeit was in my eye."
13 The mythology and poetry of ancient Ireland is older than the Welsh Taliesin poems. One of the great differences between Taliesin and the earlier Irish Bards is that Taliesin links his bardic union with nature with Celtic Christianity: "John the Divine/Called me Merlin,/ But all future kings/ Shall call me Taliesin." ('The Poems of Taliesin Pen Beirdd' in: *Taliesin and the Bardic Mysteries in Britain and Ireland* by John Matthews. The Aquarian Press 1991. page 283.) Taliesin's Celtic Christian relationship to nature is essential to Vernon Watkins's series of poems identifying himself with Taliesin.
14 Ibid. pp. 296-297. From Taliesin's poem 'Cad Goddeu'
15 'The Place and the Poem' – transcript of a BBC Broadcast, August 1949. In: GW/JT.
16 'Taliesin on the Beach' by Vernon Watkins. Gwen Watkins Archive..
17 'Taliesin in Gower' in *The Death Bell* in CP. Page 185.
18 'Poetry and Experience'. GW/JT.
19 Ibid.
20 'Poetry and the Audience' – NLW MS 22480E. Watkins wrote in some abbreviated notes: "Time-lag between experience and style. In my case six or seven years." (Notes for 'Cambridge Talk') He also gave varying lengths of time for this "time-lag", on one occasion naming it as "5 years" (Notes for 'Poetry and Experience') and on another as "eight or nine years". ('Poems and the reading of Poetry', August 1958.)
21 See endnote 253.
22 "With his quick mind and facility for figures, banking presented no problem to Vernon, who was the only person I have ever met who could add up columns of pounds, shillings and pence at a glance." DW. Page 17. Watkins said himself: "My one ability was to count figures quickly, for in those days figures passed through people's heads, not through machines." ('Address to the Poetry Society of Great Britain', 7th May, 1966 in: *Poetry Wales*, Vernon Watkins issue, Spring 1977, Vol. 12. No. 4)
23 Poetry and a Career, July 1946. In: GW/JT
24 According to Gwen Watkins this was also because Vernon Watkins had been entrusted with one of the keys needed, in combination with others, to open the bank's main safe.

25 DW. She adds that William Watkins had kept the bank informed of Vernon's progress throughout his illness and that the bank had in fact "kept his job open for him."
26 In 1959, describing how he had first become a bank clerk in 1925 he said: "*My progress in the bank was meteoric, but I was the slowest meteor on record. I am a bank clerk today.*" ('Cambridge Talk'. 22480E.)
27 Jenijoy La Belle, 'Vernon Watkins: Some Observations on Poetry', Anglo-Welsh Review, No.65, 1979.
28 Elizabeth Iorwerth Jones, shared in conversation with the author, 2000.
29 'The poet who was A1 at Lloyds'. Swansea Evening Post. 10.10. 1961.

CHAPTER SIX

SECOND APPRENTICESHIP (1930–1934)

1 Spoken by 'the girl' in *The Influences* – 1935.
2 In written form, as he did later also invent such stories out loud for his children.
3 James Cholmondley Thornton (1907-1969). Thornton had read English at Corpus Christi College, Cambridge, and so Watkins may have met him through Isherwood and Upward, at the beginning of his time at Cambridge. No details are known about how Watkins and Thornton made contact with each other over this children's book. In 1940 Dylan Thomas wrote to Watkins: "A great old friend – he's neither great nor old – came for last weekend: Jim Thornton … I gave him your address. Perhaps you've heard from him by this time." *Dylan Thomas. The Collected Letters.* ed. Ferris. p. 522.
4 "at the age of 22 I had a complete revolution in my imagination and all the poetry I had written really meant nothing to me after that … Only, I think, the very light verse that I had done up to that time meant anything more to me really." 'Insert for Spectrum'. Interview with Vernon Watkins by Dr. George Thomas. (1967) In: GW/JT. Page 122.
5 The famous folk song of the same name describes the sufferings, death and resurrection of 'John Barleycorn', who is partly the god of the corn itself, springing to new life after being buried in the earth, and partly the god in the beer made from the barley, which also gives people strange new powers of life.
6 In: *Vernon Watkins 1906-1967.* Ed. Leslie Norris. (Faber 1970) Page 94.
7 A selection of Vernon Watkins's light and occasional verses are published in *LMNTRE Poems.* (Tŷ Llên Publications 1999).
8 Dorothy Watkins says it was 6 weeks, but David Cochrane's great nephew, Tom Winnifrith, in an interesting video blog about Cochrane's death, says that it was a year before his body was discovered: http://www.tomwinnifrith.com/articles/4556/video-photos-finding-the-grave-of-great-uncle-david-cochrane-in-delphi-part-2
9 *Poetry and Experience* in GW/JT. Page 162.
10 David Cochrane wrote on the postcard: "Here I am doing Greece. It is being great fun. Venice which we saw on the way was lovely. I shall be back in Oxford about the

28th April; so write to me at Trinity College about then & tell me your life's History from where you left off last time. Then I will supply with you a further version of mine than I have time for at the moment. It is Easter Sunday today so most of the places are shut, which is rather a bore as we have not too much time. Why do you not come over to Oxford sometime next term & see Michael Balkavill (sp?) and myself. I do hope you are flourishing. I must now stop and write about six more postcards. Love David April 12th." GW archive.

11 In June, 1924 Watkins made the following 'Notes on French Poetry' (particularly in regard to Verlaine, Baudelaire and Théodor de Banville):
"Romantisme, et ses poètes ont toujours gardé la liberté de developer leur talent dans la direction qu'ils jugaient la meilleure. *Tous les Parnassiens,* malgré la diversité de leurs temperaments et de leurs tendencies, se sont assujettis à la méme discipline et ont poursuivi en commun un double but ... ils *s'opposaient nettement aux Romantiques auxquels, sans méconnaître ce qu'ils leurs devaient, ils reprochaient l'étalage de leur personnalité et leur mediocre souci d'art.*" NLW MS.

12 Letter to 'The Listener' by Vernon Watkins, Jan. 22nd, 1948.

13 In: '*Yeats and the Oracles. Sources of Yeats' Later Poetry*' by Vernon Watkins. (NLW MS.)
Just as Watkins's mature poetry may be said continually to renew the experience he went through in 1928/1929, so he says of Yeats: "I believe that this state was reproduced again and again in the latter part of Yeats's life." Ibid.

14 Diaries from Watkins's trip to Germany. NLW MS 22447B.

15 The only poem of his at this time referring to war merely looks back to the end of the First World War:
"War passed with mighty fanfaron, shame furled
Its ensign of black eagle ...
The peace of Europe had been sealed."
(Poem beginning 'War passed with mighty fanfaron' in: MS 22447B – NLW.)

16 Diary entry of June 10th. In his poem 'Farewell to Nürnberg' (1932 and 1947) Watkins attempted to encapsulate something of the 'marvels' he had experienced there. The poem was unpublished in Watkins's lifetime, but has been published in H.M. Waidson's article: 'Vernon Watkins and German Literature' in 'The Anglo-Welsh Review', Vol. 21, Summer 1972.

17 The 'Angelic Salutation' was carved by Veit Stoss and overseen by Albrecht Dürer and has hung in the Lorenzkirche since 1518. Watkins writes of it: "Great Lorenzkirche, gloom of unearthly fire,/ Raised wings of angels, poised in the trembling light./ ... Guarding a flying hush, a mute, perpetual flight ... Love, highest wisdom, a footstep from us lies;/ Truth hides, is near us, at the heart of light and sound." ('*Farewell to Nürnberg.*)

18 Untitled poem, not published in Watkins's lifetime. In: *New Selected Poems of Vernon Watkins.* (Carcanet 2006). Page 95.

19 Diary, June 13th, 1931. NLW MS 22447B.

20 Suggesting that he was dissatisfied with whatever he did write and later destroyed it.

21 'Loiterers' was published in his book 'Cypress and Acacia' in 1959. It is not particularly characteristic of his true later style, and he had special reason for publishing it in his first book that appeared after Dylan Thomas's death.

Nevertheless, he published it virtually unchanged from the 1932 version, and it must thus be seen as the earliest poem included in any of his books.

22 Included 15 years later in his third book, 'The Lady with the Unicorn'.

23 The words are from Heine's tragedy 'Almansor', where they are spoken in reference to a burning of the Koran during the conquest of Granada in Spain.

24 Gwen Watkins. Email to RR: 30/10/2015.
Dorothy Watkins also describes witnessing this event. Although her booklet about her brother contains many interesting details, her memory was often incorrect. She describes this book-burning taking place in Nuremberg, for example, whereas Watkins did not visit Nuremberg in 1933. She also recalls witnessing the book-burning on her own, which is impossible in the light of Vernon Watkins's description to Gwen Watkins. It is possible, therefore, that she was with Vernon at the event in 1933 and confused the circumstances when remembering them over 50 years later: "One night ... I followed a crowd out of curiosity, it came to a halt in a large square. I watched with horror and disgust the bestial ceremony of the burning of Jewish and Communist books by the Nazis. The night was fine and the scene might have been taken from Dante's Inferno. Uniformed men with pitchforks tossed books and papers onto a great fire, every time the flames shot up the crowd would roar its approval. I was probably the only person present when it all ended who did not give the Nazi salute and join in the singing of the Horst Wessel. I was not molested, but there were angry murmurs from the people around me. I returned to our lodgings very troubled but thankful that Vernon had not been with me, as he would almost certainly have caused a scene. This introduction to Fascism made a profound effect on us both." DW. pp. 22-23.

25 Goethe made his first 'Harzreise' in December 1777, aged 28, and had significant experiences there, both on the Harz's highest mountain, the Brocken and in the caves or mines underneath the mountains. (See *Goethe und die Rosenkreuzer*, by Frank Teichmann. Verlag Freies Geistesleben, 2007.) He wrote his poem 'Harzreise in Winter' in connection with this, and the 'Walpurgisnacht' scenes in Faust are then set in the Harz Mountains and on the Brocken.

26 Heine at a significant moment in his life had walked through the Harz and to the Brocken, resulting in his book of poems, *Die Harzreise*.

27 Watkins wrote a sequence of poems arising from the trip entitled: 'The Harz Mountains'. Some of the places he visited, named in the poems, are: Treseburg, Schienke, Altenbrak, The Brocken, Nordhausen and Goslau. MS 2249-50A. NLW.

28 "Technical Notes for a Preface to Harz Poems". MS 2249-50A. NLW.

29 'Morgen' (A translation into German of Shelley's poem 'Tomorrow'.) June 1933. Ibid.

30 DW

31 Sonnet written in Germany, June 1933. NLW MS 22464E.

32 Looking back (in 1958) at the year 1935, Vernon Watkins described W.B. Yeats as the person: "whom I regarded then and still regard as the greatest lyric poet of our age. I already owed more to Yeats than to any other poet, as he had shown me something which the others had not been able to show: that is, how a lyric poet should grow old ... It was not so much that Yeats grew old impressively, but that as he aged his poems grew better and more astonishingly fresh ... At seventy he was astonished to find

himself 'better than ever.'" ('Introduction to a Reading of Poems at Neath'. 1958. NLW MS 22480E

33   Obvious examples of this are Tennyson's 'In Memoriam' or Matthew Arnold's 'Dover Beach'.
34   'Poetry and Experience'. GW/JT.
35   From: *'Yeats and the Oracles. Sources of Yeats' Later Poetry.'* (NLW MS.) Yeats' book 'The Tower' opens with the words: "That is no country for old men". ('Sailing to Byzantium.')
36   In other words that the secret of Yeats's inspiration "did not lie only in the treatment of a theme." (*Yeats and the Oracles.*)
37   Ibid.
38   The poem ends:
Then of their honesty
I was undeceived,
Words that I cast from me,
Admit it, you thieved.
(In: NLW MS 22464E.) This poem about the need to abandon poetic borrowings ironically borrows a little too much in the end from Yeats's poem 'A Coat'. Watkins never attempted to publish it.
39   'On leaving a house'. In: NLW MS 22464E.
40   This is the ending of 'Wind and Rain', that Watkins published in 1949 (17th November) in 'The Listener'.
The original February 1934 poem, in its entirety, is as follows:
The Rootless Tree
An angry gardener took
An axe, and struck this blow.
Yet this jasmine bough,
Though it then forsook
Earth, is by genius able
To bloom, and not to fall,
Gripping the western wall
By hook or crook.
Learn from this fable:
Hope will not be slain,
Though all things rend and rive,
But quickly will revive
If it have wind and rain.
In 1962, in a poem called 'Rebirth', published in his final volume Fidelities, Watkins remembers the moment of his seeing this "resurrected" jasmine plant and suggests that this may have marked the beginning of his renewed perception of nature, which underlay much of his later poetry. He speaks of how, after the passing of his youth, he saw: "*a flower/ Rooted in ruins.*" He adds: "*From that remaking hour/ Perception begins.*"
41   MS. 22451A. (1934)
42   Sonnet. MS. 22451A. (1934)
43   "Vernon – 'The extravagant hero of night'" – notes for a talk about Vernon Watkins

by Wyn Lewis on November 27th, 1975. Gwen Watkins archive.
44   'Discovery and Adventure.' Dec. 1934. NLW. MS. 22451A.

CHAPTER SEVEN

SWANSEA'S OTHER POET (1935–1936)

1   From: 'The Poets of Swansea' by Dylan Thomas. Written in early 1932. In: *Early Prose Writings*. (Dent. 1971). Page 102.
2   Quoted in: *Dylan Thomas. The Biography*, Paul Ferris. (Phoenix, 1999.) Page 123.
3   Watkins added: "I looked to Yeats as the great living master of poetry, and I did not really want a contemporary, nor did I expect to find one." ('Notes on Dylan Thomas' in GW/JT. Page 27.) Watkins wrote elsewhere: "Also the poems of Yeats so dominated my imagination, as they came out, that I could not find room for another poet. I did, however, buy the book, and I made room for Dylan." (Handwritten notes on Dylan Thomas. NLW. Facsimile reproduced in *Portrait of a Friend* by Gwen Watkins. [Gomer 1983] Page 173.)
4   Ibid. (Emphasis added).
5   Vernon Watkins's handwritten notes for 'Notes to Dylan Thomas'. Jeff Towns archive.
6   From: 'Before I knocked' by Dylan Thomas (1933); 'True Lovers' by Vernon Watkins (1926); Notebook poem by Dylan Thomas (1st Feb. 1933); 'Poeta Caecus' by Vernon Watkins (1928).
7   From 'Innovation and Tradition' – Vernon Watkins's 1953 obituary of Dylan Thomas in 'The Times'. It is reprinted in: *Poems for Dylan* by Vernon Watkins. Ed. Gwen Watkins. (Gomer Press 2003)
8   "In a few weeks, on the day after his return, he arrived." Introduction to *Dylan Thomas: Letters to Vernon Watkins*. p.12.
9   From: 'Notes on Dylan Thomas' by Vernon Watkins – in: GW/JT, pp. 27 & 28.
10 A poem from Watkins's first book, 'Stone Footing', speaks of the lone path he had trodden since that experience, unconnected to any seeking for romantic love:
'Stopping my ear to Venus and her doves,
I steal stone footing ...
I choose this path, the rock which no man loves ...
knowing the door of my friends
Is rock, and I am exiled from their tribe'.
11 Draft of 'Poetry and Experience'. Quoted in *Portrait of a Friend* by Gwen Watkins. (Gomer 1983) Page 4.
12 'Poetry and Experience' – GW/JT, page 156.
Elsewhere Watkins wrote: "There was much that showed a love of poetry rather than an ability to write it. (Dylan's) fresh eye taught me a lot and helped to remove many archaisms" 'Notes on Dylan Thomas' – GW/JT, page, 34.
13 *Dylan Thomas: Letters to Vernon Watkins* – pp. 38-39.
14 From: 'Address to the Poetry Society of Great Britain'. 1966. In: *Poetry Wales*, Vol. 12, No. 4, Spring 1977.

15. Asked once about Dylan's influence, he replied: "*Oh, it was very great indeed ... because he showed me how very stuffy and derivative a lot of my early work was ... he helped me a great deal to show me what really belonged to my work rather than what belonged to the work of other poets.*" *Dylan Remembered. Volume 2. Interviews by Colin Edwards.* Ed. David N. Thomas. (Seren, 2004). p. 61

16. 'The Poetry of Wilfred Owen' by Vernon Watkins, written in early 1936. NLW. 22481E.

17. It is not known whether Wilfred Owen himself burned any of his early work. Among his manuscripts found after his death was "a sack which, in accordance with Owen's final wishes, his mother, Susan Owen, burned: 'it was like burning my heart'." ('Wilfred Owen' by Stella Halkyard. In: 'PN Review' 173, Volume 33, Number 3, January – February 2007. Available online.)

18. An unpublished poem by Vernon Watkins also depicts such an event:
    "Peristontilius, poet to the king,
    Tore up the whole of his collected works.
    I was a witness at that holocaust." *Peristontilius. Defecit Opus* NLW.Mss. 22464E. (The film by John Ormond about Vernon Watkins was called 'Under a Bright Heaven'.)

19. "The first poem he read to me was 'Ears in the Turrets Hear'." (In 'Notes on Dylan Thomas', GW/JT. p.28.)

20. Introduction to: *Dylan Thomas: Letters to Vernon Watkins.*

21. Quoted in PoF. Page 25.

22. *Portrait of a Friend* by Gwen Watkins.

23. 'A Note on Dylan Thomas' – GW/JT. pp. 23-24.

24. From: 'Notes on Dylan Thomas', GW/JT. p. 39

25. Notes for 'Bryanston Talk'. Jeff Towns Archive.

26. 'First meeting of Vernon Watkins with Dylan Thomas'. (Typescript.) Fascimile reproduced in: *Poems for* Dylan by Vernon Watkins. Ed. Gwen Watkins. (Gomer Press 2003)

27. From: 'The Wales Dylan Thomas knew' In: GW/JT.

28. A later version was put on stage in Swansea in 1939, and it was broadcast on radio, in its final version, in 1949. Watkins therefore remained busy with it for the next 14 years.
    Its dramatic and poetic style is Yeatsian – to such a degree that it has been seen as over-dominated by the influence of Yeats. (See for example Gwen Watkins's introduction to *The Influences* – Bran's Head Books Ltd.) This has prevented people from seeing what is of paramount importance about *The Influences* for Watkins's life – namely its *theme*.
    When one looks at Watkins's poetry immediately prior to this, one sees in fact that *The Influences*, albeit under the strict tutorship of Yeats's style, marks a huge step forward in Watkins's own mastery of poetic technique.

29. From: *The Influences* – Bran's Head Books, Ltd.
    This "moment of touch" – when "*for a moment the sunlit river and the burial-urn speak with the same music*" is what the whole Masque leads towards. -

    | 2nd Voice | **Look, look, he catches her, he is going to touch her dress!** |
    | Old Man | **Undo that cloak and let me speak to you!** |

Girl	A wise man knows the truth, but is he true?
	He feels, but can he touch the perfect thing?
	Who but the unafraid of time can sing
	Out of sheer joy, the novelty of day?
Old Man	My tender trust lies deeper than you know.
Girl	Remember, when my steps are far away,
	You caught my coloured cloak and held it – so.

30 Introduction to: *Dylan Thomas: Letters to Vernon Watkins*.
31 PoF. p. 22.
32 'Poetry and a Career'. In: GW/JT. p. 132.
33 See Alfred Janes's paintings of both Dylan Thomas and Vernon Watkins reproduced in this chapter. See also Hilly Janes's *The Three Lives of Dylan Thomas* for more about Alfred Janes (her father) and his relationship with Dylan Thomas.
34 *Dylan Remembered. Volume 2. Interviews by Colin Edwards*. Ed. David N. Thomas. (Seren, 2004). pp. 35-36.
35 'Swansea and the Arts' – 'A facsimile of the script of the 1949 BBC Radio Broadcast from Swansea.' (T Llên Publications 2000)
36 The composer Daniel Jones had also often attended the meetings at the Kardomah Café, but was away at this time and Vernon Watkins did not meet him until 1943.
37 'Return Journey' by Dylan Thomas, in: *Dylan Thomas: The Broadcasts*. Ed. Ralph Maud. (Dent 1991) Page 184.
38 'Return Journey' by Dylan Thomas, in: *Dylan Thomas: The Broadcasts*. Ed. Ralph Maud. (Dent 1991) Page 184.
39 Introduction to: *Dylan Thomas: Letters to Vernon Watkins*.
40 'Visit to Yeats in Dublin, 1938' – (transcript of Vernon Watkins's handwritten notes) – in: *Poetry Wales*, Vol. 12, No. 4, Spring 1977.
41 DT to VW, 20th April 1936, in: *Dylan Thomas: Letters to Vernon Watkins*.
42 From: 'Notes on Dylan Thomas' in: GW/JT. Page 44.
43 DT to VW, 20th April 1936, in: *Dylan Thomas: Letters to Vernon Watkins*.
44 *Dylan Remembered. Volume 2. Interviews by Colin Edwards*. Ed. David N. Thomas. (Seren, 2004). Page 38.
45 Ibid. pp. 33-34.
46 Ibid. p. 61.
47 'Dylan Thomas' by Vernon Watkins. ('Sept '64') A page and a half typescript. NLW.
48 'Introduction to a Reading of Poems at Neath'. NLW MS.
49 From draft notes for 'Notes on Dylan Thomas' – Gwen Watkins archive.
50 Introduction to Poems read at Stratford-on-Avon. NLW.
51 Introduction to: *Dylan Thomas: Letters to Vernon Watkins*.
52 Thomas Taig. Quoted in New Selected Poems of Vernon Watkins, (Carcanet, 2006). p. xv.
53 'For Whom Does a Poet Write?' in GW/JT. Page 138.
54 Ibid.
55 'Notes to DT' – GW/JT
56 Introduction to: *Dylan Thomas: Letters to Vernon Watkins*.
57 Letter to P. Hansford-Johnson, May 2nd, 1934 – in: *Dylan Thomas. The Collected Letters*. ed. Paul Ferris, (Dent 2000), pp. 147-148.

58 From Adelphi, June 1935, pp. 179-180. EPL.
59 Quoted in: *Dylan Thomas. The Biography*, Paul Ferris. (Phoenix, 1999.) Page 109.
60 Thomas's real criticism was reserved for materialistic or realistic writers, who saw words as merely signposts for things: "The realistic novelist – Bennett, for instance – sees things, hears things, imagines things, (& all things of the material world or the materially cerebral world), and then goes towards words as the most suitable medium through which to express these experiences. A romantic like Shelley, on the other hand, is his medium first, & expresses out of his medium what he sees, hears, thinks, & imagines." Letter to P. Hansford-Johnson, May 2nd, 1934 – in: *Dylan Thomas. The Collected Letters*. ed. Paul Ferris, (Dent 2000), pp. 147-148.
There is no evidence, though, that Thomas recognized a *musical*, metrical approach to poetry as an equally valid, complementary approach to his own.
61 'Swansea and the Arts' – 'Facsimile of script of 1949 BBC Radio Broadcast from Swansea'. Ty Llen Publications, 2000.
62 DT to VW, 13 Dec.1948. In *Dylan Thomas. The Collected Letters*. ed. Paul Ferris, (Dent 2000). p. 775.
63 'Introduction to a reading of poems at Neath.' NLW MS
64 From: 'Notes on Dylan Thomas' – JT/GW.
65 From draft notes for 'Notes on Dylan Thomas' – Gwen Watkins archive.
66 *Letters to VW*. Introduction. Page 16.
67 'Now, Say Nay … ' and 'How Soon the Servant Sun'.
68 Letter to Richard Church, 17th March, 1936 – in: Dylan Thomas. *The Collected Letter*s. ed. Paul Ferris, (Dent 2000).
69 Ibid. Letter to Richard Church, April 1936.
70 *Letters to VW*. 20th April, 1936. Page 25.
71 *Letters to VW*. 25th October, 1937. Page 29.
72 *Letters to VW*. Introduction.
73 'Dylan Thomas and his Poetry' by Vernon Watkins. NLW MS 22552E
74 Bryanston Talk. Jeff Towns Archive.
75 Regarding 'The Map of Love' Vernon Watkins wrote: "This book shows a very great development. The imagination is no longer, in these poems, released in a flow of imagery which can generate itself like a friction battery; it is now controlled by the religious sense." ('Dylan Thomas and his Poetry'. NLW MS 22552E.)
76 'Poetry and Experience' in GW/JT. Page 154.
77 In a poem from 1935, 'Changes', Vernon had written:
Many things we begin:
Ambition gives us a skin.
We shine through many things:
Indolence gives us wings. NLW. MS 22464E
78 The two poems are spoken at the beginning of the Masque by 'Musicians' as an overture to all that follows.
79 Jenijoy La Belle, 'Vernon Watkins: Some Observations on Poetry', Anglo-Welsh Review, No.65, 1979.
80 Ibid.
81 One of these begins with Watkins contemplating the paradox of himself – poet

through and through, yet dressed as a bank-clerk:
Posterity, know me, artist in grey trousers,
Deep love gave me my present day indifference ...
Know me, my hands along this Spanish railing, ...
Indolent, guardian of immortal values(.)
Untitled poem (MS. 22453B NLW.) Written in 1936 in Spain.
82 'Portrait of a Poet'. 1936. NLW. MS. 22464E
83 Watkins wrote to T.S. Eliot on June 1st, 1936 that "I saw Mr. de la Mare's Secretary on my return from Austria in connection with a few translations of mine." Anne Bradby, who was six years younger than Watkins, was secretary to de la Mare throughout 1936: "Late in 1935 Anne found a place as secretary to Richard de la Mare ... She started just after Christmas and a year later became Eliot's secretary." *Charles Williams: The Third Inkling* by Grevel Lindop. OUP 2015. pp. 251-252. (After their holiday in Spain in April, Dorothy and Vernon Watkins had taken a second holiday in Austria. A poem Watkins wrote in Austria is dated 'May 13th, 1936'. In NLW MS 22453E)
84 Vernon Watkins to T.S. Eliot, June 1st, 1936.
85 Letter to Francis Dufau-Labeyrie – published in Temenos 8, 1987.
86 VW to Peter Hellings. February 16th, 1942. (Privately owned.)
87 'Reading of poems to the Staff Club, Swansea University', 22 February 1967. NLW MS. 22480E
88 'The Extravagant Hero of Night' – handwritten memories of Vernon Watkins by Wyn Lewis – Nov 27th, 1975. (Gwen Watkins archive.)
89 Wyn Lewis, in conversation with the author, 2000.
90 PoF. p.16.
91 VW to FD-L – September 19th, 1938.
92 From introduction to 'Three Ballads' (by Vernon Watkins) – a BBC Radio Performance, spoken by Dylan Thomas. Recorded in 1952, broadcast in 1953. Sadly the recording has not survived.
93 Ibid.
94 *Dylan Thomas: Letters to Vernon Watkins.* Letter of 29th September, 1939.
95 Ibid. Letter of 21st March, 1938.
96 "In the middle thirties I bought an exercise book for making first drafts of poems." In: 'A Note on my own Poetry'. NLW MS 22480E. In a handwritten draft of this, he is more specific: "1935 or 6 – red school exercise book".
97 In: 'A Note on my own Poetry'. NLW MS 22480E.
98 *Dylan Remembered. Vol. 1. Interviews with Colin Edwards.* Ed. David N. Thomas. Interview with Thomas Taig. Page 103.
99 See *Dylan Thomas: The Biography.* Paul Ferris. p. 149
100 'Art Poetique' develops an extended analogy between the mastery of poetry and the mastery of the sea:
'To be the wise man and the dunce,
To be the master and the slave at once
Seems the true poet's lot;
Yet need his hands make fast from dissolute Night a knot
And his keen writing should show seamanship

Resisting slippery fingers when they grip.' 'Art Poétique'; 1936-7; NLW MS 22464E
In the poem Vernon Watkins recalls his visionary experience (described in *Poeta Caecus* and referred to in Chapter 4) of himself as a slave, in chains, rowing a great ship at sea:
> 'Son of the wave windborne, I lean on the oar of the galleon, ...
> Across the waters I their bondslave stray
> **Saved by a chain from the waste of the sea.**'

The imaginative affinity between Vernon Watkins and Dylan Thomas can hardly be better seen than in the unconscious echo of the last line quoted with the final line of Thomas's 'Fern Hill': "Though I sang in my chains like the sea."

101 "I shall be glad if you will be good enough to answer my letter about my Masque 'The Influences'. I asked what the cost would be of a small limited edition, or whether you would consider undertaking an unlimited publication." Letter to Faber's, Dec 8th, 1936. (T.S. Eliot Archive, London.)

102 "I am very sorry to have made a muddle of things; – it is all due to my ignorance of publishing ways. It is so easy to imagine five publishers excitedly poring over my manuscript and taking extensive notes, so that when I suggest printing it they will only have to refer to their notes." VW to Fabers, December 28th, 1936. (T.S. Eliot Archive.)

CHAPTER EIGHT

'WALES' AND IRELAND (1938)

1. DT to Keidrych Rhys. Feb '37. *The Collected Letters of Dylan Thomas*. Ed. Paul Ferris. Page 281. Thomas immediately saw the direction the magazine should take: "the contents should be, in the best sense, 'contemporary', new and alive and original ... (the) work should be, nearly all of it, (by) young men ... I do not think it should be stridently Welsh in tone or approach ... Keidrych Rhys should be Editor ... and Dylan Thomas ... some variety of literary advisor." (Ibid.)

2. 'Poetry and Experience' in GW/JT.

3. The place where Watkins gave his paper is unknown. Referring, no doubt, to Owen's Welshness, he comments that unlike the American audience the paper was first written for: "You have the advantage of being his countrymen." He also refers to Dylan Thomas as "a friend of mine (whom you saw not long ago)". 'Note for a Paper on Wilfred Owen. V.P.W. June 4th, 1937'. NLW. 22481E.

4. Looking back on this paper twenty-five years later Watkins wrote: "I think that it was in 1934". At the time of the paper itself, however, in June, 1937, he stated: "I wrote this paper eighteen months ago for a friend in America." It is therefore more likely to have been towards the beginning of 1936 that his unnamed 'friend in America' had approached him. (Emphasis added.)

5. In Watkins's first draft in 1936 he wrote: "He made a bonfire of all his early work." He later corrected this to: " ... *nearly* all his early work." As, fortunately, Watkins did not in the end burn *all* his juvenilia, Watkins probably made this correction based on what was true of himself. (See also endnote 19 in chapter 7.)

6. It is undoubtedly significant that the mature second poet Vernon Watkins identified himself with Wilfred Owen whereas the immature first one, at Repton, had

ENDNOTES

identified with Rupert Brooke. The difference between Brooke and Owen has certain clear parallels with the difference between the two poets named Vernon Watkins. See, for example, Owen's 'An Imperial Elegy', which begins: "Not one corner of a foreign field/ But a span as wide as Europe", in deliberate contrast to Brooke's "There is some corner of a foreign field".

7   From: 'Note for a Paper on Wilfred Owen. V.P.W. June 4th, 1937'. (NLW. 22481E)
8   Letter to Francis Dufau-Labeyrie, Macroom, June 12th, 1937.
9   "the younger men, contributors to the periodical 'Wales' & to most of the verse periodicals published in London & abroad, *who are now making what is really a renaissance in Welsh writing.*"
    DT to T. Rowland Hughes, 29 October, 1938. *Collected Letters of Dylan Thomas.* Ed. Paul Ferris.
10 *Wales* 1. Ed. Keidrych Rhys. Summer 1937.
11 *Collected Letters of Dylan Thomas.* Ed. Paul Ferris. June '37 pp. 289-290
12 The previous 3 short quotations all taken from *Letters to Vernon Watkins* by Dylan Thomas.
13 DT to VW, Cornwall, 15th July, 1937.
14 DT to Keidrych Rhys. June '37. *Collected Letters of Dylan Thoma*s. ed. Paul Ferris pp. 289-290.
15 VW to TSE, July 3rd, 1937.
16 Watkins published the poem in August in the 2nd issue of Wales, along with 4 other poems. Dylan Thomas joked a few months later from London: "By a few, your poems in 'Wales' have been admired: The Sunbather, in particular, got them on their backs." DT to VW, 7/2/1938
17 Letter from Vernon Watkins to Francis Dufau-Labeyrie. August 5th, 1937 Heatherslade.
18 Ibid
19 *Portrait of a Friend*, Gwen Watkins, (Gomer, 1983), page 52.
20 In 2016 the copyright claims over these photographs led to a court case and wide publicity: https://www.theguardian.com/books/2016/jan/22/dylan-thomas-copyright-claims-thrown-out-irish-court-photographs
21 "Dot and Marjorie and I walked back with them through the wood – Bishopston Valley wood – the way you liked so much." VW to F D-L, August 30th, 1937.
22 VW to F D-L. Friday. Summer 1937
23 Dylan Thomas to Julian Symons. 16.11. 1936. *Collected Letters of Dylan Thomas.* ed. Paul Ferris.
24 From the front page of 'New Verse', November 1937, Nos. 26-27, 'Auden Double Number'. It adds:
    "There are angles from which Mr. Eliot seems a ghost and even Mr. Yeats a gleam. Most authors still belong to … 1900 … But Auden does live in a new day."
25 Introduction to *Dylan Thomas: Letters to Vernon Watkins*.
26 DT to KR, March 10th, 1938. *Collected Letters of Dylan Thomas.* ed. Paul Ferris.
27 Review of *In Parenthesis* by Vernon Watkins. *Wales* 5. Summer 1938.
28 DT to VW, July 5th, 1938. Thomas asked Watkins again a week later: "Think about Eliot for me." 14/7/38/
29 'Harvard Advocate', December 1938 Special Issue on T.S.Eliot, containing

contributions by: Conrad Aiken, Archibald Macleish, Robert Lowell, Wallace Stevens, William Carlos Williams and others.

30   'Introduction to "The Poetry of Wilfred Owen"' by Vernon Watkins. NLW MS 22481E.
31   Introduction to *Dylan Thomas: Letters to Vernon Watkins*. The details of which poems Dylan Thomas sent to Vernon Watkins, and when, are easy to follow with the help of Watkins's notes before each letter in: *Letters to Vernon Watkins*. They are also documented in the notes at the back of Dylan Thomas's *Collected Poems*. ed. Walford Davies and Ralph Maud. (Dent 1993).
32   VW to F D-L. Friday. October 11th, 1937.
33   VW to F D-L. Friday. October 14th, 1937. Vernon continued, in the Lewis Carroll-like style in which he often wrote to Francis: "I saw a dead fish to-day – a mackerel – and it told me the last verse was wrong. It must have a perfection like the fallen sky in a fish's skin, like those dawns that break beyond the world."
34   DT to VW, 25th October, 1937.
35   VW to F D-L. Autumn 1937.
36   "It was nice of you to write to Dylan and collect another supporter for the Anti-Yeats's-Tower-Firing-Squad." (VW to F D-L. Late 1937) Vernon did not, however, merely reject the adverse comments he received, explaining to Francis: "I didn't resent your criticism ... flattery leads to apathy, you must always tell me what you feel – I want that. Applause is dreadful ... But in the world you must know that a poet has only one need, that his poetry shall be loved. So failure rankles." (VW to F D-L, November, 1937.)
37   VW to F D-L. Autumn 1937.
38   Keidrych Rhys to VW, 22nd October, 1937. In the same letter Rhys said to Watkins: "It is only by being unpure that we can achieve a Pure Whole." A few months later Rhys said a little more of what he meant: "I think a few 'unpure' images would help you ... Living at Heatherslade one's apt to forget drab valleys, the Welsh Sunday, fish and chip shops and 'pictures' 2 years late that continually break down and so on to the Great Strike 1926 ... " Keidrych Rhys to VW, 5th Feb 1938. NLW MS.
39   DT to VW, Nov 10th, 1939. A later version of the poem, 'The Eastern Window', is in: CP. Page 36.
40   DT to VW, April 1st, 1938.
41   VW. Letter to The Observer. 1st Dec. 1957.
42   VW to FDL, 18th November, 1938.
43   VW to F D-L. April 11th 1938
44   DT to VW, 7th Feb. '38
45   "Envy the beggar in your book-fed glut.
     Crooked is the conduit of immortal song."
     From 'Quatrains',1935. NLW MS 22464E
46   Keidrych Rhys to VW, 22nd October, 1937.
47   DT to VW, Nov. 10th, 1939
48   "Yeats's Singing School" in: *Yeats the Initiate* by Kathleen Raine. The Dolmen Press/George Allen & Unwin. 1986. p.446
49   *W.B. Yeats – The Poems*, ed. Daniel Albright. (Everyman, Dent. 1994.) pp. lv – lvi.
50   "I suggested that perhaps one of the tests of a good poem was whether it was

accurately remembered over a long period of time. I said I found that after six or seven years I could remember every single word of a poem of his without reading it again ... I said I found that where I remembered a whole poem except for one indistinct line, that line usually turned out to be a bad one." VW to W.B. Yeats. As reported in 'Visit to Yeats in Dublin, 1938' – (transcript of Vernon Watkins's notes after his visit) – in: Poetry Wales, Vol. 12, No. 4, Spring 1977.

51 VW to FDL (February 14th 1938): "I sent Wales No 3 to Yeats, to show him my poem and the photo I took of his town. But I only addressed it to Yeats – Dublin – or else Yeats – Ireland. Could it have got there? I've had no reply."
52 W.B. Yeats to Vernon Watkins. March 19th, 1938.
53 VW to FD-L. From a letter of – "Monday night" which FDL dates: 'probably early 1939'
54 Before receiving Yeats's letter Watkins had already planned to return to Ireland in May. In his letter to FDL on February 14th 1938 he had said: "I'm going on holiday ... if in May, would you like to go and see Yeats with me? I've asked permission, but of course he won't get the letter unless the postman knows where he lives. Or we might disguise ourselves as postmen."
55 VW to F D-L, May 9th, 1938.
56 Ibid.
57 Ibid.
58 Ibid.
59 VW to F D-L, May 15th, 1938.
60 'Notes in Memory of Vernon Watkins' by Francis Dufau-Labeyrie. (Gwen Watkins Archive.) A shortened version was published in *Poetry Wales*, Vol. 12, No. 4, Spring 1977.
61 (VW to F D-L, Jan 6th, 1938.) Francis being a lover not just of poetry but also of women, Vernon added: "I think the last sect must be yours, a very naughty one. P.S. Please illustrate this poem for me."
62 Vernon's letters to Francis are also where Vernon expressed his confidence in his own poetry more freely than anywhere else, writing, for example, about one of Shelley's poems that Francis was translating: "I like the translation from Shelley (which, by the way, is a mediocre poem in English, not nearly as good as Dylan) (or me!)" VW to F D-L, April 11th, 1938. He did, however, also tell Francis: "I ought to confess that I place in things that I write a quite immoderate faith. You are more sensible and are able to see things in better perspective. I can never see things with cold eyes." (VW to FDL – 'Thursday night' – prob. late 1938 or early 1939.)
63 VW to F D-L. Friday. October 11th, 1937.
64 This probably contributed to the difficulties that arose between Watkins and Dufau-Labeyrie, as the issue in which Labeyrie's translation was to have appeared was the only issue which Vernon helped to edit: "Keidrych came here the weekend before last ... We prepared Wales No. 4 together." Dufau-Labeyrie must surely have been hurt by the omission, even if Watkins assured him that he had had no part in the decision: "He's not printing 'The Bad Lads' – (my suggestions were vain) – because he's confining himself to Welsh work." (VW to F D-L, Feb 14th, 1938.)
65 The letter has not survived and was therefore presumably destroyed by Dufau-Labeyrie.

66 VW to F D-L, March 18th, 1938.
67 'L'ami de Dax' [V.P.W. March 1938] Unpublished poem. Gwen Watkins archive.
68 VW to F D-L, March 18th, 1938.

CHAPTER NINE
A DEATH AND A BIRTH (1938–39)

1 W.B. Yeats to Vernon Watkins, June 2 1938
"I am glad to hear that you will be in Dublin in June … Unless I hear to the contrary I will look forward to seeing you on Thursday 23rd about 4 pm."
2 Vernon and Dorothy Watkins went to Camaret, Morgat, Douarnenez, Audierne, Concarneau and Pont-Aven. Vernon wrote a detailed prose-description of this holiday, called 'Finistere and Ireland'. (NLW Ms). Vernon Watkins was also a keen amateur photographer, with what Franics Dufau-Labeyrie called his "voluminous camera". One of his photographs of this holiday was exhibited that Autumn in London, as he told Francis: "my photo of fishing-boats at Audierne is being exhibited this week in the United Banks Art Exhibition at the Guildhall." (VW to FDL, 25th October 1938.)
3 From Vernon Watkins's prose description of his June 1938 holiday, entitled: 'Finistere and Ireland'. Typescript. NLW MS.
4 "As Mrs. Yeats undid the paper from the flowers she remarked to W.B. 'How wonderful it was for them to know that your favourite colours are these, pink and blue.' She came to him, handed them to him and he smelt them. He said nothing, smiled … We noticed afterwards that all the flowers in the room were just those colours: 3 vases of pink and blue flowers." ('Visit to Yeats in Dublin, 1938' – (transcript of Vernon Watkins's notes after his visit) – in: *Poetry Wales*, Vol. 12, No. 4, Spring 1977.)
5 As well as receiving a copy of 'Wales' from Vernon Watkins, Yeats may also have been alerted to the magazine by the highly positive review T.S. Eliot's journal 'The Criterion' had just given it, describing it as excelling anything similar from Ireland (or Scotland): "*Wales* is distinguished by poems and criticism that could stand on their own legs anywhere, in Peking or Paris or Peru as well as in Pontypridd … . Scotland and Ireland, except as represented in the periodicals of metropolitan intellectuals, have lately produced nothing so vital and novel as *Wales*." (April, 1938)
6 Yeats elaborated: "Where poetry was left to the intellect alone it degenerated into a box of tricks. But the intellectual toil was necessary; any moment the unexpected reward might come."
7 'Articulations, May 1955' by Vernon Watkins. In: *Temenos* 8, 1987.
8 'Though to Please Man'. CP. Page 478.
9 Francis Dufau-Labeyrie, "Notes in Memory of Vernon Watkins", Jeff Towns Archive.
10 "Yeats asked what sort of literary circle there was in Swansea – he asked twice where Swansea was. I said vaguely 'Between Cardiff and Fishguard on the sea.' I said there wasn't much of a literary circle in Swansea. There had been Dylan whom I was friendly with and used to see three times a week revising each other's poems, but now he had gone to Laugharne & was married."

11 From: 'The Tragic Generation' in: Autobiographies. Macmillan, 1980. Page 292. (Emphasis added.)
12 'Visit to Yeats in Dublin, 1938' – (transcript of Vernon Watkins's notes after his visit) – in: *Poetry Wales*, Vol. 12, No. 4, Spring 1977.
13 See endnote 499 for the review in 'The Criterion', for example, praising 'Wales' over anything similar being produced in Ireland.
14 Watkins, for others than himself, "suggested drama was a good contrast" and Yeats agreed.
15 When Vernon Watkins sent the photograph to Yeats's sister after his death, she wrote: "I like your photograph of our brother very much only spoilt by that black eye shield … the same oculist wanted me to wear one – I said decidedly "no" … But W.B. was always too anxious to do what experts told him – he wanted so badly to have health – I think he hated invalidism – so I try to think it was well he went like he did – with no lingering illness." Elizabeth Corbet Yeats to VW, April 3 1939. Gwen Watkins archive.
16 'Notes in Memory of the Dublin Visit' by Francis Dufau-Labeyrie in: *Poetry Wales*, Vol. 12, No. 4, Spring 1977.
17 Letter to FDL, Jan. 21st, 1941.
18 The very first statement by Yeats that Watkins jotted down in his notebook was: "There must always be a quality of nonchalance to make a poem permanent". It was almost certainly no accident that these were the first words by Yeats that Vernon quoted to Dylan Thomas. Watkins must surely still have had on his mind Dylan Thomas's severe criticism, a few months earlier, of his own use of the word 'nonchalance' in a poem. Dylan had written: "the awkwardness of '*poppy's nonchalance*' is obvious: it sounds like a man with a lisp & a stutter trying to gargle." When Vernon had defended his phrase Dylan had merely reiterated: "In one thing you are still wrong: 'poppy's nonchalance' is bad; it cannot be anything but bad; and I refute your criticism from the bottom of my catarrh."
19 'Introduction to a Reading of Poems at Neath.' NLW MS 22480E.
20 Dylan Thomas sent 'On no work of words' to Vernon Watkins in September 1938.
21 "I wanted to know whether he would object to my reproducing his conversation because had he objected I should not have published the poem." Interview with Vernon Watkins by Dr. George Thomas. 'Insert for Spectrum'. In: GW/JT.
22 VW to FDL – 'Tuesday evening.' FDL added: 'Probably late 1938'.
23 WBY to VW, Oct. 23rd, 1938. Yeats thanked Watkins for "those poems you sent me a month ago. Forgive that long delay."
24 "The whole of last week-end was spent doing the new and final version of the Yeats poem. This I've sent to Eliot … I'm very pleased with it now." VW to FDL 'Sunday night'. FDL added: 'Autumn or Winter 1938.'
25 "the poems on Yeats are very good, and if THE CRITERION had continued, I should have thought it most suitable to have published one of them in it." TSE to VW, 21st March 1939. In: the Berg Collection, New York Public Library.
26 Ibid.
27 VW to TSE. March 22nd, 1939.
28 TSE to VW. 15th May 1939.
29 VW to FDL, September 19th, 1938.

30 *Letters to Vernon Watkins*, page 95.
31 DT to VW. 29th December, 1938.
32 VW to FDL. 'Wednesday night' – 'prob. late 1938 or early 1939'
33 In: 'Life And Letters' April, 1939. Vernon Watkins sent a copy of this to W.B. Yeats's sister, Elizabeth Yeats, who wrote to thank him: "*very much indeed* for … your long and difficult poem 'Yeats in Dublin' – I have read it many times and each time I read it I do get more from it … I do feel that the whole poem is like my brother – a kind of essence of William Butler Yeats the man … you will think me very unlettered & so I am – but I get from the whole poem a beautiful serenity – & my brother's quiet room at Rathfarnham rises up before me." E.C. Yeats to VW, 15th May, 1939.
34 The leaders of Russia and Czechoslovakia had not been invited to Munich.
35 "Thank you for 'Poem in the Ninth Month'. It's fine. I'll use it, of course." DT to VW. December 20th, 1938.
36 DT to VW – letter sent on 19th October, 1938.
37 Dylan Thomas's recording of 'The Hand that Signed the Paper' from 1938 is available online.
38 VW to FDL. 'Wednesday evening'. FDL added: "probably Autumn 1938". Correct dating: 26th October, 1938.
39 Dylan Thomas to Henry Treece, July 6th, 1938.
40 VW to FDL. 26th October, 1938.
41 VW to FDL "Tuesday evening – probably late 1938"
42 Pearl White died on August 4th, 1938.
43 From "Soroptimist Reading" – 2nd Feb. 1965. NLW MS 22480E
44 From: *Authors take sides on the Vietnam War*, ed. Cecil Woolf and John Bagguley, Peter Owen, London, 1967.
45 VW to FDL. Nov 18th, 1938. He added: "I'm so much an individualist that I feel that improvement is hardly ever organized except in educational things. I wish there were no poor, no very poor people, & I wish there were no sick people. But if there are – and there are – it is people who will help them most, whatever government there is."
46 According to Gwen Watkins: "Frau Hechinger or some member of her family contacted Vernon in the mid-thirties to ask if she could be accepted as a refugee in Britain. But Jews could only be accepted if someone would sponsor them (i.e. be responsible for their lodging and support, or could offer them a job.) Vernon tried desperately to find someone who would do this, but without success, and though he wrote several times, he heard no more of any of the family." Email to the author, 30/10/2015
47 VW to FDL – Wednesday 26th October– 'Autumn 1938'
48 VW to FDL. Nov 18th, 1938.
49 By Dr. Gerhard Schacher, former economic adviser to the German Reichbank and significant anti-Nazi political spokesman.
50 Gwen Watkins refers to this dream in *Portrait of a Friend*, page 68. (See also *Collected Poems of Dylan Thomas*, Dent 1993, page 215.) Gwen Watkins does not state that Dylan Thomas had the dream on New Year's Eve, but it is highly likely that he did so, in that the whole poem takes place "on the tip of the tongue of the year."
Vernon Watkins's notes on Dylan Thomas's life state: "1938 Caruso – Horse &

Pleasure-bird". (Notes for 'Notes on Dylan Thomas'). He never explained 'Caruso', which he must have heard from Dylan Thomas. Perhaps the man in Dylan's dream who said 'He sings better now' was Caruso. Or perhaps the man called out: 'He sings better than Caruso now'. If the latter is true, the story would have a humorous afterword, when Bob Dylan, who took his name from Dylan Thomas, stated in 1965: "I'm just as good a singer as Caruso ... I hit all those notes. And I can hold my breath three times as long if I want to."

51   See *Dylan Thomas: The Biography*. Paul Ferris. (Phoenix Books, Orion, 2000) p. 186.
52   *Collected Letters of Dylan Thomas*. DT to Desmond Hawkins. Page 396.
53   *Poetry and Experience*. Vernon Watkins. GW and JT.
54   'New Year, 1965' by Vernon Watkins. NLW MS.
55   Ibid.
56   "Eight Poems by Dylan Thomas" by Vernon Watkins. In GW/JT.
57   Bryanston Talk. Jeff Towns Archive.
58   Ibid. "I really think that this little poem, written in 1938, marks the turning-point in DT's work, after which he was unable and unwilling to write in his early style. It is the equivalent of Yeats' poem 'A Coat' in which he announced the bare style of his later poetry and the death of his early, ornate style."
59   Dylan Thomas's original title for '*The Map of Love*' was: '*In the Direction of the Beginning*'. See DT to VW, December 20th, 1938: "I'm making it an odd book: 15 poems & 5 stories: all to be called *In the Direction of the Beginning*."
60   NLW MS. 22479E, p. 49.
61   "Hound Voice"; "John Kinsella's Lament for Mrs. Mary Moore"; "High Talk"; "The Apparitions"; and "A Nativity" were published in 'The Mercury' in December 1938. Watkins wrote to Francis Dufau-Labeyrie: "Yeats has 5 new poems in the Christmas number of the Mercury, which I've got. There's a beautiful one 'A Nativity' and a grand one 'High Talk' which I'll copy for you." VW to FDL, 15th December, 1938.
62   Ibid. 'High Talk' had been written in July, 1938 – soon after the visit of Vernon Watkins and Francis Dufau-Labeyrie to W.B. Yeats on June 23rd, 1938.

In March 1939, when Watkins read Yeats's late poem 'A Bronze Head', he wondered whether Yeats – consciously or unconsciously – might have taken his title-phrase from Watkins's 'Yeats in Dublin'. Watkins wrote to Dufau-Labeyrie: "The most lovely poems of Yeats in the Mercury. But the last one 'A Bronze Head' *(he may have taken the title from my poem)* is the best, I think. Yet, when I read them, each is best." (VW to FDL, 29th March 1939.) 'Yeats in Dublin' begins: "A rich lupin-garden,/ A long amber room,/ A bronze head, bookshelves/ Glittering in that gloom". Yeats's 'A Bronze Head' begins: "Here at right of entrance this bronze head".
63   "Yeats has more poems in the January Mercury – 3. Really they are wonderful. 'Politics' is a very slight thing, but the other two: 'Man and the Echo' and 'The Circus Animal's Desertion' are really splendid." VW to FDL. January, 1939.
64   VW to FDL. 30th January, 1938.
65   A mutual friend of Watkins and Francis Dufau-Labeyrie.
66   VW to FDL. 30th January, 1938.
67   VW to FDL, Jan 30th, 1939. Watkins described Roquebrune as: "a lovely place with rocky walls, cobbled streets, a hill and narrow passages, exciting as it grew dark."
68   In: *The Ballad of the Mari Lwyd*, where Watkins placed it immediately after his poem

for Dylan Thomas, 'Portrait of a Friend'.
69 'The Mummy' ... was suggested to me ... by the death of someone I knew." In: 'Poetry and the Reading of Poetry. Introduction to poems read at Stratford-upon-Avon.' August 1958. NLW MS 22480E.
70 From:'The Mummy' by Vernon Watkins.
71 DT to VW. February 1st, 1939.
72 Caitlin Thomas to Vernon Watkins, 4th February, 1939. In: *Dylan Thomas: Letters to Vernon Watkins.*
73 'The Dalai Lama's sacred skill;
Now his voice is in the stream,
His footprint sunk into the hill;
You were gathered in the seam
That sewed the great man's burial shroud,
Dropped by a swan's or a heron's bill
Frightened by a sudden scream
And gathered to the moving cloud.'
From: 'Poems for Llewellyn' in 'Life and Letters Today', March 1940. Vol. 24. No. 31.
74 DT to VW, March 1940.

CHAPTER TEN

'SAILORS ON THE MOVING LAND' (1939–1941)

1 In Welsh: "Cymdeithas Cymru Newydd".
2 Dylan Thomas to W.T. Davies, July 1939. *Collected Letters of Dylan Thomas.* Page 441.
3 Immediately after his meeting with Yeats, Watkins recorded Yeats's answer (beside the heading 'Welsh Nationals') as: "Poetry must not be nationalist, but must be national. The rebellion must be against casual mechanical lifelessness." ('Visit to Yeats in Dublin, 1938' – transcript of Vernon Watkins's notes after his visit – in: *Poetry Wales,* Vol. 12, No. 4, Spring 1977.)
4 Letter from Vernon Watkins to W.T. Davies of 19th July, 1939, in Welsh Arts Council Mss in NLW. Extracts of Watkins's letter are quoted in: 'Yr Academi Gymreig and Cymdeithas Cymru Newydd' by Meic Stephens, in: 'Poetry Wales', Winter 1968, Vol. A, No. 2.
5 'War and Poetry: The Reactions of Owen and Yeats'. In: *Yeats and Owen: Two Essays.* By Vernon Watkins. The Hunting Raven Press. 1981.
6 See endnote 4. Regarding friendship, Watkins had said earlier in the letter: "I have always believed very strongly in friendship, but never in groups of any kind." A good example of Watkins refusing to let a difference of views interfere with friendship was in his relationship with Keidyrch Rhys. He wrote to Peter Hellings: "I've heard from Keidrych, angry letters saying how grossly I misjudge him and Welsh Nationalism. In spite of quarrelling we get on pretty well ... " April 22nd, 1943.
7 In 'Wales' 23, Autumn 1946.
The third question in the questionnaire was: "*Should 'Anglo-Welsh literature' express a Welsh attitude to life* ... ?" Watkins answered: "The best Anglo-Welsh literature will always be that which abhors Anglo-Welsh limitations." To the final question, about

'Welsh Nationhood' and its special attributes, Watkins humorously refused to support any feelings of patriotic pride: "I think Wales should be proud of being the humblest country in the world."

8 Dylan Thomas at this time had also lost patience with Rhys's editorship of 'Wales'. He wrote to Rhys on 7th January 1939: "You … have lacked drive & firmness, you've let the possibility of a possibly *great* magazine almost slip away. It mustn't slip away altogether. Whatever I can do, let me know." Dylan also continued to lambast Rhys for the inclusion in 'Wales' of writers like Nigel Heseltine: "Heseltine should receive the recognition due to him: complete silence. I'm not going to mention him again ever in a letter to you."

9 "We do sometimes take orders for privately printing a book for the author – in that case we do not publish the book – we merely print it." E.C. Yeats to V.W. – Feb. 7th, 1939.

10 Watkins's first 'port of call' with 'Yeats in Dublin' had been the 'London Mercury', no doubt because it had published and was still publishing all of Yeats' most recent poems. Watkins told Francis Dufau-Labeyrie: "The poem on the Dublin visit is finished & has already been to London, but the 'Mercury' have refused to publish it – It's immensely long – that may have been a reason. And perhaps too intimate a poem for a magazine. However, it is the best poem of its kind in the world." (VW to FDL. 'Wednesday night' – 'prob late 1938 or early 1939'.) The poem was, however, published in the successor to 'The London Mercury': 'Life And Letters' (or: 'Life and Letters Today continuing the London Mercury ').

11 In March 1939 'Wales' published 'The Collier' – which was not only fitting, the poem being set in the Welsh hills, but had also been sent by Watkins to Keidrych Rhys over a year before, in February 1938. In October 1938 'Wales' published his short poem 'Pit-Boy', which also fitted the Welsh themes of 'Wales', but apart from these all of Watkins's published poems at this time appeared in London journals.

12 In: 'Life and Letters', Vol. 21/20, April 1939.
13 VW to TSE. May 16th,1939.
14 VW to FDL, Mid-March 1939
15 VW to FDL, March 12th, 1939
16 VW to TSE, May 16th, 1939.
17 VW to FDL. Monday night. Prob. Early '39
18 VW to FDL, Jan 29th, 1939.
19 VW to FDL, April 26th, 1939.
20 VW to FDL, April 15th, 1939.
21 Watkins wrote Llewellyn many another poem also: 'The Mother and Child'; 'Infant Noah'; 'Llewellyn's Spoon'; 'Llewellyn Asleep'; 'Llewellyn's Chariot'; 'A Child's Birthday'; 'Leaven's Eleven'.
22 DT to VW. 13th Dec. 1939
23 DT to VW. Letter of Jan 30th, 1940.
24 'The LONDON MERCURY. Incorporating the Bookman', Volume XXXIX, Number 233, March 1939 included "The Statues"; "News for the Delphic Oracle"; "Long-Legged Fly" and "A Bronze Head" by W. B. Yeats.
25 VW to FDL, April 15th, 1939.
26 VW to FDL, 'Thursday', 'probably early 1939'. Published in: 'Temenos 8'. pp. 151-152.

27. *Letters to Vernon Watkins*, Dylan Thomas, p.17.
28. As these letters are dated in *Dylan Thomas: Letters to Vernon Watkins*: 3rd March, 20th March, April, May, 12th May 1939.
29. DT to VW, 12th May, 1939.
30. VW to FDL, 21st May, 1939.
31. DT to VW, 21st May, 1939.
32. VW to FDL, early 1939.
33. Ibid.
34. The 'Wales' editorial in August 1939 asked: "When will our poets feel the need for social change before anything else?" (This would either have been written by Keidrych Rhys or Nigel Heseltine.)
35. VW to TSE, July 14th, '41
36. VW to F D-L. 'Tuesday'. 'Probably early 1939'.
37. VW to FDL, 15th Dec. 1938.
38. VW to TSE, June 5th, 1939.
39. VW to Peter Hellings, July 2nd, 1939.
40. DT to VW: May/June 1939. p.67.
41. DT to VW, July '39.
42. VW to FDL, July 6th, 1939
43. VW to FDL. July 7th, 1939.
44. Broadcast interview with Robin Holmes, 1957. NLW. 2552E.
45. VW to TSE, July 19th, '39.
    Watkins also told Dufau-Labeyrie: "Last night was momentous. The Masque was glorious. It was beautifully produced & most sensitively spoken. Also it was very well received by a fine audience." VW to FDL. July 7th, 1939.
46. Undated review in 'Swansea Evening Post' – by "C.F." (This may have been Dylan Thomas's friend, the journalist Charlie Fisher.)
47. VW to W.T. Davies. July 19th, 1939.
48. DT to VW, 25th August, 1939.
49. DT to VW. 25th August 1939. p.70.
50. *Dylan Remembered*. Vol. 2. Ed. Colin Edwards. Interview with Thomas Taig. Page 103.
51. *Dylan Thomas: Letters to Vernon Watkins*, p. 19.
52. Nigel Heseltine in his editorial, written on Sept 7th 1939, clearly expressed his social and political views, by strongly warning against Fascism not only in Europe but also in Britain: "Our fight will be against any establishment of Fascist principles in this country. When we have finished the war there are forces which will gladly set up such a system in this country. That is what we shall have to fight if we are to live." ('WALES' 10 – October 1939.)
53. *Dylan Thomas: Letters to Vernon Watkins*, p. 19.
54. *Vernon Watkins: The Early Years*. Dorothy Watkins. (Privately Printed.)
55. See *Dylan Thomas: The Biography*. Paul Ferris. Page 188. Dylan Thomas approached several writers in October and November 1939, but the attempt came to nothing and Thomas abandoned the idea.
56. Vernon was unable to attend the wedding, as he was working. Though Keidrych Rhys joked: "Do come to the wedding. We arranged it specially for your lunch

ENDNOTES 281

hour!" (Rhys to VW, 21st July, 1938.) In the same letter, along the same lines, Rhys wrote about one point of disagreement he had with Vernon's Masque: "I do believe in its integrity & in its being a part of yourself – except for the praise of indolence. You're anything but indolent, Vernon."

57 The day after the Masque Vernon had had his last holiday with his sister Dorothy, to Scotland: "We shall start at Loch Lomond & go through the Pass of Glencoe I expect, but we never decide until we get there – leave everything to chance. We may meet Anyone & see Anything." (July 7th, 1939. To FDL.) Vernon describes, however, that he had stayed with Dylan in Laugharne "on my way back from a holiday abroad". (*Dylan Thomas: Letters to Vernon Watkins*, page 75.) Watkins probably, therefore, had a second short holiday to France, after which he went on to Laugharne.

58 VW to TSE. May 16th, 1939.

59 VW to FDL. Quoted in Temenos 8, 1987.
This quotation has until now erroneously been seen to relate to Watkins's much longer poem: 'Yeats in Dublin'. This error was first made by Francis Dufau-Labeyrie in 'Temenos 8' – and was then repeated by the present author in the introduction to 'New Selected Poems of Vernon Watkins.' (Carcanet 2004). Watkins, however, is unquestionably referring to 'The Last Poems of Yeats'.

60 On April 28th, 1940, Watkins asked T.S. Eliot: "I wonder whether you would like to read a paper on Yeats' Last Poems which I wrote last Autumn." He initially called the paper 'Cuchulain Comforted' and also sent a copy to George Yeats. She wrote back on August 10 1940: "I am puzzled at your reference to 'my paper, 'Cuchulain Comforted'. I wonder where you sent it?" Six months later Watkins then offered the revised version to George Yeats, who replied: "I should be very glad to see 'Yeats and the Oracles'. I never got the original version – the new tenants of the house probably destroyed it." (March 9th, 1941.) When Eliot did eventually see it he was extremely positive: "*I find your Yeats essay the best examination of his style that I have seen.*" (TSE to VW, June 21st 1941.)

61 VW to TSE, November 10th, 1940: "I would like to keep 'Yeats in Dublin' and 'The Last Poems of Yeats' (both printed in 'Life and Letters Today') back for possible publication with my Yeats paper some day."

62 DT to Henry Treece, December, 1939.

63 DT to VW, December 13th, 1939.

64 Ibid. The "ridiculous cigarettes" Vernon very occasionally smoked were black Balkan 'Sobranies'.

65 Introduction to *Poetry Wales*, Vol. 12, No. 4, Spring 1977.

66 Glyn Jones, 'Whose Flight is Toil', in: *Vernon Watkins 1906-1967*, ed. Leslie Norris, Faber 1970.

67 '*Yeats said that a poem will suddenly fall into place like the click of a box. I say the good artificer makes the box.*" Vernon Watkins: Some Observations on Poetry. Ed. Jenijoy La Belle. The Anglo-Welsh Review. 1979. No. 65.

68 'New Year, 1965' by Vernon Watkins. Gwen Watkins Archive.

69 VW to FDL. March 12th, 1939.

70 'Poetry and Experience' in *Vernon Watkins on Dylan Thomas and Other Poets and Poetry*. Parthian 2013. Ed. Gwen Watkins and Jeff Towns.

71 'Return to a house where one had Died' (Nov 6th, 1926). NLW.

72 Note to 'Ballad of the Mari Lwyd' in *Collected Poems of Vernon Watkins*.
73 VW to TSE, March 7th. 1940.
74 VW to FDL, 'Thursday', 'probably early 1939'. Published in: 'Temenos 8'. pp. 151-152.
75 VW to Elizabeth Iorwerth. November 17th 1941.
76 DT to VW, March 6th 1940.
77 *Dylan Thomas: Letters to Vernon Watkins*. Page 83.
78 VW to TSE, April 28th, 1940. "On May 11th I shall be going to Paris ... I am wondering whether you could possibly manage an interview on Friday May 10th or Thursday May 9th."
79 VW to FDL, Jan 21st, 1940.
80 Ibid.
81 DT to VW, 5th June, 1940.
82 'Taliesin in Gower: Vernon Watkins – a Retrospect' by Gwen Watkins. 'Gower', Vol XLVIII. 1997. (The Journal of the Gower Society.)
83 DT to VW, "probably August 1940".
84 'Unveiling the Statue (for a French Friend before the Fall of France)' – in *The Lady with the Unicorn*.
85 "Thursday, June 27th, 1940. 6 High Explosive bombs dropped on Danygraig Road and a further 4 bombs on Kilvey Hill at 3.30am. The four bombs that landed on Kilvey Hill all failed to explode. No casualties." See: 'The Three Nights Blitz. Swansea and the Second World War.' https://802525liran.wordpress.com
86 Ibid.
87 DT to VW, early September 1940. *Collected Letters of Dylan Thomas*. Ed. Paul Ferris. Page 524,
88 Ibid.
89 Ibid.
90 *Dylan Thomas: Letters to Vernon Watkins*. Page 95.
91 Ibid.
92 Ibid. Page 96.
93 DT to VW. 1940. *Collected Letters of Dylan Thomas*. Ed. Paul Ferris. Page.509.
94 DT to VW. *Collected Letters of Dylan Thomas*. Ed. Paul Ferris. Page.526. Vernon Watkins dates this letter 'probably August 1940' in *Dylan Thomas: Letters to Vernon Watkins*.
95 DT to VW. Early September 1940. *Collected Letters of Dylan Thomas*. Ed. Paul Ferris. Page.524.
96 VW to TSE. November 10th, 1940.
97 VW to TSE, June 16th, '41.
98 'Articulations'. May 1955. In: Poetry Wales. Vernon Watkins issue. Spring 1977. Vol. 12. No. 4. Page 56.
99 'Ballad of the Equinox'. ("Equinoctial Ballads" – 13). Eventually published in Watkins's fourth book *The Death Bell – Poems and Ballads*. (1954).
100 'The Tyranny of the Equinox' – No. 14 of his 'Equinoctial Ballads'). Eventually published in Watkins's fourth book *The Death Bell* as 'Ballad of the Three Coins'.
101 'Ballad of the Gravestone'. October 1940. (A ballad written at the same time as the 'Equinoctial Ballads' sequence.) Gwen Watkins Archive.
102 The poem was published once in *Life and Letters* in May 1949 (Vol. 61, No. 141) and

extracts of it are included in Gwen Watkins's *Portrait of a Friend*. Vernon Watkins, however, continued to work on the poem after 1949 and produced a later version of the poem which has never been published. It is published here for the first time in the appendix.

[103] Gwen Watkins has written that the poem describes a meeting soon after Vernon Watkins and Dylan Thomas met for the first time, in 1936, on Dylan's 22nd birthday. The poem does perhaps look back to earlier meetings, but the emphasis on war, and the state of the relationship between the two men clearly relate to the years of the Second World War and fit well with Dylan's and Vernon's situation in January 1941, when the first draft of the poem was written. Vernon Watkins's final version names "London and Townhill falling", thereby giving the poem a validity also for all Vernon's wartime encounters with Dylan in pubs in London.

[104] "I had a hell of a week, working till 11 every night & then biking home – I've given up buses." VW to FDL, July 6th 1939.

[105] Dylan Thomas in 'Because the Pleasure-Bird Whistles' had also written of being able to speak, through inspiration, but of being unable to know anything about the source of this inspiration:
"An enamoured man alone …
Savours the lick of the times …
Nor ever, as the wild tongue breaks its tombs,
Rounds to look at the red, wagged root."

[106] Vernon's reply in the finished version is more opaque, but finishes with his saying that although language does indeed seem unable to speak at this moment, the "beak of air" can never be silenced:
    To-night all words are deluged from the slate:
    When will the shell close on the beak of air?

[107] *Dylan Thomas: Letters to Vernon Watkins*, p. 19.

[108] Afterword to *Adventures in the Skin Trade*, Signet Classics, New York, 1961.

[109] 'Essay on Vernon Watkins', David Wright, *Nimbus*, Vol. 3, No. 1, Spring 1955.

[110] Not only did Dylan fail to turn up at the Masque, but there is also no evidence that he ever appreciated it. Having promised to review it for 'Life and Letters' he never did so – and he later returned it to Watkins without comment.

[111] The planned London event at the Mercury Theatre in London in 1939 was made impossible by the outbreak of war. The event was then planned for a year later, in Autumn 1940, but this too was unable to happen. On July 12th, 1940 Watkins wrote to Eliot about his 'Ballad of the Mari Lwyd': "But for the intensification of air raids it would probably have been performed at the Mercury Theatre in August or September, with my Masque, but everything fell through."

[112] After Dylan's death, the experience of this night would strangely repeat itself, or re-echo, in a highly disturbing dream Vernon had of Dylan. (Described in Part Two, Chapter 5.)

[113] Watkins sent the poem to Eliot (with the title 'Footprints at Oystermouth') with his war-time poem 'Sea-Music' on June 23rd, 1941: "*Another, in somewhat the same form, but less liquid, 'Footprints at Oystermouth' was written in January and is a record of one evening with Dylan Thomas, to whom it is dedicated. I should like you to see this, too*".

[114] 'Poetry and Experience' in JT/GW.

115 Written in April 1941. Included in: *The Lady with the Unicorn*. After the poem had been published in 'The Listener' Watkins sent the poem to Eliot on June 23rd, 1941, saying: "The incident is a true one. It is the only war poem I have done or shall do, as I have thrown all my feeling into it."
116 *Other People's Children* by Dorothy Watkins. Page 35. The Cromwell Press. UK. 1993.
117 Vernon had already written about Ulysses in his poem before Dorothy took this ship: "Her ship coming back was the 'Ulysses' which was a coincidence or telepathy, perhaps, as that was not one of the new parts." VW to FDL. 27.11.1945.
118 *Other People's Children* by Dorothy Watkins. Page 52.
119 VW to TSE. 23rd June 1941. Watkins sent 'Sea-Music' to Eliot, together with 'Sailors on the Moving Land' and 'The Spoils of War'.
120 DT to VW, June 21st, 1941.
121 When Dylan Thomas sent Watkins the poem on 27th July 1944, he wrote: "It really is a Ceremony, and the third part of the poem is the music at the end."
122 VW to TSE. April 24th, 1941.
123 VW to TSE. June 1st, 1941.
124 DT to VW. 28th May, 1941.
125 VW to TSE. July 12th, 1940.
126 VW to TSE, Oct 25th, 1940.
127 "if the other poems showed variety and were very different from [the 'Ballad of the Mari Lwyd'] so much the better (…) when you are ready to let me see a volume I shall be very glad to consider it." TSE to VW, 31st October, 1940.
128 VW to TSE, Nov 10th, 1940.
129 VW to TSE, Dec 12th, 1940.
130 TSE to VW, Dec 9th, 1940. Eliot added: "some poems might have to be omitted. Difficult to decide which, because even your secondary verse has an opulence of phrase, and an originality of rhythm – qualities perhaps more Welsh than English".
131 VW to TSE, April 24th, 1941.
132 VW to TSE, April 26th, 1941.
133 "And one of them, when he saw that he was healed, turned back, and with a loud voice glorified God, And fell down on his face at his feet, giving him thanks: and he was a Samaritan. And Jesus answering said, Were there not ten cleansed? but where are the nine?" *The Gospel of Luke*, Chapter 17, verses 15-17.
134 *Gratitude of a Leper*. NLW. 22464E.
135 VW to FDL, 1939.
136 VW to TSE, May 7th, 1941.
137 TSE to VW, 30th May, 1941.
138 DT to VW, 22nd May, 1941. Watkins told Eliot on June 16th: "Dylan Thomas thought there was too much 'self-disgust' in 'Gratitude of a Leper', perhaps. I myself can't see that."
139 VW to TSE, 31st May, 1941. Eliot sympathized with Watkins, but made clear it was not in his hands: "I also like the leper title myself, but that seems unpopular." (TSE to VW, 5th June, 1941.)
140 VW to TSE, June 16th, 1941.
141 TSE to VW, 21 June 1941.
142 VW to TSE, 23 June 1941.

143 Eliot completed the first draft of 'Little Gidding' at the beginning of July, 1941. He completed the final version of the poem in September 1942. (See *The Composition of the Four Quartets* by Helen Gardner; Faber 1979.)
144 *The Dry Salvages*, Part II. T.S. Eliot.
145 VW to TSE. July 1st, 1941. Eliot replied: "Your one criticism of the poem interests me very much. It is very likely that you are right: all that I can say about it at the present time is that as my phrase was quite deliberate and conscious I don't propose to change it now. I still mean what I meant then, but such a criticism may make a difference to some poem in the future." (TSE to VW, 9th July 1941.)
146 DT to VW, 22nd May, 1941.
147 DT to VW, 28th May, 1941.
148 DT to VW, 28th August, 1941.
149 VW to TSE, 8th October, 1941. Translation of proverb:
"What takes a long time will, in the end, be beautiful."
150 *The Spectator*, January 2nd, 1942. '*Walter de la Mare and a New Poet*.' Sheila Shannon. The review went on: "Mr. Vernon Watkins combines unusual lyrical qualities, a seeing eye, and active imagination, a sensitive use of language, and a subtle ear for rhyme and rhythm."
151 *The Listener*. 25th January, 1945. '*Poetry in War Time*.' Henry Reed.
152 'On the Publication of my book' (October 1941). It later became 'Prometheus' (Aug. 1946).
153 VW to Peter Hellings. Nov. 17th, 1941.
154 VW to Elizabeth Iorwerth, November 17th, 1941.
155 VW to TSE, June 13th, 1942.
156 *Ur of the Chaldees – Seven Years of Excavation* by Sir Leonard Woolley. Pelican Books 1938. Reprinted 1940.
157 VW to FDL. Feb 16th. 1942. Watkins tried as hard as he could to reapply for some more suitable task – "but even the C.O. saw a Policeman in me and saw nothing else."
158 VW to TSE, August 22nd, 1941.

www.ingramcontent.com/pod-product-compliance
Lightning Source LLC
Chambersburg PA
CBHW040309170426
43195CB00020B/2899